D1713210

Diversity in a Youth Correctional System

Series on Massachusetts Youth Correction Reforms

Center for Criminal Justice
Harvard Law School

- Reforming Juvenile Corrections: The Massachusetts Experience by Lloyd E. Ohlin, Robert B. Coates and Alden D. Miller

- A Theory of Social Reform: Correctional Change Processes in Two States by Alden D. Miller, Lloyd E. Ohlin and Robert B. Coates

- Diversity in a Youth Correctional System: Handling Delinquents in Massachusetts by Robert B. Coates, Alden D. Miller and Lloyd E. Ohlin

- Designing Correctional Organizations for Youths: Dilemmas of Subcultural Development by Craig A. McEwen

- Neutralizing Inmate Violence: Juvenile Offenders in Institutions by Barry C. Feld

Diversity in a Youth Correctional System

Handling Delinquents in Massachusetts

Robert B. Coates
Alden D. Miller
Lloyd E. Ohlin
Harvard University

Center for Criminal Justice
Harvard Law School

Ballinger Publishing Company • Cambridge, Massachusetts
A Subsidiary of J.B. Lippincott Company

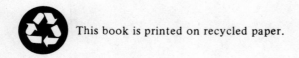 This book is printed on recycled paper.

Prepared under grant numbers 72−NI−99−00096, 73−NI−99−00556, and 74−NI−99−0176 in the National Institute of Law Enforcement and Criminal Justice, grant numbers 76−JN−99−0003 and 76−JJ−99−0452 in the National Institute of Juvenile Justice and Delinquency Prevention, both in the Law Enforcement Assistance Administration, U.S. Department of Justice, and under grant numbers 71−35X−905A1, 71−35X−905A0, 73C−060,231, 74C−084,2332, and 75C−047,2391 in the Massachusetts Committee on Criminal Justice, and with help from the Center for Criminal Justice using funds from Ford Foundation grant 690−0122. Points of view or opinions stated are those of the authors and do not necessarily represent the official position of the U.S. Department of Justice, the Massachusetts Committee on Criminal Justice, or the Ford Foundation.

International Standard Book Number: 0−88410−787−6

Library of Congress Catalog Card Number: 78−7311

Printed in the United States of America

Library of Congress Cataloging in Publication Data

Coates, Robert B
  Diversity in a youth correctional system.

  (Series on Massachusetts youth correction reforms)
  Includes bibliographical recerences and index.
  1. Juvenile corrections—Massachusetts.
2. Massachusetts. Dept. of Youth Services.
3. Community-based corrections—Massachusetts.
I. Miller, Alden D., joint author. II. Ohlin, Lloyd E., joint author.
III. Title. IV. Series.
HV9105.M4C6   364.6'09744   78−7311
ISBN 0−88410−787−6

To Jimmy, Joel and Jeremy

Contents

List of Figures and Tables

Foreword

During the seven-year period from 1969 to 1976, some of the most sweeping reforms in youth corrections in the United States took place in Massachusetts. The state's Department of Youth Services became a highly visible national symbol of a new approach to juvenile corrections through its repudiation of training schools and its advocacy of community-based services. Over the same period the study of these reforms by the Center for Criminal Justice, Harvard Law School, generated a detailed and extensive body of data about the processes of change and their impact. The five books that make up this series are based on that data. In a time of increasing concern about the extent and seriousness of youth crime, this work is of special importance. The books are intended not only to constitute a comprehensive case study but also to explore significant issues of theory and policy and to present an analytic record of experience that will serve as a useful guide to other states that seek to improve the effectiveness of their youth corrections system. More broadly, these books provide important insights into the process and problems of effecting change in human service agencies.

*   *   *

Traditional public training schools have been the focus of criticism for several decades, with attacks coming from three major sources. First, critics have argued that these institutions are partly responsible for high rates of recidivism because of their criminalizing effects on the young people who emerge from them. A second source of criticism has come from proponents of treatment ideologies. They argue that counseling and therapy should replace traditional custodial care, and that youthful offenders should be dealt with at home and in their communities. A third challenge to training schools has come from advocates of the civil rights of children, and has focused on due process, the "right to treatment," and the "right to be left alone." These challenges have put strains on the correctional systems in many states and have raised important questions about whether programs can help young people and still meet a community's demand for protection.

These questions were confronted during a period of crisis, reform, and reaction in Massachusetts correctional policy that made the state a unique site for observation and evaluation. It was at the beginning of this period that the Harvard Center for Criminal Justice inaugurated its study of the reform process. A brief review of the events surrounding the Massachusetts reforms will allow for a better perspective on the scope of this project.

*   *   *

A series of crises in youth correctional services in Massachusetts was followed in 1969 by the resignation of the long-time Director of Youth Services who had strongly supported the use of traditional training schools. Recidivism rates for youth ranged from 40 to 70 percent, and investigations of the system, with accompanying newspaper coverage of its dramatic shortcomings, led civic and professional groups and the public to support reforms.

When Francis Sargent became Governor in 1969, he expressed his strong support for reforming youth services. In the fall of that year he appointed a new commissioner, Dr. Jerome Miller, to head a reorganized Department of Youth Services. Miller took charge with a mandate from the legislative and executive branches of state government and from liberal reform groups to develop new programs, although the scope of the mandate was broad and undefined.

For the first two years Miller sought to create a humanized and therapeutic climate within the existing institutions. Visible symbols of the old system such as dress and haircut requirements were abandoned. This raised a storm of protest from old-line staff who resented such attacks on their absolute control. Miller's order not to strike a youth brought similar outcries. In the early months Miller's efforts were hampered by financial limitations and the tradition-minded bureaucracy he inherited. Nonetheless, by the spring of 1971 Miller and his new planning unit had prepared a reform plan which focused on decentralized, community-based treatment centers—both residential and non-residential.

These moves were met with resistance from the adherents of the old philosophy. Many of them were close to influential legislators and community leaders in the small towns close to the training schools. And they had relationships with judges, probation officers, and public officials, many of whom shared their views about the proper function of the training schools. During his first two years, Miller was faced with two legislative investigations of his reforms.

Meanwhile, Miller decided that therapeutic communities could not be run successfully in the existing institutions, particularly in view of the resistance from old guard personnel. In the most dramatic stage of the reform process, he moved to close the old training schools, to establish a network of decentralized community-based services, and virtually to end locked facilities for youth. He took steps to establish a structure more closely tied to community life: regionalization of services; new court liaisons; diagnostic and referral policies; individual case decisions; the monitoring of services increasingly purchased from private agencies; and staff development programs to reassign, retrain, or discharge former personnel.

Suddenly in January 1973, after three hectic years of change, Miller resigned to become the new director of Family and Children's Services in Illinois. He believed that administrators initiating major reforms invariably become expendable because the hostility which focuses on them creates a barrier to completing the process of reforms and that a new commissioner could best finish the job. When Miller left, financial and personnel problems had not yet been resolved, and a new system of residential and non-residential services had not yet fully replaced the old.

Under Miller's successors as Commissioner, Joseph Leavey and John Calhoun, the Department has consolidated the new network of community-based programs and resolved many of its administrative problems. It has had to contend, however, with a sizable amount of public counter-reaction, including strong pressure to increase the availability of secure facilities to the courts.

Massachusetts has demonstrated that radical changes in official ideology and programs can be achieved over a comparatively short period of time, but the traditional training school system that existed in Massachusetts is still the dominant pattern throughout the country. In light of this situation, it is clear that the Massachusetts reforms, and the political and organizational upheavals that accompanied them, have presented to policy makers and scholars a rich opportunity to study a crucial issue in human services and to learn something as well about complex change in process.

The Center for Criminal Justice at Harvard Law School has taken advantage of this opportunity for the past seven years. This project was undertaken shortly after the Center was established. One of our principal goals in creating the Center was to engage in major empirical projects that would provide data and analytical insights to guide policy makers in the administration of criminal justice. The work reflected in this series of books has been the largest by far of our projects. Under the leadership of Professor Lloyd Ohlin a remarkable group of scholars—the authors of the books in this series—have combined their varied backgrounds and skills to make a major advance in knowledge and theory in a field that has traditionally been dominated by fads, fashions, and untested dogma. This collaborative effort by Ohlin, Miller, Coates, Feld, and McEwen had the benefit of the work of a fine supporting staff and profited from the advisory and critical roles played by other staff members of the Center, our Criminal Justice Fellows and visiting Research Fellows.

Only time tells which intellectual undertakings have a major impact on the development of social institutions. I can only record my sense that this volume—and the others in the series—reflect a rare convergence of a fascinating and significant set of social changes with the tireless, objective and imaginative efforts of a unique group of scholars.

James Vorenberg
Harvard Law School

Preface

This project began in the winter of 1969–70 in anticipation of major reforms in the Massachusetts youth correctional system. From a personal standpoint it represented a fresh opportunity to study two important correctional problems previously explored to some degree in two separate projects: the process and impact of significant changes in correctional policy and the relationship between the organizational structure of correctional programs and peer group subcultures among inmates. An earlier opportunity to study the first issue, change in correctional organizations, occurred from 1953 to 1956 when I directed a study at the University of Chicago of a major change in the Wisconsin prison probation and parole system as a consequence of transfer of corrections to the welfare system. This project, supported by the Russell Sage Foundation, was carried out with the assistance of Donnel M. Pappenfort and Herman Piven and, in the final year, Donald R. Cressey. It yielded many insights into problems of organizational change and the internal dynamics of prison life which have found reflection at various points in the present study. Extensive use has been made of the Wisconsin data to test the generalizability of new theoretical perspectives developed in the analysis of the Massachusetts data and reported most fully in the second book in the series, Miller *et al.*, *A Theory of Social Reform.*

An earlier opportunity to undertake a comparative analysis of the second issue, relating to the effect of organizational differences on peer group subcultures and inmate response to program intervention, occurred from 1957 to 1960 when I codirected with Richard A. Cloward at Columbia University a study of a public and private training school for boys in New York State. The results of this project were never fully developed but generated theoretical insights which were incorporated into our book on *Delinquency and Opportunity* (1960), and into the program of Mobilization for Youth project on the Lower East Side of Manhattan. The Massachusetts data has provided an excellent opportunity to explore much more intensively the sources of subcultural variation, and the books by Feld and McEwen report the results of this objective. In addition, more probing study of inmate response to programs was possible through the analysis of cohort data reported in the volume by Coates *et al.*

Initial explorations in 1969 utilizing staff and fellows of the Center for Criminal Justice led to intensive participant observation and formal interviewing of Department of Youth Services staff and youth in the summer of 1970. The direction of the total project crystallized when I was joined by my associates Alden Miller, late in 1970, and Robert Coates, in 1971. Barry Feld, who had been one of the observer-interviewers in 1970, directed a subculture study in selected institutional cottages in the summer of 1971. This type of study was extended to the community-based programs of the deinstitutionalized system by Craig McEwen in the summer of 1973. Barbara Stolz, who participated in the subculture study of the summer of 1971, began in 1972 a doctoral study of the state-level political process external to DYS. This study was complemented by a parallel dissertation analysis of organizational and political process in the central office of DYS by Arlette Klein.

In approaching the project as a whole, Miller, Coates and I developed a general conceptual framework, an observation guide which was employed throughout most of the study, and a system-oriented strategy of program evaluation. While we worked closely as a team, sharing most decisions in a collegial fashion, there was some specialization in terms of principal interest. I was particularly interested in the construction of a case analysis of the entire reform effort and its relevance to broader trends of correctional policy. Miller was especially interested in the system-wide analysis of the process of change, with an emphasis on the effectiveness of interest group tactics. Coates was particularly concerned with issues of program evaluation in the context of active change, and in the conceptualization of community-based corrections.

During the course of the Harvard study, seventeen separate data-gathering efforts took place, focusing on recidivism, program dynamics, the relations between youth and correctional staff in various settings, and the politics of the reform and counter-reform movements. These components of the overall study are shown in the accompanying diagram in relation to the major historical events of the reform. They combine variously in the present series to form the perspectives from which the authors of the five books viewed the day-to-day reform process in the Massachusetts youth correctional system and in other systems that faced similar upheavals. Each book has important implications for the study, promotion, or restraint of change in other social service settings as well. As briefly summarized here, they range from the most comprehensive perspective to the most particular.

Reforming Juvenile Corrections: The Massachusetts Experience (Ohlin, Coates & Miller) provides a description and analysis of the entire Massachusetts youth correctional reform process and a comparative assessment of the effectiveness of successive correctional policies. The presentation sets the analysis in the context of ideological conflicts about youth in trouble. We discuss successive phases of the reform process and the conditions leading to it, using an analytical structure that guides narrative development and critical discussion while employing data from all seventeen components of the Harvard study. We thus seek to explain from a broad policy perspective not only why and how the changes occurred but what effects they had on youth, staff, and other involved groups.

The series proceeds to a more detailed analysis of the process of change. *A Theory of Social Reform: Correctional Change Processes in Two States* (Miller, Ohlin & Coates) draws extensively on classic sociological literature while using the events in Massachusetts and the earlier correctional reform movement in Wisconsin to develop a conceptual model that identifies key interest group constellations, their critical characteristics and interrelationships, and the dimensions of their impact upon correctional systems. Conclusions based on an analysis of largely qualitative data are tested in the development of a mathematical simulation. The book addresses policy issues centering on ways to promote or hinder reform.

The diversity of programs developed during the reform years offered a natural laboratory for the testing of policy. As some five hundred youths moved through the complex network of Massachusetts correctional programs, including non-residential programs, foster care, forestry, group homes, boarding schools, secure programs, and adult jails, the research staff followed and documented their progress. In *Diversity in a Youth Correctional System: Handling Delinquents in Massachuestts* (Coates, Miller & Ohlin), both the short-run and long-run impact of such program sequences become

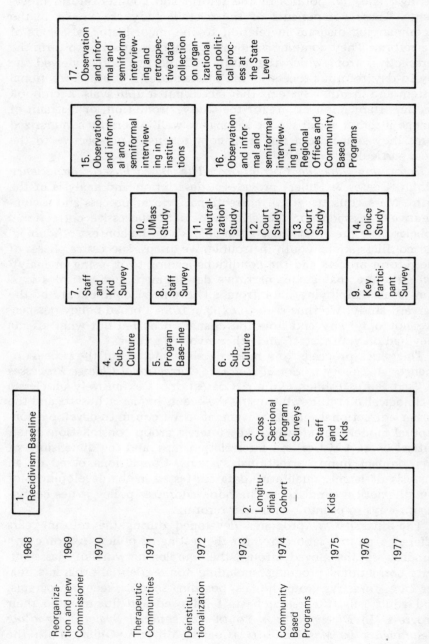

BLOCK PLAN OF STUDY CORRELATED WITH MAJOR CHANGES IN DYS

Components of the Study

1. *Recidivism Baseline:* A study of official records of youth paroled before the reforms to provide a comparison baseline for recidivism of youth passing through the new programs.

2. *Longitudinal Youth Cohort:* Repeated interviewing of youth at different points in their progress through the system from intake to return to the community, along with official records checks of recidivism for comparison with the recidivism baseline.

3. *Cross-Sectional Program Surveys, Staff and Youth:* Interviews to further characterize programs through which youth in the cohort had to pass.

4. *Subculture, 1971:* Interviewing and participant observation in selected programs before the closing of the institutions.

5. *Program Baseline:* Interviewing in institutions immediately prior to the closing.

6. *Subculture, 1973:* Interviewing and participant observation in selected programs after the closing of the institutions.

7. *Staff and Youth Survey:* Interviewing in institutions during the first year after reorganization.

8. *Staff Survey:* Informal interviews of remaining staff in the institutions after most of them had already closed.

9. *Key Participant Survey:* Interviews of staff throughout the reform system after consolidation of the reforms.

10. *University of Massachusetts Study:* Interviews and observation at the University of Massachusetts conference used to place youth taken from the closing institutions.

11. *Neutralization Study:* Interviews with participants and observation of the process of setting up group homes in specific communities, during which attempts were made to neutralize community resistance.

12. *Court Study, 1973:* Interviews and observation to assess the interface between the courts and the Department of Youth Services.

13. *Court Study, 1974:* Continuation of Court Study of 1973.

14. *Police Study:* Interviews, questionnaires, and observation to assess the interface between the police and potential DYS youth.

15. *Observation and Informal and Semiformal Interviewing in Institutions:* Monitoring of the day-to-day process.

16. *Observation and Informal and Semiformal Interviewing in Regional Offices and Community-Based Programs:* Monitoring of the day-to-day process.

17. *Observation and Informal and Semiformal Interviewing and Retrospective Data Collection of Organization and Political Processes at the State Level:* Monitoring of the day-to-day process.

clearly visible through quantitative analysis of longitudinal data characterized by approximately 2,500 variables. By synthesizing and cross-testing various theoretical perspectives on the youth correctional process, we were able to focus important policy issues concerning the quality of life within programs and the extent and quality of linkages to the community, all of which vitally affect the youths' future relationship to society.

A detailed look at the problems of both innovative and more traditional youth program settings is provided in *Designing Correctional Organizations for Youths: Dilemmas of Subcultural Development* (McEwen). Using participant observation and survey methods the author contrasts ten institutional program settings for youth with thirteen others that were part of a community-based system developed to replace the training school system. In calling upon a range of settings unusual in previous subcultural research, McEwen presents a detailed analysis of day-to-day interaction patterns that reflect different policies of community contact, egalitarianism, youth participation in decision-making, degree of supervision, and selection of youth with special background characteristics. These policies and patterns of interaction are then related to outcomes in youth subcultural beliefs, youth behavior, and the relations between youth and staff.

The final volume in the series, *Neutralizing Inmate Violence: Juvenile Offenders in Institutions* (Feld), focuses on a subset of ten program settings for youth, ranged across a custody-treatment continuum within the confines of training school institutions. In this more intensive look at a traditional group of institutions, also used for other comparative purposes in the preceding volume by McEwen, participant observation and survey methods are combined to examine in closer perspective the connection between the official correctional organization and inmate subcultures. The study explores ways of creating diverse patterns of official programs and subcultural responses within the confines of the same institution. Feld focuses sharply on policy issues concerning organizational means for the control of violence in institutional settings and contributes to more general theory of complex organizations.

The series thus offers an opportunity to examine a broad range of theoretical and practical concerns, the interrelationships of which are virtually impossible to perceive in a less comprehensive study. The project was originally designed to do this and was supplemented by special studies as new issues and problems developed in the reform process.

Since the Massachusetts study focused on controversial issues, every effort was made to encompass as wide a range of perspectives on these issues as possible. The theoretical structure of the project was designed to articulate the different interests that coalesced into support or criticism of various reform measures or their consequences. This led us to search out persons holding widely divergent views and, where necessary, to undertake special studies of some groups like judges and police to make sure their perspectives were adequately represented. Our own research staff was composed in such a way as to assure sympathetic understanding of opposing points of view. In fact we encountered the common research experience of staff identification with their respondents, particularly in the course of participant observation. This required special attention to the problem of achieving a balanced assessment over-all by having a variety of interviewers collect data on the same topics.

It should be kept in mind that problems of change and policy implementation in youth corrections have much in common with problems in other human service organizations—adult corrections, mental health, retardation, and welfare social services. The theories and strategies of change, the methods of evaluating service systems and the development and implementation of new policies represent forms of knowledge and insight of equal utility and transferability to these other types of service organizations.

A large number of people have been involved in this study between its inception and the completion of the manuscripts in this series. In addition to Ohlin, Miller, Coates, Feld, McEwen, Stolz, and Klein, whose roles were described above, there has been a large field staff ranging at times up to twenty people. It is not possible to fully state our indebtedness to the dedication and enterprise the field staff displayed or to acknowledge fully their contribution. Here we can only list their names:

Nathaniel Ackerman	Elizabeth Farrell
Henry J. Albach IV	Robert Fitzgerald
Wendy S. Allen	John H. Fleming
Mark E. Ashburn	Gail Garinger
Ira M. Baline	David D. Garwood
William Bazzy	Paula A. Garwood
Bonnie B. Boswell	Geoffrey Ginis
Judith H. Caldwell	Preston B. Grandin
Robert Chilvers	John Greenthal
Roy Cramer	Nancy Hall
Diane C. Engster	Elinor C. Halprin
Finn-Aage Esbensen	Kenneth Hausman
John R. Faith	William Hill

Albert R. Johnson
Stewart W. Kemp
David R. King
Gwen Kinkaid
Neil Koslowe
Cheryl A. La Fleur
Thomas Manley
Jacqueline Miller
Andrea Mintz
Mary Morton
Fern Nesson
Susan Nyman
Gail A. Page
Linda Perle
Clifford Robinson
Wendell P. Russell, Jr.
Kurt L. Schmoke

Fern Selesnick
James R. Shea
Carol Sherman
Shelley Stahl
Mary Strohschein
Kip R. Sullivan
Hollis Sutherland
Arthur R. Swann
Blue Tabor
Eva Teichner
Christian S. Schley
Jane E. Tewksbury
John Troubh
Helene Whittaker
Elizabeth Williams
Anne Yates
Alma Young

Judith Auerbach and Jan Schreiber joined the project during the final year and a half as editors. Though special acknowledgement is included in the author's note to the individual volumes which they edited, the wealth of experience and professionally sound judgment they brought to the overall project proved of enormous help in identifying and clarifying the special contributions of each of the books and the series as an articulated whole. Marion Coates did most of the computer programming after 1971 and brought to this task great patience and perseverance in setting up and checking out complicated forms of data processing. An expert consulting team from the firm of Peat, Marwick, Mitchell and Co., led by Robert Nielson, undertook the very difficult task of a comparative cost analysis of the old and new correctional programs.

Secretaries who worked on the project included Christine Conniff, Deborah Cooper, Lorna Dumapias, James Franklin, Kathleen T. Gardner, Nancy Le Massena, Nancy J. March, Darnney L. Proudfoot, and Lucille Young.

Throughout the course of the project we received support and useful suggestions from Center staff members and directors of other projects at the Center. Most of all, however, we are deeply indebted to Professor James Vorenberg, Director of the Center. From the beginning Jim provided constant encouragement, criticism, and professional judgment, especially when trouble-shooting was needed in periods of crisis. Rosanne Kumins, Administrative Assistant of the Center, could always be counted on for help in moving the project along through innumerable hazards, but she also managed our budgets and accounts despite the exasperating complexities of coordinating funds from different sources. I am personally grateful to Harvard Law School Dean Albert M. Sacks for his encouragement and generous grants of research leave so that I might remain deeply involved in the research effort.

Special assistance was provided by staff of the funding agencies, especially James Howell of the Office of Juvenile Justice and Delinquency Prevention, Law Enforcement Assistance Administration, U.S. Department of Justice, and Robert Cole and Karen Joerg of the Massachusetts Committee on Criminal Justice. The Massachusetts Office of the Commissioner of Probation, under the direction of Elliot Sands, Commissioner, Joseph Foley, Assistant Commissioner, and Mark Santapio, in charge of the records, was of great help in securing data on recidivism.

Obviously, the study could not have been done at all without the generous cooperation of the staff and youth of the Massachusetts Department of Youth Services throughout the project with the constant support of Commissioner Jerome Miller, his successor Commissioner Joseph Leavey, and finally the present Commissioner John Calhoun.

Funding for the project came from several sources. The project was begun using the Center's own funds from its original Ford Foundation grant. Beginning in 1971 the project was funded in large part by the Massachusetts Committee on Criminal Justice, and aided by matching funds from the Center's Ford Foundation grant. In 1972 additional funds were granted by the National Institute of Law Enforcement and Criminal Justice, Law Enforcement Assistance Administration, U.S. Department of Justice. This support was later taken over by the Office of Juvenile Justice and Delinquency Prevention, when that office was founded and eventually became the principal source of funds for the project as a whole in its final two years.

Lloyd E. Ohlin
Harvard Law School

Authors' Note

This book and the research on which it is based has benefited from the talents and efforts of many individuals.
Conducting a seven year study of a rapidly changing service agency required openness and cooperation on the part of central
office, regional and program staff. Without their assistance in gaining
access to programs, tracking youth, and developing insights into the
day-to-day problems of dealing with youth, the project could not
have been completed. Equally important has been the readiness of
youths in our samples to share their understandings and feelings
about what was happening in their world. In many instances, particularly when interviewing youths on the street, youngsters would
be able to help us find others in the sample about whom we lacked
follow-up information. Such occasions demonstrated their belief
that what we were doing might some day make a difference, if not
for them, at least for others in similar circumstances.

A special word of thanks is due our field research staff. Their
schedules had to be fitted to those of staff members and youths.
Many interviews were conducted in the evenings and on weekends.
Their tasks were fraught with frustration by broken appointments,
scanty information on where to locate youths, and travel conditions.
However, they brought to their jobs high energy and dedication
which enabled them to take these difficulties in stride.

The actual preparation of this book was also helped immensely by
the contributions of several individuals. The programming skills and
patience of Marion Coates allowed us to take a massive amount of
data and break it down into meaningful and interpretable blocks.

Discussion of the relationships between youths engaged in delinquent activity and the public schools was greatly enhanced by reaction to early drafts by Peg Billings. We are especially grateful to Barbara McDonald who expended a lot of time and energy responding to the rough drafts of each chapter providing insights, stimulation and editorial assistance. Finally, we appreciate the skills of Jan Schrieber who edited the chapters in their final stages.

Robert B. Coates
Alden D. Miller
Lloyd E. Ohlin
April 27, 1978

**Diversity in a Youth
Correctional System**

Introduction

During the past fifteen years much rhetoric, considerable financial resources, and substantial efforts have been expended in diverse sections of this country to replace institutions with community-based programs as the primary means of handling juvenile delinquents. Today, more youths are placed in community settings than in the past. A few states now place less reliance on training schools and more on networks of community-based programs.

While the nation has garnered considerable experience with community-based corrections and has seen some limited success in the reduction of crime, much of that experience remains inconclusive because in most instances the scope of the intended change was indeed small. Typically, community-based programs have operated as appendages to a much larger training-school system [1]. That such programs have had little impact should not be surprising. Too frequently the programs have only been allowed to handle either the less serious youth offenders or youngsters who would not have originally been in the correctional system (e.g., some school truants or "disobedient" children have been admitted in order to participate in new model programs) [2].

As a result, many issues concerning the potential of community-based programming for juvenile corrections as a whole remain unresolved. In the first place, there is little consensus about what actually constitutes community-based corrections. Second, little is known about the impact of community-based programming when

2 Diversity in a Youth Correctional System

implemented on a large scale. Third, the question of how one evaluates the new programs remains largely unanswered. Fourth, little is actually known about what kinds of programs work best with what kinds of youths. Finally, very little work has been devoted to understanding the process of successfully reintegrating youths into communities. These are but a few of the issues to be addressed in this book, and it appears unlikely that these issues will be resolved in the near future. However, the data and analyses presented here should provide the reader with the tools to grapple more intelligently with these important theoretical and policy issues.

The research on which this book is based comprised a seven-year effort to document and analyze the changes taking place since 1969 in the Massachusetts Department of Youth Services (DYS). Massachusetts provides a unique opportunity for probing issues of community-based corrections because it has gone further than any other state toward actually replacing a training-school system with a community based system [3].

Rather than focusing on a single program or a small number of programs, this research has focused on a single state's entire network of programs for delinquent youths committed through the courts to correctional facilities. As noted in the preface, other volumes stemming from this overall project have concentrated on a small set of programs, providing fairly rich detail on their day-to-day operations [4]. This book, like the research project itself, directly addresses the system or network of some 150 programs. The emphasis here, therefore, is on developing typologies and conceptual schema that permit one to look at a large number of programs and see how they fit together rather than singling out a model program effort. We will examine issues confronting the management of the system, the impact of the system on youths, and to a lesser extent the intricacies of individual programming.

Accordingly, we shall address five central questions: (1) To what extent is the reformed system in Massachusetts community based? (2) Compared to the institutional system, what is the effect of the reformed system on the youths being processed through it? (3) Within the reformed system, what are the differential impacts on youths of experiencing programs of different types and to varying degrees community based? (4) What factors tend to impede or facilitate reintegration? (5) What policy implications for managing a community-based system can be drawn from closely observing the Massachusetts effort? Our primary focus is on the impact of changes on youths. Therefore, the principal data sources analyzed in this book are a series of interviews with youths. However, throughout the book and especially in the concluding chapter, interviews with staff and observations of program operations will be drawn upon to extend our analysis and interpretations. Observations and findings contained in other volumes of this series will be drawn on occasionally to set this analysis and the resulting policy recommendations in the broadest possible context.

The Massachusetts Department of Youth Services is not being held up as a system to be replicated intact elsewhere. It has had some successes and some failures. But most importantly from our perspective, it has provided an opportunity to study closely the deinstitutionalization process and the difficulties of putting together and managing a community-based system. Thus, other states have the chance to learn from the experience in Massachusetts how to avoid certain common pitfalls.

This book contains eight chapters plus appendices. Chapter 1 lays out the conceptual model used for describing community-based services and presents a case for expanding the traditional conception of the corrections arena. Chapter 2 briefly describes the reform efforts undertaken to modify the training schools, the actions taken to actually close them, and the steps taken to form an alternative community-based system. This chapter also compares the quality of life within the institutions with that in the community-based system. Chapter 3 lays out the research design of the study in a nontechnical manner, sharing with the reader some of the practical problems that faced this project. An evaluation model is constructed that should prove valuable to others who are attempting to evaluate action programs undergoing change. Chapter 4 is the first chapter that presents data based on the core sample described in this book: a longitudinal sample of nearly 500 youths who were repeatedly interviewed from detention through the DYS programs until they had been in the community for six months. This chapter focuses on the detention decisions and the short-run consequences of detention. Chapter 5 identifies the factors that tended to influence where individual youths were placed within the mix of programs available through DYS. Chapter 6 looks at the short-run and long-run consequences of having been in different kinds of program settings. Factors such as self-image and relations with significant others are considered. Chapter 7 contains an analysis of recidivism data. System rates and program rates are compared, and an attempt is made to identify those factors most critical for hindering or facilitating reintegration. Chapter 8 takes all of the data presented and draws on the foregoing analysis to identify policy implications for the management of a community-based system.

Chapter 1

Looking Anew at the Corrections Arena

Every reform can be studied from a variety of perspectives. It should be clear to any reader of the various books in this series that a number of theoretical perspectives and research questions have converged within the larger framework of the study. In this chapter and in the next two chapters we will try to explain why certain issues and not others are addressed as we look at the impact of the reforms on youths. We will also specify some of the assumptions that guided the formulation of questions and the choice among research designs.

Given the major reform effort made in the Massachusetts Department of Youth Services (DYS) to shift from institutional care to community-based care, we will begin this chapter by exploring what is meant by the concept of community-based corrections. From that discussion we will make a case for expanding the correctional framework to correspond to the practicalities of providing community-based care. We will briefly describe how an interactionist perspective has influenced our manner of looking at the outcomes of the reform. We will introduce the reader to the institutionalization-normalization continuum—a theoretical construct that guides much of our analysis of programs and program outcomes. Finally, we will consider how the continuum can be applied at various levels to human services.

THE MEANING OF COMMUNITY-BASED CORRECTIONS [1]

During the past decade, human services, including corrections, have gradually moved away from institution-based to community-based services. Some observers would describe this movement as a passing fad or a surface "bandwagon" phenomenon. The movement is probably not a fad; it seems likely to persist. But it certainly has benefited from the bandwagon effect. Nearly every state now has its showcase programs to publicize its progressive approach to serving human needs, and many states are moving at a fairly rapid pace to reduce the number of youths housed in institutions.

"Community-based services" remains, however, an ill-defined term connoting a heterogeneous collection of strategies for handling juvenile and adult offenders. For example, a halfway house may mean halfway in or halfway out. In what ways does a halfway house differ from a group home, a shelter care facility, a camp, or a ranch? What dimensions discriminate among community-based and institution-based programs? Is it location, level of control, public vs. private administration, or range of services provided? There is little common understanding among those who work in the field as to the appropriate answers to these questions. This lack of agreement detracts from public acceptance and effectiveness of policies promoting community-based care, and it makes systematic research, planning, and implementation difficult.

Because of the emphasis in Massachusetts on closing institutions and establishing community-based care as well as our own objective of evaluating the extent to which the new system impeded or facilitated reintegration, we have been forced to try to bring some clarity to the question. We begin by focusing directly on the implications of the words "community" and "based."

The word community is currently overworked in everyday conversation since it seems to capture what so many of us find lacking. It can mean many things: a small number of people sharing similar ideas; a specific territory in which a number of people reside; a "we" spirit. In this book, community means *the smallest local territory that incorporates a network of relationships providing most of the goods and services required by persons living within the boundaries of the territory* [2]. These services include such things as schools, employment, markets, banks, churches, and sanitation services.

This definition of community is helpful to our concept of community-based services in two ways. First, it differentiates a neighborhood as a subcomponent part of a community, for neighborhoods do not have networks of relationships to provide a sufficient number of goods and services. Second, the restriction of the term to the smallest localized territory providing such a network means that we can talk of smaller units than metropolitan areas if necessary.

Given this definition of community with its focus on relationships, how should we conceive of community-based corrections? Specifically, how do we isolate those essential qualities that make some programs more community based than others?

The words community based focus our attention on the nature of the linkages between programs and the network of relationships comprising a community. For example, we are interested in knowing to what extent programs are able to gain access to community services such as schools, work opportunities, and recreational facilities. A key set of variables that provides a basis for differentiating among programs is the *extent* and *quality* of relationships between program staff, clients, and the community in which the program is located. (If clients come from outside the program community itself, relationships need to be considered with both the community in which the program is located and the community from which the client comes or to which the client will return.) The nature of these client and staff relationships with the community provides the underpinning for a continuum of services ranging from the least to the most community based. Generally, as frequency, duration, and quality of community relationships increase, the program becomes more community based [3]. Before discussing the implications of that continuum, let us further explore variations in these community relationships.

Frequency and duration of community relationships are important in this concept of community-based corrections, but the quality of relationships is especially so. The chain gangs of an earlier era set inmates to work in the community outside the prison walls but did not yield the kind of relationships with the community that are envisioned here. The relationships of particular interest to us are those which support offenders' efforts at becoming reestablished and functioning in legitimate roles. Included, among others, are relationships that encourage clients, enable clients to appreciate their self-worth, match community resources to client needs, and advocate for better community resources and freer access to those resources.

From a pragmatic point of view, a wide range of actions may be taken by a program to create supportive client relationships with a community. Those actions may be directed toward at least four levels of community intervention. First, actions may be directed at private and public agencies to encourage support for a client and his family. This may entail efforts to cause a neighborhood youth corps or state employment agency to supply jobs, a YMCA or YWCA to provide a place of residence, or a public welfare agency to provide financial help for family assistance. Second, actions may be designed to cause community institutions such as schools and churches to provide alternative educational programs, lay counseling, emergency shelters, or hot lines. Third, efforts may be directed at formal and informal voluntary community groups to educate the public about client needs and about ways in which civic groups may provide supportive assistance. Fourth, actions may be directed toward local residents to elicit the residents' support for the program, the clients, and a redirection of the community's response to youth and adult offenders.

This concept of *extent* (i.e., frequency and duration) and *quality* of the relationships to the community as the key indicators helps to distinguish the degree to which services are community based. The continuum composed of the variable dimensions of community relationships adds more realism to the concept of community corrections than would a classification with mutually exclusive categories that would sacrifice information and be less workable and useful. It also reflects the reality that, given the varying needs of specific offenders and specific communities, no system can afford to have all of its programs lodged at either end of the continuum.

The underlying continua, that is, relationships, are tangible and thereby subject to measurement. Relationships between program clients, staff, and the community can be counted and assigned priority. For example, relationships may involve community residents participating in "in-house" activities, but a higher priority should be placed on clients developing relationships that permit exchange within the *larger* community. The quality of relationships can also be measured. For example, they can be evaluated as helpful or harmful and further classified as to how they are helpful or harmful.

Consider job training programs. Programs that offer only job training could be compared to those programs that offer job placement along with training. The latter programs are likely to reflect greater emphasis on generating supportive linkages between the client and the community. The continuum could be used specifically to compare the relative merits of different group homes or probation departments. More generally, data might be collected to compare broad strategies of treatment ranging from maximum security institutions to nonresidential services. A data base could also be developed to allow for comparing systems from state to state. Thus the concept developed here, which focuses on relationships, has considerable import for research, quality control, and system-wide policy-making.

Knowing the treatment model being used in a facility does not necessarily tell us whether or not it is community-based. For example, if we know that program A employs guided group interaction, that fact tells us nothing about the program's relationship to the community. With its emphasis on community relationships, our continuum helps the practitioner identify those aspects of a program that make it genuinely community-based. In short, the continuum concept underscores the idea that even a "happy, caring" group residence is not enough unless it affects relationships with the larger community. Thus pinpointing community relationships as the key set of variables emphasizes consideration of two staff responsibilities, whatever the specific treatment model may be: (1) matching clients with existing community resources and (2) working with the community to generate resources where they are lacking.

We believe that this conceptualization of community based represents a step beyond some of the more simplistic definitions current in the field. By using the above conceptualization, one cannot assume that a correctional facility that is neither a training school nor an institution with bars is necessarily a community-based program. That remains an empirical question that can be answered only by looking at the extent and quality of relationships with the community. Similarly, locating a program in an urban setting instead of a distant rural region is no guarantee that it will develop any linkages with the community. We all know of too many programs that are merely islands within the community—small institutions, but nonetheless institutions.

Looking at the extent and quality of relationships of program staff, clients, and the local community provides a basis for differentiation. The concept of relationship is concrete and measurable. It can be dealt with on a general level that permits broad comparison, or it can be measured in a fairly specific and exacting way that permits comparison among individual programs. The utility of this concept does not depend on our ability to categorize programs neatly as groups homes, foster care, or nonresidential services because the label of the program is unimportant. The more a program involves clients in community activities, the more it is community based [4].

BROADENING THE CONCEPT
OF THE CORRECTIONS ARENA

Using this notion of community-based services as a standard, how do youth corrections in general measure up? Poorly! Traditionally, the arena of corrections has embraced a narrow and restrictive view of its clients. It has fostered a client-centered emphasis, whether with individual- or group-oriented treatment. Lip service is sometimes paid to acting directly upon the panoply of forces affecting a youngster, but all too often the action taken by correctional staff is directed solely at the youth. Action directed at families, peer groups, schools, community elites, and others who make important decisions about the youth is viewed as politically much more sensitive than actions directed at the youth alone.

While it is true that over the past several decades some decision-makers have experimented with greater community emphasis, it is equally true that the primary mode of working with youths has remained focused on the individual youngster, typically within a training school setting and largely divorced from the networks within which the youth normally functions and to which he or she will most likely return [5]. For the most part, research has also ignored the vast arena in which a youth lives out his or her day-to-day experiences. Typically a research approach will look at the specific treatment modality of a program, attempt to determine the effect it has had on the particular youngster, and then obtain some kind of recidivism measure. This approach often ignores any unintended consequences of the treatment, including positive consequences that may be indirect gains of the treatment, and places the responsibility for recidivism solely on the correctional program.

The theoretical model developed in this chapter takes the perspective that the correctional arena is much broader than generally acknowledged. Beyond the individual youngster, it takes into consideration and directs action toward families, peers, schools, and other youth-serving groups in the community. In short, the arena of youth corrections thus defined encompasses the youth in the youth's total life situation.

This position has emerged gradually under two principal influences. First, it is shaped by the authors' experience with the delinquency phenomenon and their understanding of the delinquency literature [6]. Second, it has come about in response to the reform effort within DYS, which had as its overriding purpose the goal of reaching out to youths in their communities.

The reform objectives were far-reaching and affected many youth-service systems. First and probably foremost was the desire to change a training-school system into a community-based system. Among other things, this entailed setting up program and staffing arrangements that would take advantage of existing community resources or, where they were lacking, advocating for resources for youths. It involved interacting with other systems to define more sharply which youths should be served in the department. Younger youths were screened out to be handled by the welfare department. Limits were placed on the number of youths in detention, especially secure detention. Court liaison officers worked in the courts to influence the adjudication and disposition process directly. Removal of status offenders from the DYS system was supported. DYS officials took an active role in advocating the closing of the county-operated training schools, which primarily served a truant population. In addition, throughout the early years of reform a campaign was waged to influence public opinion at the state and local levels to be more favorably disposed toward the rights and needs of children.

Thus, to have narrowly interpreted the original objective of the reform effort as specifically focused only on youths in the correctional system, apart from their networks, or on the ability of individual programs to bring about specific individual change, or as affecting only the correctional system would have been a grave misreading of reformist intentions in this situation.

THEORETICAL FRAMEWORK:
THE INSTITUTIONALIZATION-
NORMALIZATION CONTINUUM

Our theoretical model was developed to clarify the parameters of the correctional issues we were observing and to provide a basis for evaluating in broad terms the correctional system under study. The theoretical framework underpinning our conceptualization of deviance in general and the correctional arena specifically is interactionist in character. Youths are viewed not only as being acted upon by other persons and social institutions, but also as actors in their own right [7]. These joint actions are critically important. Interactions with parents, siblings, peers, teachers, police, and significant others shape to a large extent their involvement in deviant and conforming acts. Actions by various gatekeepers including teachers, youth workers, police, and judges play an important role in determining which behaviors are officially regarded as delinquent and which youths committing such acts will be formally processed as delinquents. Neither their participation in delinquency nor their categorization as delinquents is treated as a given, but it remains a product of a complex set of relationships.

A youngster is frequently pulled in several different directions with competing groups in conflict for the youth's allegiance and commitment to their sets of values and expectations [8]. A classic conflict may develop over parental values and those of the peer group. Or conflict may emerge between peers, each of whom wants the youth to adopt a different course of action. The youngster in question may very well capitalize on the conflicts by playing one group off against another—here again the youth is not simply being acted upon.

Even if two youngsters commit the same act, officially defined as delinquent, they may not be handled in the same manner. One may have been typically described as a "good kid," and this youth's act, seen as constituting a rare event, may be attributed to the need to "let off steam." The other youth may have been seen as a failure in school, may come from a "bad family," or have had other negative experiences and therefore may be regarded as embarking on a delinquent career, thus requiring formal processing through the juvenile justice system [9]. Two youths exhibiting similar behavior may also be treated differently because one family is presumed to have more power to deflect formal processing.

Recognizing the importance of viewing deviance and conformity as consequences of an interaction process, we have broadened our view of the correctional arena. We now take into account the nature of relationships in which the youngster was enmeshed before being committed to DYS, look carefully at the sets of relationships in which youths are engaged while in DYS, and consider as best we can the unfolding sets of relationships that characterize a youth's situation as the youth returns to the community.

The core of our theoretical model is the institutionalization-normalization continuum, which is used to distinguish among different kinds of relationships. The term institution in correctional parlance calls up images of prison buildings isolated by distance or high walls from the surrounding community. As the community-based movement has progressed, many people have realized that even such facilities as group homes can share with the old-walled institutions an isolation that, it turns out, does not necessarily depend upon physical barriers. Thus, institutionalization, a term reflecting process, is commonly used in corrections to refer to the effect of institutional settings such as maximum security prisons and secure mental hospitals on its clients.

We view institutionalization as a term that represents in essence a qualitative description of a set of relationships within the setting and across the boundaries of the setting. According to Goffman, the "encompassing or total character [of total institution] is symbolized by the barrier to social intercourse with the outside and to departure that is often built right into the physical plant, such as locked doors, high walls, barbed wire, cliffs, water, forests, or moors" [10]. The physical plant itself becomes less critical for differentiating among relationships when we realize that across societies and throughout history various groups of people have been systematically denied access to social intercourse and resources because of social class, race, and religion. Being locked in a physical space may be a characteristic of only some forms of institutionalization. Thus in our framework we consider institutionalization to imply relationships that generally seek to exclude youths from resources potentially available in other relationship networks or systems. The exclusion may be controlled by the use or threat of force, or it may be much more subtly brought about by the application of labels such as "hard-core delinquent," "intractable," "slow learner," or "retarded."

We believe that the institutionalization-normalization continuum with its emphasis on relationships can be generalized to apply to relationship sets other than simply correctional programs. One can imagine, falling on our extreme institutionalization pole, relationships within families, schools, peer groups, and correctional programs that attempt to restrict a youngster's access to resources outside the boundaries of the principal relationship set being analyzed. An example might be a family that has turned inward to keep a retarded child isolated at home. The archetype remains the maximum security prison, which is tightly monitored and cuts off nearly all contact with relationship networks outside its walls. Still other examples of institutional relationships such as monasteries may be cited, which are considered benign though equally divorced from external networks [11]. Similarly the theocracies and other attempts to build utopian communities today and in centuries past were also very isolated, depending upon tight controls to maintain the internal community spirit that was so critical for the survival of the experiment. Examples today would include the Hare Krishna movement and Synanon groups.

In yet another setting and at a more microscopic level, we can consider the institutional effects of some tracking systems within a school building. Those youths of whom teachers expect little are set aside in their own classes and classrooms. Within the school system they may rarely meet students from other tracks. Because they are in different classes, recesses and lunches are taken at different times. They may encounter one another through organized sports, but even there many in the lower tracks will, almost by definition, be ineligible to participate.

A family that will not send its children to an accredited school, that tightly monitors the social intercourse of its offspring, and that denies its youngsters access to health care can be regarded qualitatively as fostering a form of institutionalization. While these youngsters are not physically locked in the house, they are denied the opportunities for social and physical development available to others.

The other pole of the continuum, normalization, represents a situation in which a youth has fairly open access to resources both within the specific relationship set under study—be it family, school, peer group, or correctional program—and within the larger relationship networks. A family setting where youths are supported and respected and allowed to have open access to the community with appropriate controls would typify a normalized situation. We would also expect that the caring within the family would spill over into the relationships that the youths have outside the family. That is, if a youngster is having difficulty at school, a parent would attempt to sort out and negotiate the problem with the child and the teacher. A more normalized school setting would provide for a variety of interests of students, would foster fluid movement of students in and out of specialized programs without categorizing or labeling, and would encourage involvement of parents.

For churches, a normalized church setting would not be ingrown but would engage in active exchange with persons and issues outside its physical boundaries. In this sense both the congregation oriented toward social action and the more fundamental proselytizing congregation may be more normalized than the congregation that does not want to "become involved" and simply perpetuates its weekly rituals. Within the correctional arena the more normalized settings maintain linkages with the larger community and attempt to nurture constructive relationships for youths with significant others such as parents, teachers, and employers.

It should be clear to the reader that while our primary objective in this book is to look at how youths are processed through correctional programs and the longer run consequences of that experience, the qualitative character of relationships in those programs have many similarities with other sets of relationships in which youths participate. The institutionalization-normalization continuum can, therefore, be generalized to apply to relationship sets outside correctional programs.

We will now turn to a discussion of the dimensions that underpin our continuum. Because our primary focus is in the corrections arena most of the illustrative material will be drawn from that field. As we proceed, the reader can note that one could just as easily adopt examples from other relationship sets such as schools, families, or peer groups.

We can define the continuum as having three dimensions. The first is *social climate* or the nature and quality of the relationships within an interaction or relationship set, be it a family, peer group, or correctional program. The second is the *extent* of relationships permitted outside the relationship set. The third is the *quality* of interaction outside the relationship set. In the correctional world, this perspective would place considerable emphasis on looking at what happens to a youth outside a specific correctional setting, thus permitting one to determine to what extent the program is community based and what types of community interaction and participation are encouraged. Each of these dimensions and their subdimensions will be discussed in some detail below.

For illustrative purposes, the dimensions and subdimensions as they apply to the correctional arena are presented in Table 1−1, which depicts the ideal type of institutionalized setting and the ideal type of normalized setting. Although the continuum is bounded by ideal polar types, it is important to note that actual relationship sets in general and actual correctional programs are more likely to be found at intermediate points between these two types.

Social Climate [12]

The social climate of correctional settings is defined by the nature and quality of relationships among youths and between youths and staff. In families it would be among siblings and between children and parents. In schools it would be among students and between students and teachers and administrators, and so on, depending on the relationship set. The first subdimension we will consider, communication, is the flow of information within the program. Do youths feel that they are adequately informed about what is happening to them in the context of the relationships? How is communication between youths and others in and outside the setting monitored and controlled? Earlier research on institutions has shown that considerable strain may arise within correctional settings because residents do not know what is happening and are unable to predict what will happen [13]. In addition, the monitoring of communications has been shown to be an integral part of institutionalization, which strips away one's sense of privacy. To the extent that one's behavior and communications are known to others in these settings, the situation approximates what Lofland describes as an integrated round [14]. A segregated round is a situation in which individuals have opportunity for private communications and a sense of privacy.

The second subdimension, *decision-making*, is the extent to which youths exercise some control over what happens to them. While it is unlikely that youngsters will be dealt with as the equals of staff in correctional settings, some settings foster more decision-making by

Table 1–1. Poles of the Institutionalization-Normalization Continuum Represented by Ideal Types

Dimensions and Subdimensions	Institutionalized Setting	Normalized Setting
I. Social Climate		
A. Communication	Communications within facility closely monitored. Institutional personnel determine what will be communicated to whom.	Persons are free to communicate to whomever they wish about what-ever they wish.
B. Decision-making	Very little shared decisions. Where shared decisions exist they are frequently the result of negotiations with the inmate subculture. The inmate subculture has its own pecking order and limited participa-tion in decision-making. Thus some inmates feel isolated from both the formal and informal control systems.	Clients are encouraged to play an active role in decision-making. Clients are able to reject aspects of the program without negative consequences.
C. Nature of control	Strong-arm tactics by inmates and staff. Threat of physical abuse. Stripping away of routine rewards. Using parole date as a means of control.	More reliance on rewarding positive behavior. Identification with staff and program. No hammer; if client decides to leave program he will not be hassled.
D. Client perception of fairness	Likely to perceive system as abusive and unjust. System caters to a few. Where perceived as fair, perception rests on consistency and predict-ability, not on justice.	Different clients handled equally, or if uniquely, then with clearly explained reasons flowing from universally applied just principles.

II. Extent of Community Linkage		
A. Frequency	Infrequent contacts with people from the outside. Contacts occur within institution.	Frequency depends on the client, but is encouraged.
B. Duration	Brief, transitory.	Duration depends on the client, but is encouraged.
III. Quality of Community Linkage		
A. Communication	Communications with people on the outside are monitored.	Communications are not physically monitored. Staff may talk to client about his communications.
B. Decision-making	Decisions about whom one can talk to subject to approval by institution administrators.	Clients are encouraged to make decisions about the kinds of linkages they want.
C. Nature of control	Actual contact inside is observed. People from outside searched.	Little direct punishment if client fails to fully develop linkages. Contacts not directly observed. Ultimate control: if client fails to work his situation out and gets into further trouble, he will be back in the justice system.
D. Fairness	Community does not give client a "fair break."	Community gives client a fair chance of "making it."
E. Access to community resources	Largely determined by institution administrators; they must approve the use of any resources—inmates in some cases legitimately refuse resources.	Only limit to access to community are the abilities of clients and staff or significant others to encourage the community to respond on his behalf—a limitation that should not be minimized.

youths than others. Prior research has pointed out the importance for residents of having some sense of control over their own destinies [15]. The total institution is often characterized as holding to a minimum the involvement of inmates in decision-making. Frequently in these kinds of settings, inmates resort to setting up a peer subculture to govern their affairs. Within these subcultures some inmates have more freedom to exercise their decisions than do others. Within the more normalized correctional settings much more emphasis is placed on interactions with the larger community, thus reducing the frequency of contact among clients and the necessity of having a highly structured client subculture for ordering the distribution of rewards and punishments [16].

The subdimension *nature of control* refers to the manner in which persons are rewarded or punished for their behavior. Participants in any social system experience various kinds of rewards and sanctions. In a correctional setting, the nature of control and the need for it are frequently intense. Control mechanisms can be very explicit, such as the use or threat of physical force, or more subtle, for example, the setting of parole dates or the implementation of a specific treatment model such as the therapeutic community approach [17].

The subdimension *fairness* refers to youth's assessment of the justness of relationships within the setting. Does the youngster believe that he or she is being treated fairly? Does the youngster believe that the setting favors some youths more than others? In corrections, the fairness issue has taken on more relative importance in recent years as more policy-makers have recognized the marginal impact of specific treatment strategies [18]. The consensus seems to be that, whether or not treatment proves effective, the system should at least function fairly for all who are processed through it [19].

Extent of Community Linkage

The second major dimension, extent of community linkage, is the amount of contact between youths and persons in the larger community, occurring either in the community or in the relationship setting (correctional programs, family, school, or church). The subdimensions, which are self-evident, are *frequency* and *duration*. Our assumption is that the more frequent and durable the contacts the more significant are a youngster's relationships with outside persons.

Quality of Community Linkage

The third major dimension focuses attention on the quality of community linkage. In an attempt to synthesize several theoretical positions, Friday and Hagen identify five major patterns of role relationships—family, community or neighbor, school, work, and peers—that largely determine delinquency involvement. They hypothesize that "if youth have intimate role relationships in all five areas or kinds, they are much less likely to engage in youth crime [20]. The intimacy or quality of these kinds of role relationships is what we have in mind as we look at the nature of community linkage. For the most part, the subdimensions parallel those describing the social climate of the program. Here we again look at the *communication* process, however, now between the youth and the people in the community outside the principal relationship under consideration. Likewise youth participation in *decision-making* in the outside community, the manner by which the outside community attempts to *control* youth behavior, and the youngster's perception of *fairness* by the outside community will help to differentiate the overall nature of the relationship setting.

In addition to these subdimensions, *access to community resources* is also considered. Here we have in mind two concerns. First, what kinds of resources are brought to bear on the youth's circumstance? And second, what is being done by adults in the relationship set to generate new resources or at least access to resources heretofore restricted from the youth? It is at this point that the level of advocacy by the adults comes under close scrutiny. We contend that even small amounts of data on these dimensions and subdimensions will permit researchers and policy-makers to differentiate among various kinds of relationship settings along a continuum ranging from the total institution to a normalized setting.

We have stated the underlying characteristics of the institutionalization-normalization continuum in general terms, drawing illustrations from diverse social settings such as the family, school, church, and correctional programs, because we believe that this conceptual scheme is useful in analyzing and evaluating the quality of interaction across a broad range of social settings and relationships. The three dimensions and their subdimensions can be used to compare the degree to which some structural arrangements facilitate more normalized environments than others. The continuum can also be used to make comparisons across relationship settings: for example, in general how do schools compare to churches or correctional programs in normalization? What are the strengths of each type of setting? On which dimensions do they yield normalized scores? What are their weaknesses?

The continuum can also be used to compare different types of structural arrangements within one kind of relationship set. For example, this book has a primary focus on differences across programs

in a correctional system. One could, however, compare an open classroom with a more traditionally run classroom. Or one could look at
comparative normalization scores between so-called establishment
churches and the newer gatherings associated with the Jesus movement. Furthermore, the continuum can be used to draw comparisons
within subsets—differences among groups within the Jesus movement
or differences among group homes in the correctional arena. As has
been suggested by some who have reviewed this model, the continuum also has considerable potential as both a monitoring and training tool at the individual staff level. A teacher, an advocate, or a
foster parent can be rated on the extent to which he or she facilitates
positive scores on each of the dimensions and subdimensions.

We contend, therefore, that serious consideration of what actually
constitutes community-based services forces us to think anew about
the scope of corrections. Much of what has heretofore passed as community based must be recognized for what it is—the establishment of
small institutions that nevertheless remain just as isolated as the
larger institutions they were designed to augment or replace.

Chapter 2

The Massachusetts Department of Youth Services: The Emergence of Diversity Out of Chaos

Over a period of years, the Massachusetts Department of Youth Services (DYS) has moved further and at a faster pace toward deinstitutionalization and the establishment of a community-based network of services for delinquent youths than any other state. The unique facet of this reform effort has been its system-wide focus. Rather than merely setting up some showcase community-based programs, the reformers attacked the backbone of the institutional system, beginning with the most secure facility available for juveniles and eventually including all of the major training schools. In their place they established a vast network of programs primarily purchased from the private sector. Most of these new settings handled a varied population of youths instead of working only with the DYS youngster. As we will see, the network of programs provided a range of diverse settings and services never available or envisioned within the institutional system.

A detailed history of the change process and the factors that made possible the radical restructuring of a bureaucracy such as DYS is available elsewhere in this series [1]. Here we are principally interested in showing historically what the institutional system was like. We shall describe settings and programs and point to some of the indicators of the quality of life in the system. The new system will likewise be described and some of the pivotal decisions involved in shaping it will be outlined. The impact of this system as compared with the institutional system will be analyzed throughout the remaining chapters of the book.

AN OVERVIEW OF THE REFORM EFFORT

The following is a brief account of the major efforts that directly affected programming for youths. The seven-year period is divided somewhat arbitrarily into four time periods for illustrative purposes.

The Training-School System and Pressures for Change in 1969

The institution-based system that Jerome Miller, the new commissioner of DYS, inherited in October of 1969 was ripe for modest reform. It was not, however, prepared for the massive changes that would occur over the next three to four years. In 1969 the system consisted of three detention and reception units for boys; a detention and reception center for girls; a forestry camp; an institution, Oakdale, for boys 7 to 11; a cottage-based training school, Lyman, for boys between 12 and 14; a cottage-based training school, Shirley, for older boys; a secure psychiatric wing, Bridgewater, for the most "dangerous acting-out youth"; and a cottage-based training school, Lancaster, for girls. As one can see, where a youth was placed was largely determined by age and sex with exceptions made for youths who posed security problems.

While the detention centers were surrounded with traditional hurricane fences, the training schools were not. They tended to be located in rural areas; the cottages housed up to thirty youths, and doors were locked at night. Girls were locked in their rooms at night with pails to serve toilet needs. Standard uniforms were generally used, and cottage groups were highly regimented to maintain control; groups marched to and from the cafeteria and the school. Haircuts and the regulation of cigarettes were routinely used for control purposes, as was the age-old tradition of keeping youngsters guessing about when they would be eligible for parole. Threats and the use of physical force were also part of the daily set of manipulations to maintain control within the institutions. Those who did not respond to these pressures were ultimately "shipped out" to a more secure, more repressive cottage or institution. The psychiatric wing of the Bridgewater Institute of Juvenile Guidance was the ultimate "hammer."

At these institutions custodial efforts outweighed treatment or program efforts. Lancaster and Lyman did operate schools in the traditional mode but as much effort had to go into maintaining control as into educating. Shirley had a nominal vocational training program. A few youths were taught barbering. Others learned to paint and acquired minor carpentry skills by helping maintenance men.

Still others worked in the cafeteria or on the garbage truck. Individual counseling also prevailed. Although life in the training schools was highly structured, idleness characterized much of the day. Playing tough or "bogarting" and planning escapes provided some excitement for the more adventurous youths. There was very little contact with the community. For example, at Lyman parents could visit on two Sundays a month for two hours. Lancaster probably enjoyed the most community contact, with some of the girls participating in a day-care nursery set up on the institution's grounds.

It would be unfair to stress only the harmful features of these training schools. These facilities were undoubtedly less destructive than many others existing in the United States at the time. Many staff members were well intentioned though convinced that they were engaged in a losing battle to help their charges. Certainly there were success stories. Staff members fondly recall the youngster who went straight and continues to correspond with them each holiday season. However, the structure in which both staff members and youths were forced to exist worked against the likelihood of much success. The large number of youths made some regimentation a necessary condition for maintaining control. When that regimentation was violated, it was not hard to justify the use of force to maintain order assuring the staff at least a minimal chance of being able to work together. The need for order squelched more than one innovative program idea. Furthermore, these institutions were so isolated from the youngsters' home communities that there was little opportunity to have any impact on the situation to which all youths would ultimately return. While the institutional settings may not have been totally hopeless, they were fraught with frustration for both youths and the staff.

Demands for change came from within and without. Some staff members were fed up with the physical abuses that they observed daily and with which they were at times unwillingly associated. Some were weary of the lack of support from the Boston office or institutional administrations for desired changes. During the last half of the sixties no less than a half dozen investigations were conducted by outside groups including the Children's Bureau of the Department of Health, Education and Welfare. These investigations generally deplored the abusive conditions under which the youths lived, the lack of programming, and the lack of training and administrative support for the staff.

Physical abuse of a youngster by a staff person at Bridgewater became the final catalyst for the toppling of the DYS commissioner preceding Miller. A number of private interest groups and members of the press coalesced to urge the resignation of the commissioner and to campaign for significant changes within the youth corrections system. The governor responded early in 1969 by appointing a blue ribbon committee to select a reform-oriented commissioner who would implement changes and would thereby alleviate a politically embarrassing situation. The legislature responded in turn with fairly progressive-sounding legislation designed to improve the system. Into this challenge stepped the apparently mild-mannered, reform-oriented Jerome Miller. He entered a climate prepared for change with a mandate for change. But no one, including Miller, envisaged the kind of change that would take place over the next few years.

Reshaping and Closing the Training Schools in the Winter of 1971 to 1972

The existing climate for change allowed the Miller administration to close the Bridgewater institution within his first year. But this was not enough. The new commissioner and his top aides were convinced that the other training schools needed to be humanized. Steps were taken early to reduce the regimentation and harrassment within the institutions. Youths were permitted to wear their own clothing. Disciplinary haircuts were forbidden. Regulation of cigarettes as a control mechanism was disallowed. And use of force was deplored.

Staff members were outraged. This outside interference from the Boston office was seen as an attempt to undermine their authority. Without these traditional control measures, chaos would result. The rift between Miller and many members of his institutional staff began immediately.

The changes in treatment policies reflected a movement toward group work. Selected cottages began to develop therapeutic communities that allowed for more youth participation in deciding what would happen in each cottage. Experts in group process visited the state to conduct training sessions for the staff. The therapeutic community approach, as implemented, was not simply a treatment device; it was also a control device replacing the traditionally harsher control measures. While implementation of the device received enthusiastic support from some staff members it was resisted by many. Sabotage was attempted at many levels, and abuses of authority continued. Staff sought out their state representatives, insisting that the training schools were being turned into country clubs, that delinquents, not staff, would soon be running the institutions. Within some programs, escapes were subtly supported. In one cottage an escape plan with routes through the local town was left hanging on the bulletin board for all to study. During a surprise visit to the discipline cottage at Shirley, Miller discovered that a newly purchased TV was being watched by the staff but the residents were sitting on a row of chairs placed behind the set.

By the end of 1970, Miller was already disillusioned about significantly changing the institutions, and he had little faith in the abilities of the bulk of his staff. There was a growing sense that to alter the situation for youth corrections the institutions would have to go. In early 1971, an abortive attempt to close Shirley was made. The attempt failed largely because institutional staff members were able to reach their state representatives, who then intervened. Many of these legislators were already miffed because Miller had not gone through the proper legislative and administrative channels.

Miller was not deterred. The cottages adopting the therapeutic community model were redefined as staging cottages. After sufficient time for solidifying the program and stabilizing the subculture, each would be moved intact to a local community. This gradual approach to deinstitutionalization also met with resistance. By late 1971 that plan was scrapped. More determined than ever to get out of the institution business, the Miller administration adopted a three-prong strategy. First, federal Law Enforcement Assistance Administration (LEAA) money would be used to set up as many as twenty group homes run by private agencies. Second, the state would be divided into seven regions, each having its own regional administration to manage program development, monitor the movement of youths, and operate the day-to-day program affairs of the department. Third, the training schools would be closed as soon as possible. In November 1971, a top-level meeting was held to discuss the phasing out of the training schools.

After considerable debate Miller's top assistants had worked out a gradual phase-out plan calling for the closing of the three training schools by late spring or early summer. This plan was displayed on the conference room blackboard. Miller was asked to join the group and give his approval. He never sat down. He was obviously distressed at the idea of a gradual pullout that would be open to incessant attack and possible rebuff by recalcitrant staff members and their supporters in the legislature. His response to the plan was, "Hell no!" He believed such a prolonged fight would place the youths in the middle and that the staff would take their frustrations out on them. He wanted an immediate pullout centering on Shirley and Lyman, and he wanted it done in January while the legislature was out of session.

The scene was not unlike a scramble on an aircraft carrier under fire. A decision had been made. Now the search was on for the most effective way of bringing about the actual closings. Should it be low key? Should it be dramatic? Were there some youths who could not go to community settings? Where were the youths to go? Would federal funding come through quickly enough to allow the establishment of group homes?

In order to move quickly, arrangements had to be made to house those youths who could not immediately be paroled. Detention and reception centers were used, and Oakdale, which had been closed for young boys in 1971, was made into a reception center to provide more options. Only a few group homes were available. The federal money had not come through quickly enough and would only trickle in during the next several months. No mechanism had been set up for processing youths into new facilities. To most people it appeared that the department needed to buy more time.

A novel solution came from the University of Massachusetts School of Education. A conference was planned for an entire month—January 15 to February 15—for some 100 DYS youths. The purpose of the conference was to provide a place for these youths while alternative placements were worked out. While at the university each youth was linked with a student advocate. The idea was not as strange as some might think because there existed at the University of Massachusetts a nucleus of people in the School of Education, under the direction of Larry Dye, who had had considerable experience working with DYS youths at the Westfield Detention Center and on the university grounds. In addition to providing a mechanism to facilitate the closing of the training schools, this experience provided one of the initial opportunities for the system to experiment with one-to-one advocacy [2].

In early January and February preparations were made in the training schools and at the university. A team screened the youths at the institutions and segregated them into those who could be paroled, those who had to be retained in the detention reception centers until more structured group home programs were in place, and those who could go to the University of Massachusetts. At the university screening of advocates was in progress at the same time.

The week before the fifteenth of January saw both Miller and the governor wavering. But final approval of the deinstitutionalization plan was given. On the fifteenth a curious drama was played out at Lyman and Shirley: a caravan of nearly one hundred cars, one for each youth, paraded out of the training schools before television cameras to begin their trek to Amherst. The first state-operated training school for boys in the United States was going out of business.

The Shaping of a Community-based System in 1972 to 1974

The spring of 1972 was chaotic at best. Adequate placements in sufficient numbers did not exist. The new regional administrators were still trying to figure out what they were supposed to be doing. There was a backlog of youths in the detention and reception centers, and a legislative committee was mounting an investigation of Miller's administration of DYS.

The spring of 1972, however, also marked the beginning of an innovative period of program development, a period that would continue at least through 1973. Staff members were faced with an urgent situation. They had responsibility for placing youths in community-based programs, but only a handful of such programs existed. At one of their weekly meetings, the regional directors, who had spent much of the fall bickering among themselves about office size, staff size, and their own salaries, complained bitterly to an assistant commissioner from Boston office that once the training schools had closed Boston no longer supported the regional offices. The question on everyone's mind was "What are we supposed to do with the kids on our doorstep"? The response was that the haggling over power among the regions had to be set aside for a time. As far as programs were concerned, the regional directors were told to "be creative."

Regional staff members were exasperated, but they did become creative. They sought out existing resources in their regions. With the assistance of Boston office personnel and private vendors, a number of nonresidential programs were developed. Many of them were alternative schools. Others provided work experience and renumeration, for example, by establishing an ice cream parlor and a pizza shop. Neighborhood youth corps positions were used. Some of the regions set up extensive foster care networks operated by private agencies. Boarding schools were tapped and as funds became available the group home network was enlarged [3]. Many of these also attempted to develop linkages with local schools and employers. Personnel involved at that time now look back and believe that the slowness with which enough group homes were set up to handle all the youths coming out of the training schools was fortunate because it forced them to construct a much more diverse range of options for youths than originally conceived.

By late 1972, the backlog in the detention centers had eased some. Youths were scattered through a vast network of programs, all but a handful operated by private vendors. A few of these programs were run on a contractual basis; that is, a program potentially housing twelve youngsters was paid for by DYS whether or not twelve youths actually occupied the residence. Most of the programs, however, operated on a purchase-of-service basis; that is, DYS would pay for services rendered. This meant that a specific program would generally be serving different categories of youths in order to remain operational. Along with DYS youths would be youths from the

Massachusetts Department of Children and Family Services, and some youngsters whose families were paying directly for their treatment. The purchase-of-service system greatly enhanced the department's flexibility in providing services to its charges—and it expanded the range of services available.

The delivery of services still faced major obstacles. Youths had been dispersed widely across the state without a uniform day-to-day tracking system that permitted administrative staff to know where many youths were. In such a situation it was easy for some industrious program directors to abuse the lack of fiscal accountability. However, a federal audit looking into possible abuse concluded that most abuses that were documented could be attributed to lack of training in bookkeeping rather than fraud. The extensive use of purchase-of-service arrangements placed a great burden on a state bureaucracy not equipped to establish rates of payment and quickly process the payments to the private vendors. By the summer of 1973, reasonable order had been brought to this complex problem of payment for services rendered. Vendors began to indicate that they preferred to work with the department because it paid its bills faster than others. While welcomed, the improvement in processing was too late for some. Several of the smaller programs had already gone bankrupt. One long-run consequence was to reduce the competition among the private vendors, thus pointing to the danger that a few larger vendors could at some time in the future monopolize the youth service area.

During this period central office personnel in charge of service delivery were bothered by the problem of quality control. How could the department be certain that the youths spread across some 100 to 150 programs were being properly cared for? Several efforts were attempted to set up some kind of monitoring system. But usually staff members were diverted to other crises, and routine quality control efforts were forsaken as a result.

Programs for girls were badly needed. Lancaster actually held on as a girls' institution with three cottages operating until the spring of 1974. The question of whether those youths needing secure care were being properly detained was becoming a major political issue.

In 1973 and 1974 there were a number of personnel changes that necessarily had an impact on the development of the community-based system. In January 1973, Commissioner Miller accepted a job in Illinois. His deputy commissioner, Joseph Leavey, became acting commissioner but was not confirmed until late in 1974. Leavey had been a chief architect of the development of regionalization and was certainly dedicated to carrying out the policies of the community-based system. Through his aides and his leadership rationality was brought to the chaotic fiscal problems confronting the newly re-formed system. His administration was plagued, however, by con-tinual controversy over how best to organize to serve youths. From the staff point of view Leavey took little action to resolve these con-troversies, which were enveloping his administration and the system [4].

During the course of 1973 and 1974 more than ten top and mid-dle management personnel in the Boston office departed. Most of these persons had some responsibilities for program development and the operation of the overall program effort. Many of them were not replaced, thus creating a leadership vacuum. The system could cer-tainly tolerate the departure of a commissioner who had drawn too much political fire, but the loss of so many people who had played key roles in developing the ideas and procedures of a makeshift com-munity system had a far-reaching demoralizing effect within the Boston office and on those persons in the regional offices and the private agencies who had begun to depend on them.

Consolidation in 1975 to 1976

One of the bleakest years for DYS during this study period was 1975. Much of the year was taken up with rear-guard action against conservative coalitions who wanted to set up large secure facilities for the many youngsters whom they regarded as dangerous. Much time had to be spent lobbying to maintain the department's annual budget. The commissioner was also coming under increasing fire for mismanagement and insensitivity to the issue of secure care. Regional offices and private vendors often felt at sea. They were receiving little direction or support from the beleaguered Boston office. Far too often, youths had to be terminated from programs because con-tinued funding was not possible. Again, some of the smaller programs either went bankrupt or decided not to serve DYS youths because of the uncertainties surrounding the department. After an extensive media attack in the fall of 1975, Leavey was forced to resign.

In January 1976, Jack Calhoun took over the reins of the depart-ment. Although he came from the outside, Calhoun had extensive experience in the Boston area with justice programs, and he had good relationships with conservatives and liberals alike. He immediately took some of the heat out of the issue of secure care by having the attorney general set up a blue ribbon committee to study the issue and make recommendations. That committee functioned for a year.

Steps were taken quickly to strengthen the fiscal accountability of the system. For the first time it seemed likely that the department could say where each youngster was on a given day. Still problems remained. Many staff members in the regions questioned the administration's commitments to innovative programming. The numbers of youngsters being served by a few agencies continued to increase, threatening to reduce competition and program options. Commitment to quality control also remained a serious question.

BROAD COMPARISONS OF THE QUALITY OF LIFE BETWEEN THE INSTITUTION-BASED SYSTEM AND THE COMMUNITY-BASED SYSTEM

In order to complete this brief sketch of the reform effort, we will sketch in broad strokes some comparisons between the institution-based system and the community-based system.

In June 1968, on a typical day, the system handled 2,443 youths. Eight hundred and thirty-three were in the institutions; the remainder of them were on parole status. In July of 1974, on a typical day, there were 132 youths in secure care, 399 in group care, 171 in foster care, 724 in nonresidential care (61 of the 724 also being in residential care), and 941 on traditional parole (minimal supervision in the community). While the reform apparently did not increase the total number of youths handled on a given day by the department, the nature of the youths being served did change somewhat. The percentage over sixteen years of age had increased from 33 to 58 percent, while the average age of youths in some of the other social service agencies in the state had declined. Although only a small percentage (10 percent) of the youths were in the system because they had committed crimes against persons, this percentage marked a change over the fiscal 1968 period when 2 percent had committed such crimes [5].

Both of these factors may reflect in part the Children in Need of Services (CHINS) legislation passed in December 1973. This legislation forbade the department from handling those youths who were in the court because of status offenses. (The department remained responsible for detention of these youngsters prior to court appearance until 1977.) In the course of our own study, the effects of the CHINS legislation were not observed until the early fall of 1974. At that point, the number of girls committed or referred to some of the regions dropped off dramatically. Until 1976, many CHINS youngsters were still remanded to DYS because the larger child-care system did not have enough alternatives to handle them.

But what about the quality of life in the two systems? Efforts to reform the institutions and then later set up the community-based system were undertaken after all to humanize the process of handling youths in trouble. In late 1971, a sample of youths in the training schools was interviewed to explore the quality of life perceived in those settings. Later a similar sample was drawn between 1973 and 1975 to document the quality of life perceived in the community-based settings. The interviews focused particularly on the process of communication, punishment patterns, reward patterns, and the presence of a negative youth subculture. Table 2—1 displays the results. The training school cottages are separated into two columns. One represents the cottages that were not particularly affected by the efforts to modify the training schools. The other represents the staging cottages—the settings that adapted the therapeutic community model and were for a time seen as the precursors of the community-based programs [6]. The new system in the third column represents the complete range of program options from secure care to nonresidential programs [7].

The findings suggest that significant changes had been made within the training-school settings. On the whole, the staging cottages showed a marked improvement in the quality of life that they provided for their residents. While the community-based system generally yielded similar results even when including programs that handled the most seriously acting-out youngsters, the system as a whole does not show improvement over the staging cottages. Very little difference appears between the three types of settings in terms of information flow. Youths in all settings seemed to believe that they were kept informed. However, punishment was deemphasized in the staging and community-based settings in contrast to the institutional settings. Conversely, rewards were emphasized. The institutional settings were characterized as yielding more negative subcultures than were the staging and community-based settings.

Although the staging cottages were able to modify the institutional environment (no mean achievement in itself), they remained isolated from the larger community. Only 6 percent of the institution-based sample indicated that they had any routine contact with people outside the institution. Treatment approaches in the staging cottages focused almost entirely on the individual through group work. Thus, little attention was focused directly on a youngster's network of relationships in the community. Because of the isolation of the cottages and the individual treatment, those relationships were only dealt with indirectly. The youths became the sole object of interven-

Table 2-1. Quality of Life Within Training School Cottages and Community-based System

Social Climate Item [7]	Groups					
	Training School Staging Cottages		Training School Institutional Cottages		Community-based System	
	Percent	(N)	Percent	(N)	Percent	(N)
The staff members try to keep you informed about what's happening with the cottage.	84	(89)	79	(86)	86	(246)
The staff makes changes in the cottage without consulting the kids.	37	(87)	43	(82)	35	(245)
If the kids really want to, they can share in decisions about how this cottage is run.	94	(88)	85	(84)	77	(246)
Most of the rules here are fair.	83		76		75	(246)
If a kid messes up, the staff will punish him/her.	66	(86)	81	(83)	55	(244)
If a kid messes up, other kids will punish him.	42	(89)	41	(85)	22	(243)
Kids in this cottage usually tell someone when they think he's done something wrong.	89	(89)	78	(84)	78	(246)

Statement		(N)		(N)		(N)
If a kid does well, the staff will tell him so personally.	90	(89)	81	(85)	87	(246)
If a kid does well, the other kids will tell him so personally.	61	(89)	34	(85)	60	(246)
The staff will reward a kid for good behavior.	78	(89)	77	(85)	76	(246)
Other kids will reward a kid for good behavior.	60	(87)	37	(82)	55	(246)
This cottage is pretty much split into two different groups, with staff in one and kids in the other.	19	(88)	55	(84)	25	(246)
The kids in this cottage have their own set of rules on how to behave that are different from those of the staff.	36	(88)	57	(85)	42	(245)
There are too many kids here who push other kids around.	33	(89)	62	(86)	27	(245)
This cottage is more concerned with keeping kids under control than with helping them with their problems.	30	(87)	61	(85)	28	(245)

tion. It was expected that if youngsters had a better understanding of themselves and their situation, the youngsters would be better able to handle pressures after returning home.

By contrast, over half of the youths in the reformed system were in nonresidential and foster care programs. In this system a mix of program strategies prevailed. A few programs continued to focus almost entirely on the individual. These programs tended to be tightly controlled therapeutic community models. Other programs attempted to focus on both the individual and the youth's situation. This involved working with families, helping youths to enter or stay in public schools, and providing work skills and employment. However, even programs with the desire to focus on the youth's situation often found it easier simply to work with the youth; community work became secondary and frequently muted. Even so, the community-based system can be seen as maintaining the humanitarian gains of the staging cottages while attempting to reach out more effectively to the youngster's real life situation in the community. We will see in the remainder of this book that efforts to establish constructive community ties need to be regarded as a continuing high priority.

Chapter 3

In Search of Answers:
How the Study Was Done [1]

Chapters on the methodology of a research study are too often overly technical and are frequently skipped by the reader who is not particularly interested in methodological nuances. However, the way in which a study was done should be of importance to any discerning reader. For it is in such a chapter that the reader can discover what kinds of questions and issues received highest priority, what kinds of trade-offs were made to complete the study (and almost every study is faced with important trade-offs), and what kinds of problems were encountered and handled in what ways. For these reasons, we have tried to provide in this chapter a straightforward presentation that is as nontechnical as possible of our procedures in evaluating the reform efforts under study. A more technical discussion of our use of sampling and regression techniques can be found in Appendix A.

RESEARCH DESIGN ISSUES

The immediate problem confronting the study was the fact that it was focused on a corrections system that was contemplating massive change. No one knew for sure where the changes would take place, when they would occur, or what they would be. In 1969, deinstitutionalization was not a common word like it is today. Although the new commissioner had received a broad mandate for change, he was not talking of deinstitutionalization. The immediate objectives seemed to follow fairly traditional lines of improving the institution-based system while considering some options for expanding the range of treatment settings by developing some community-based alternatives to the training schools. By the winter of 1970, however, it was clear that the chief administrators had become disenchanted with revamping the training schools. An abortive attempt was made to close one training school. Still there seemed to be no clear-cut decision to dismantle the entire training-school system. Yet by late 1971 such a decision had been reached.

Evaluation in the Context of a Changing System

Thus our most immediate and pressing problem (as it would have been with any social service agency) was that the conditions of stability frequently thought necessary for evaluation seemed incompatible with the flexibility required to attain the action goals of the agency. Nevertheless, there is a special need for evaluation studies when an agency is engaged in a process of major change or reform. That is the time when important decisions are being made. Studying the agency during such a state of flux provides an opportunity to look at the impact of major decisions on agency programs at various levels and to observe the interaction of the agency system with other systems. Furthermore, evaluation of the agency's array of programs at various stages in the process of reform will be more useful to other agencies considering similar reforms than would an evaluation of agency programs somehow insulated from the pressures and effects of change. The latter kind of evaluation ignores the reality that programs are implemented in a political arena where adaptive actions are constantly required to achieve program goals.

Evaluation research on systems that are changing must cope with the fact that traditional models of research involving controlled experiments require stable conditions until the results are in. The process of reform in the agency must "hold still to have its picture taken," so to speak. Yet if the agency "holds still," reform may not take place at all because reform is largely a matter of seizing the right moment and moving quickly. Even if the agency is not breaking ground, but merely consolidating its program, "holding still" for the period of evaluation may expose it to serious setbacks resulting from a failure to adapt to the fluctuating political pressures surrounding it. Thus the social scientist is confronted with the problem of constructing more improved flexible means for evaluating such systems as they function and change in the real world. This certainly was one of the principal problems confronting us as we sought to evaluate the reforms of the Massachusetts Department of Youth Services (DYS).

Throughout the past decade evaluation research has prospered principally because of the increased funds made available by such programs as the War on Poverty and the War on Crime. Evaluation projects in mental health, corrections, employment, and other social service areas have proliferated. In most instances, specific "treatment" programs of one sort or another have been selected, goals identified, and success or failure assessed. The net effect on the programs studied has been quite variable. In some cases, information gleaned from the evaluation study has been used to modify and improve the program. In other cases, the findings have had no impact at all. A major defect of these evaluation studies is that they have tended to concentrate on the impact of specific programs without sufficient regard for the systemic context in which they functioned. Therefore they have yielded little in the way of generalizations that might be applied to similar programs elsewhere. Yet it is apparent that the social service fields are becoming more systemic in their attempt to provide a wide range of alternative services to a varied client population. Judgments are less often made now than earlier about the effect of specific programs in isolation from ancillary supporting or alternative services to which the client group may also be exposed.

In criminal justice it is particularly important to perceive the operations of a system and the interrelatedness of its various component parts and programs. For example, there exist in most states correctional systems responsible for providing a range of services to criminal offenders from classification and diagnosis to education, vocational training, group and individual therapy, and aftercare. Furthermore, correctional systems are themselves only one set of programs in a more comprehensive system of criminal justice that also includes the police, prosecution and defense, and the courts. Alternatively, correctional systems are also often regarded as a part of another more encompassing social service system. For example, a modern department of human services may include mental health, alcoholic clinics, children's services, and vocational rehabilitation in addition to corrections.

We were convinced that large-scale evaluation must involve, in addition to the evaluation of specific programs, the consideration of programs from a broader systemic viewpoint. Administrators of correctional systems, for example, needed to know if their total program or system, either as it was or as it could be reconstituted, was having any positive impact on its clients. These administrators needed to make rational decisions about system change, for instance about the advisability of maintaining some programs while scrubbing others. Evaluation of programs *in their systemic context* and comparison of programs *across the system* were therefore considered necessary to provide much of the information needed to make these policy decisions.

The issue boils down to a distinction between two evaluation models that prevail at this time: the goal-model approach that is more widely used and the system-model approach that is more comprehensive and informative. Sherwood, working with the goal-model approach, suggests that three sets of variables are needed for an adequate assessment of whether a program is actually attaining its goals [2]. These variables are the program, intermediate variables, and dependent variables. The program variables include the types of service provided by the program; intermediate variables include such effects as improvement of client self-esteem; and dependent variables include the primary goals such as employment or reintegration. The goal-model approach thus proceeds in linear fashion from program inputs to program outputs.

By contrast, the system-model approach, although incorporating features of the goal model, also includes the relationship and impact of various intra- and extra-system linkages. Whereas the goal-model approach assesses specific programs simply in relation to outcome (i.e., whether certain goals are attained), the system-model approach compares the effect of specific programs within different systems and assesses relative success given the constraints of each operating system.

Levinson aptly points out that an 18 percent success rate for a work training program may be viewed as a drastic failure if one is only using the goal-model approach, but it may be defined as being successful if additional system factors are acknowledged [3]. For example, if the clients were notoriously untreatable, an 18 percent success rate would be a great improvement over other programs within the same or similar systems.

Levinson further suggests, thus opening up a new area of inquiry, that program staff and other clients may be encouraged by even an 18 percent success rate to apply even greater efforts to the program or to other programs, which is to say that a program may affect the system in ways other than its so-called success rates might imply. Or to raise still different questions, the system model may show that links with other programs or systems are not adequately coordinated to serve the client as the client leaves the program, and thus whatever good the program has done is lost, perhaps accounting for a low success rate in the end.

The hallmark of the system-model approach is the attempt, by increasing the number of variables under consideration, to depict the interrelationships of programs being evaluated within the larger social service system and other impinging systems. Evaluation then becomes the analysis of the shifting balance of forces impinging on a system's clients, including both those forces under the control of the agency and those not under the agency's control.

Thus in evaluating programs in systems, it is very important to consider the various linkages within the social services system and the linkages between the social service system and the larger system of the community that is being served. Figure 3−1 depicts the typical commitment or referral path of a client. By following the client along this path, we may point out a number of such system linkages. We begin with a particular community. Either by referral or commitment the community or its representatives determine that one of its members is in need of specific services that the social service agency can provide. The agency receives the individual, looks at his history, and determines that the client should be placed in program G. The staff of program G, and perhaps the other program clients, determine whether the client should become a part of their operation. This process of entry into the program may take very little time or it might take some weeks. Once accepted in the specific program the client is affected by the social climate of the program, that is, the nature of relationships between staff and client, among staff, and among clients. The client is also affected by the program components that have been devised to "treat" him or her. If the client is to learn a skill, the client is affected by (say) the auto mechanics component. The nature and extent of relationships with the community represent yet another linkup between systems. Program staff may actively intervene within the community on behalf of their clients. Staff may argue for a youth to be accepted back in the local high school on a trial basis while the youth continues to be supported by the social service program. Community support may also be present within the program through the volunteer aid of skilled craftsman or tutors.

At some point, whether the program is residential or nonresidential, the client will be discharged. The determination of discharge may be a joint decision reached by program staff, the social service agency, and perhaps even representatives of the community. Once the client is released, linkages are still possible. The program staff may recognize an obligation to continue working with the client through follow-up support and intervention within the community. In addition, other community groups may seek to assist or hinder the client's reintegration into the community.

Figure 3–1.   Typical Commitment or Referral Path of Client with System Linkages

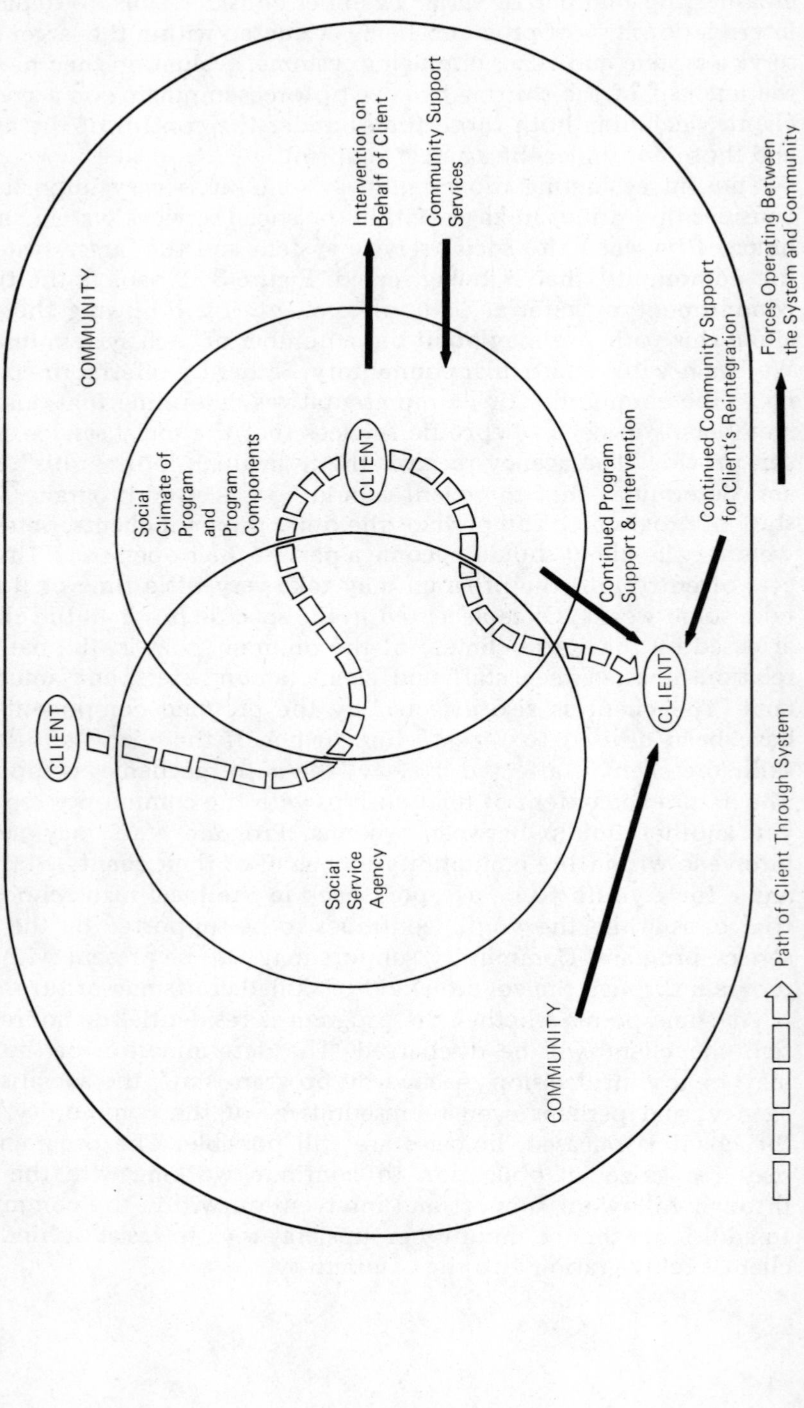

COMMUNITY

COMMUNITY

Social
Climate of
Program
and
Program
Components

Social
Service
Agency

CLIENT

CLIENT

CLIENT

Intervention on
Behalf of Client

Community Support
Services

Continued Program
Support & Intervention

Continued Community Support
for Client's Reintegration

Forces Operating Between
the System and Community

Path of Client Through System

In this book we have used a methodology for evaluation that allows the analysis of these "systems" issues *in changing situations*—where the issues are most important. Much of what we have done poses an alternative to the classical experimental approach to evaluation. Yet by doing so we are not proposing a rejection of the principles underlying the experimental method. Instead, the point is to harness those principles more effectively for the job at hand than has been possible with the classical experimental control method.

CONCEPTUALIZING PROGRAM SETTINGS FOR EVALUATION IN A CHANGING SYSTEM

During the first years of this evaluation project, research efforts were low keyed. Research proceeded with a skeletal staff to keep abreast of decisions being made in the central office. Two extensive efforts were undertaken in the summers of 1970 to 1971 to survey opinions of staff and youths about existing programs and directions for change and to document through subculture studies the day-to-day life of selected cottages within the training school system. By the fall of 1971 the research staff was enlarged, and plans were made for a full-scale evaluation of programs for youths.

We learned very quickly what it meant to be studying a system undergoing rapid change. Anticipating the closing of the training schools at some future date, we took steps to conduct a survey of youths and staff in the training schools to learn about the quality of relationships and the kinds of program experiences they were having. This would provide a systematic baseline of data that could later be compared to data gathered in a community-based system if such a system were to become an actuality. We proceeded in a fairly traditional manner to construct questionnaires and pretest them. After setting up an appointment to talk with administrators of a program that was to be the first to receive the survey, we visited the program to make final arrangements. On the way into the building we met several youths leaving the building with staff. This seemed strange because this particular program was supposed to be quite secure. However, the administrator was rather embarrassed to inform us that his program had just been closed and the youths were being transferred to another facility. We learned quickly that a specific program might not be there when we arrived and that the programs that were surveyed might not exist six months later.

As we completed the pretest phase, we began to make plans for the actual survey. At the same time we were asked to attend an important meeting at the Boston office. There the decision was made to close the training schools and to do it quickly. We hastily acquired more staff to permit us to complete the baseline survey before the training schools were closed.

The ebb and flow of program settings clearly indicated that we could not rely on entirely traditional evaluation approaches—we could not always expect to be able to collect data on a youth entering a program and then again as that youth left the program in order to evaluate the specific program. We needed to generalize at a broader level so as not to be vulnerable because of the demise of any particular program. Originally we devised an approach to focus on program strategies. We planned to compare and contrast tutorial education strategies with group education strategies and traditional classroom strategies. Strategies of vocational training, work experience, and counseling were also delineated. The assumption was that while specific programs would come and go the treatment strategies would remain fairly constant.

However, as the study proceeded, we found such an approach to be forcing a certain kind of treatment rationale on a system that really had no such rationale. Treatment per se had been replaced with a desire to set up programs that created atmospheres quite distinct from institutional environments. Through talks with staff and administrators it became apparent that the model in vogue was the creation of a familylike setting that provided some specific resources to the youth such as counseling and remedial education but which also tapped the resources of the larger community. We therefore began to think through more extensive elaborations of the kinds of information that would permit us to compare and contrast *program settings* across a large number of such settings. For this phase of our work we did not try to get the same detailed, in-depth information that could be obtained in the more narrowly focused subculture studies by Feld and McEwen of a dozen cottages or program settings, but we did obtain enough day-to-day information to permit us to describe the full range of programs operating across the system. By recognizing that these programs could be broken down into subgroups, we also minimized our difficulties with specific programs not surviving throughout the life of the study.

As we sought to establish a general model for evaluating program settings, we developed what we describe as a tri-level evaluation model. The model is described here in its comprehensive form, although certain elements had to be deemphasized in the course of this study. For example, detail on program strategies did not remain a primary focus for the reasons cited above. What we could do with questions requiring departmental records (e.g., concerning costs) was limited by the existence and quality of the necessary records. We were able to obtain systematic data on most of the issues raised in the model. For other issues we had to rely on more fragmentary and qualitative information. This book for the most part focuses on the systematic data.

In developing the model it was useful to think in terms of three levels of consequences: immediate, short run, and long run. The immediate level consists of system inputs and outcomes that occur while the client is actually in the program. The short-run level consists of outcomes that can be detected in the client as the client leaves the program. The long-run level consists of the continued inputs, whether from the system or not, and outcomes that occur after the client has left the correctional system. The evaluation criteria included in each level are shown in Table 3–1 and discussed below.

Level One

Level one includes three areas of consideration: resources, social climate, and system linkages.

Resources. Within level one our first consideration was to identify criteria connected with the quality of resources from the larger system available to the program and the program's use of them. One set of criteria concerned the background characteristics of staff; professional skills, prior experience, orientation toward clients, age, and race were some of the indicators considered. To determine if the program simply took the best clients and also to identify the changes that took place within the clients over time, it was useful to look at some of the background characteristics of clients. Self-image indicators, age, sex, aspirations, risks to the program, and target characteristics (such as the type of offense committed) were included. Interest and participation in in-service training may be considered another gauge of program staff willingness to utilize available resources. Obviously, system administrators will be interested in the costs of the program, but costs may be determined by several methods. One can compare total costs, cost per client, and cost per reintegrated client. Location may be another concern. Is the program located in an area accessible to program clients? The administrators will also want to know whether there is adequate physical space for the functioning of the program.

Social Climate. Our second task within level one was to operationalize the social climate of the program. Some would suggest that the environment of the program is at least as important for the success of the program as the program components themselves.

Table 3-1. The Tri-Level Evaluation Model with Examples of Operational Indicators

Evaluation Levels	Operational Indicators
I. Immediate	
A. Utilization and quality of resources from the larger system	
1. Background characteristics of staff	1. Orientation toward clients 2. Age 3. Race 4. Professional skills 5. Experience
2. Background characteristics of clients	1. Age 2. Sex 3. Self-image 4. Aspirations 5. Target characteristic, e.g., type of offense 6. Client risk
3. In-service training components	1. Interest in continued training 2. Participation in continued training
4. Costs	1. Total 2. Cost per client 3. Cost per reintegrated offender
5. Location	1. Community based
6. Physical structure and space	1. Adequate space and facility
B. Social climate of the program	
1. Relationships *among staff*	
a. Nature and distribution of responsibility in relationships among staff	1. Responsibility for "treatment" 2. Responsibility for "control"
b. Nature and distribution of power in relationships among staff	1. Line staff more influence over who goes home on weekends than treatment staff

c. Nature and distribution of rewards in relationships among staff

1. Who is rewarded for what, e.g., rewards for reducing runs
2. Intrinsic rewards for working with clients

d. Actions taken by staff affecting the distributions of responsibility, power, and rewards in the relationships among staff

1. Staff split and attempting to secure influence and rewards
2. Seek outside help to take over custodial functions

2. Relationships between staff and clients

a. Nature and distribution of responsibility in the relationships between staff and clients

1. Shared responsibility for "treating" clients
2. Some clients are given responsibility to exercise punitive control over clients

b. Nature and distribution of power in the relationship between staff and clients

1. Staff and clients share equal vote on which clients progress to new level
2. Staff can make all decisions

c. Nature and distribution of rewards in the relationship between staff and clients

1. Staff reward clients for helping one another adjust to the program
2. Clients reward staff by keeping the lid on

d. Actions taken by staff or clients affecting the distribution of responsibility, power, and rewards in the relationship between staff and clients

1. Staff meetings to articulate program goals and responsibilities
2. Routinization of accountability by utilizing logs
3. Reprimands for staff or client for misdemeanor

3. Relationships among clients

a. Nature and distribution of responsibility in the relationships among clients

1. Some clients have responsibility to welcome and socialize newcomers

b. Nature and distribution of power in the relationship among clients

1. There are leaders among clients
2. Some clients decide when others are to be discharged

c. Nature and distribution of rewards in the relationships among clients

1. Clients punish other clients for misbehavior
2. Tough clients are rewarded (weekend passes) by other clients

d. Actions taken by staff or clients affecting the distribution of responsibility, power, and rewards in the relationships among clients

1. Clients hold kangaroo court to implement control
2. Staff place clients in position to act on other client behavior

(Table 3–1. continued overleaf)

Table 3-1. continued

Evaluation Levels	*Operational Indicators*

I. Immediate (*continued*)
 	
  C. Linkages with the larger system
 	
    1. Process of entry
	1. Length of time required to make selection
	2. Type of client selected
	3. Screening techniques
	4. Presence of probationary period; how long, how many clients have been rejected
	5. Number clients leaving program within first week

2. Quality and extent of client and staff contact with community a. Nature and distribution of, aspired-to, actual, or expected responsibility in the relationship between the clients, staff, and the rest of the community	1. Client has responsibility for initiating any contact with community 2. X number of clients set up weekly tasks for improving ecology of neighborhood
b. Nature and distribution of aspired-to, expected, or actual power in the relationship between the client, staff, and the rest of the community	1. Community persons advocate in the community for clients 2. Clients can determine the kind of communication link with the programs, e.g., vocational, institutional, church volunteers, etc.
c. Nature of distribution of aspired-to, expected, or actual reward in the relationship between clients, staff, and the rest of the community	1. Clients want legitimate jobs 2. X number of clients develop worthwhile interpersonal relationship with community residents
d. Actions taken by staff, clients, or other affecting the distributions aspired-to, expected, or actual responsibility, power, and rewards in the relationship between the client, staff, and the rest of the community	1. Community contact is retrained or encouraged by program staff 2. Public schools prohibit clients from participating 3. Police encourage clients to participate in community activities

3. Discharge process

   1. Typical length of stay
   2. Who determines when a client is ready to be discharged
   3. Criteria for discharging clients
   4. Attempts to develop community supportive services prior to release

II. Short Run

A. State of the client at completion of program with respect to specific objectives of specific components of program

   1. Reading skill
   2. Self-image
   3. Initial placement in community, etc.

III. Long Run

A. Relationship of clients with the community after discharge

1. Nature and distribution of responsibility in the relationship between clients and the rest of the community

   1. Follow-up responsibility of program staff for client
   2. Community institutions give employment to support client in reintegration

2. Nature and distribution of power in the relationship between the client and the rest of the community

   1. Client may resist
   2. Nature of social control agency response and impact

3. Nature and distribution of rewards in the relationship between the client and the rest of the community

   1. Client receives legitimate job
   2. Client is returned to correctional agency due to continued acting out—length of time out—seriousness of acting out overtime

4. Actions taken by staff: clients or others affecting the distributions of responsibility, power, and rewards in the relationship between the client and the rest of the community

   1. Intervention with community agencies on part of program staff for client
   2. Harrassment by social control agency to impede reintegration of client
   3. Apathetic response of community institutions and employers

First we were interested in knowing about the nature and distribution of responsibility, power, and rewards among the staff—and the actions taken by staff to maintain or alter those distributions. (This particular concern receives more attention in other products of the overall project.) Thus we wanted to know whether responsibility for treatment and responsibility for control were shared by all staff or whether there was a line staff and a treatment staff. Who really made treatment decisions? Who really made control decisions? Who determined whether a client could be home on a weekend? Among the staff, who was rewarded for what? Were there rewards for reducing runs? What were the rewards for successfully handling a client? What actions by groups of staff were taken to improve their position of authority? Was there a split between staff over issues of control, and was one group seeking outside help to improve its position?

Our second area of concern in this category was the relationships between staff and clients. Again we focused on the nature and distributions of responsibility, power, and rewards, this time between staff and clients, and on the actions taken by staff or clients affecting those distributions. Was there a shared responsibility to exercise punitive control over other clients? Did the staff make all decisions or did clients participate in decision-making? Did staff reward clients for helping one another, and did clients reward staff by "keeping the lid on"? Were there regular staff meetings to articulate program goals and responsibilities? Was accountability scrutinized by using daily logs?

A third area of concern was the relationships among clients. Once again, we looked at the nature and distribution of responsibility, power, and rewards, this time among clients, and at action taken by clients affecting the distributions. Did clients have a responsibility to protect one another from staff or persons from the community? Were some clients seen by other clients as being more responsible to the staff than others? Did the clients have dominant and minority groups with their own leaders? Were new clients socialized in such a way as to insure present power relationships? Were some clients expected by other clients to "educate" new staff about the rules of the program? These and other social climate indicators could be applied both through observation of the program in operation and by talking with program staff and clients.

System Linkages.   The third consideration under level one was the linkages between the program and the larger correctional and community systems. The first critical area of concern under linkages was the process of entry into the program. The system administrators might want to achieve certain norms for this process that would become criteria for evaluating and setting up quality controls. Indicators included the typical length of time required to make a selection of clients, the type of client selected, screening techniques, presence or absence of a probationary period, and the number of clients leaving the program within the first week.

A second area of concern under this category was the quality and extent of client/staff contact with the community while the client was still in the program. Because the ultimate goal of any correctional agency is to reintegrate the client successfully into a community, the impact of the program at this level is crucial. Here we were interested in the nature and distribution of responsibility, power, and rewards, whether aspired to, expected, or actual, and in actions taken by staff, clients, or others affecting the distributions between the client, the staff, and the rest of the community. Was there a shared responsibility among program staff, the social service agency, and other community groups to improve contact between the client and the community? Did program staff have the authority to require family participation in the program? Could program staff influence schools to accept program clients while they were still in the program? What did clients want to do within the community while participating in the program; what sorts of rewards were they looking for? Were clients hassled by the police while they were in the program? Did the staff members become advocates for the client within the community or were they only "program oriented"?

The third area of interest within the linkages between the program and the larger systems was the discharge process. This was of particular interest since in some instances it was known that the less well-behaved clients were dismissed because they disturbed the program while the better behaved clients were retained to foster a positive subculture. Some indicators included who determined when a client was ready to be discharged, criteria for discharging clients, and attempts to develop community supportive services prior to release.

Level Two

Level two, the short-run effects, deals with the state of the client upon completion of the program with respect to specific objectives connected with specific program components. While the indicators of success varied according to the program strategy, one can set forth appropriate steps for evaluating this level. Whether the program component be educational, vocational, or of a counseling nature, the evaluator had to determine the specific goals and strategies used to achieve these goals. The evaluator could then put together criteria for measuring goal achievement. For example, if the specific goals of a structured recreational program were to improve the client's motor skills and self-image, we could measure the client's motor skills and self-image before the client entered the program and after finishing it. Effect of the specific program on self-image could be confounded with effect of social climate and contact with the community; however, these confounding effects could be accounted for by comparison of programs that had similar social climate or contact with the community, but which differed in strategy for developing motor skills and self-image.

Level Three

The third evaluation level, long-term effects, focused on the relationship of the client with the community after discharge from the program. We were interested in the long-range consequences of the client's experiences within the program for the client's successful reintegration into the community. We were also interested in how the program staff and other community groups or persons facilitated or hindered the reintegration process.

For this reason we directed our attention to the nature and distribution of responsibility, power, and rewards and the actions taken by staff, clients, and others affecting those distributions. Did community institutions acknowledge responsibility for assisting the client during the reintegration process after the client had left the program? Were the program staff members continuing to follow up their clients with support? What was the nature of influence by the client's peers? Had the client's self-esteem improved, and therefore his or her expectations of a place in the distributions of responsibility, power, and rewards? Had the community undertaken to offer the client a legitimate, responsible job? Had the client been able to accept the responsibilities offered to him or her and to influence his or her own progress after leaving the program? Had community representatives returned the client to the social service agency? What responsibilities did community representatives fulfill by returning the client? How long before being returned had the client been out? What responsibilities, if any, had the client failed to meet—what was the level of acting-out behavior before the client's return compared to the acting-out behavior for which the client was committed or referred previously? Did social control agents exercise their power by harassing the client? Were the program staff still intervening on the client's behalf? Did they have the resources to intervene effectively? What was the family doing, and with what results, to effect the client's successful reintegration after the client had left the program? What did the client, his or her family, community members, and social control agents stand to gain if the client succeeded? If the client failed?

The tri-level evaluation model is summarized in Table 3–1. Taken as a whole, it should expand the kinds of criteria used for addressing the issue of success in the context of a changing system because it enables the evaluator to look at a wide variety of criteria that reflect not only change occurring within the client per se but also change occurring within the system and system linkages that affect client outcomes.

DATA COLLECTION

Consistent with our emphasis on a systemic approach to evaluation, the primary principle underlying the data-collection strategies was one of triangulation. That is, wherever possible we tried to gather data concerning a given issue from a variety of actors (many having different points of view) and at different time periods throughout the study [4]. Furthermore, a variety of data-collection techniques were employed, including structured interviewing, informal interviewing, observation, reviewing documents, and aggregation of official data available from police, courts, DYS, adult corrections, and the welfare department. This triangulation approach permitted us to validate many of our findings from a variety of sources and through more than one data-collection technique. It also has provided us with insights into the conflicts over specific program policies and has provided a foundation for understanding some of the practical problems encountered when attempting to implement new programmatic policies.

The range of data sources generated for this book will be enumerated and briefly described below. That discussion will be followed by brief discussions of our procedure for pretesting the primary data-collection instruments.

Data Sources

Data for the study are drawn from several samples gathered over the length of the seven-year project, as can be seen in the diagram in the preface. The principal data source for this book is a longitudinal sample of youths begun in 1973. Another primary source is a cross-sectional survey of youths in programs from 1973 to 1975. Other data sources include cross-sectional baseline data reconstructed for recidivism comparisons in 1968 and gathered on samples in 1970 and 1971 to 1972. In addition, data are also available from two sub-culture studies, the first completed in the summer of 1971 and the second in the summer of 1973. Each of these data sources will be described below. Following a description of the data sources will be a discussion of the modes of analysis employed in this study.

The Longitudinal Sample
The structure of the longitudinal sample is a series of four inter-views with a cohort of youths entering the department between January 1973 and December 1974. These youths were followed with a succession of interviews from detention, if any, through program experience and return to the community.

A youth may come into contact with the department in several ways and at several stages of the youth's contact with the criminal justice system. Some youths are detained prior to court appearance. Youths detained for more than two days were interviewed to obtain information about individual background, current relationships, aspirations, and self-image. Some of these youths were released without being put into further contact with DYS. Others were committed or referred to DYS.

Youths who were either committed or referred to DYS were then interviewed after going through court. Referred youths remained under the jurisdiction of the court while committed youths were completely under the control of DYS. This distinction was frequently not understood by the youth or program staff. In subsequent analysis, whether a youth was referred or committed did not generally emerge as a variable that predicted different outcomes. The interview at this stage focused on the court and detention experiences and on relationships, aspirations, and self-image. Some youths, particularly referred youths, reached this stage without going through detention. These youths were then being interviewed for the first time as they entered a program. They were not asked about detention because they had not been through it, but they were asked about their individual background experiences because they had not been asked before. In addition, a small sample of youths going through detention but not committed or referred to DYS were interviewed a second time for comparison purposes, just like the youths who were committed or referred.

Youths who were committed or referred were then interviewed again prior to the termination of a residential program or after a period of three months in a nonresidential or foster care program [5]. This interview concerned the experience in the program, relationships, aspirations, and self-image.

The final interview was held after the youth had been out of residential programs for about six months, or had been in nonresidential or foster care programs about nine months, or when a youth had recidivated. This interview focused heavily on relationships between the youth and members of the community as well as upon aspirations and self-image. It was supplemented by information from DYS staff and by official record checks. The official record checks covered a period for one year after program termination. The youths in the comparison samples (i.e., youths who were detained but were not committed or referred, which was described at the second stage above) were given the same interview and record checks at this point as were the youths who were committed and referred and who had gone through the DYS programs [6].

Of course, some youths did not follow clear paths through DYS such as the youths described above. The sequence of interviewing was adapted to the course they did follow. For example, youths who kept moving from program to program were additionally interviewed as they left each program unless this happened more frequently than monthly intervals.

Thus the chief categories of data involved were the individual backgrounds of youths, their experiences in programs, their relationships, their aspirations, their self-images, the impressions they made on staff, and their official records. The youths involved were primarily served by DYS as contrasted with a small comparison sample of youths in the criminal justice system who were not served by the department.

Cross-Sectional Sample

The longitudinal sample permits a close look at the effect on youths of being processed through the juvenile justice system over time. However, for program evaluation, the longitudinal sample is somewhat limited by itself. This is so because the sample of youngsters was so widely dispersed across so many programs that one did not have enough youths from any one program to determine the specific character of different programs. Our way of dealing with this problem was to group individual programs into program types. In order to obtain an even more complete picture of what was going on within specific programs and program types, a cross-sectional survey was administered within each region during the time that the youths from the longitudinal sample were in the program. Thus the cross-sectional sample permits us to describe more fully the experience of being processed through specific types of programs, and the longitudinal data in conjunction with these data enable us to assess impact.

Programs were included in the cross-sectional sample if they were being frequently used by the department and also had some of the youths from our longitudinal sample. Programs that only worked with one or two DYS youths during the course of a year were omitted for this survey. In programs with fewer than twenty youths, all participants were interviewed. In programs with more than twenty youths, a sample was taken. The interviews were devised to emphasize the social climate of the program facility, the extent and quality of linkages with the community, and the youngster's participation in various program strategies.

Observations of Program Interactions

A third set of data that we drew upon to categorize programs and explain outcomes consists of the day-to-day observations that study staff recorded as they followed the longitudinal sample of youths in and out of programs. These data focus on the interactions among the program participants, the nature of activities within the various program settings, and the extent and quality of linkages with the community. Incorporated within this data set are informal interviews with youths and staff.

Staff Interviews

A fourth set of data was generated by systematically interviewing staff at the program, regional, and central office levels. Here again, for purposes of this analysis, the pertinent questions revolved around the nature of interactions among the program participants, the nature of activities within the various program settings, and the extent and quality of linkages with the community. In addition to the above data sources, which we relied on most heavily, other sources were also used to make across-time comparisons, enrich the description of programs, and more fully flesh out the processing of youngsters through the early stages of the juvenile justice system.

1968 Baseline Sample

A sample of youths paroled from the training schools during fiscal 1968 was drawn to provide a skeletal description of the kinds of youths treated prior to deinstitutionalization. This sample also served as a baseline sample of youths for whom one could gather recidivism data and make comparisons with the longitudinal sample flowing through the restructured community-based system.

1970 Survey

An extensive survey of staff and a smaller group of youths was conducted to establish opinions concerning the institutional system and attitudes toward change. This survey was relied on more heavily in our analysis of organizational change.

1971 and 1972 Baseline Sample

Prior to the closing of the training schools in 1972 all youths were interviewed. The interview schedule was essentially the same as that used for the cross-sectional sample administered from 1973 to 1975. Although some reforms had been implemented in the training schools, this data set provided us with comparable information on the social climate, the nature of activities, and the extent of time spent in the open community before the major reforms took place.

1971 and 1973 Subculture Studies

During the summer of 1971 and the summer of 1973, intensive subculture studies were done in selected cottages and programs. These observation and interview data were used to describe more fully the quality of life within programs and according to the program typologies. These studies thus enlarge our analysis of the longitudinal and cross-sectional data.

1973 and 1974 Court Studies

During the summer of 1973 and the summer of 1974, interviews were conducted with selected judges, probation officers, lawyers, and DYS court liaison officers to determine the process of handling youths at the detention and court stages as well as obtaining the respondents' opinions on the DYS reforms and the impacts of those reforms on other parts of the juvenile justice system. These data were used to flesh out the process data that we obtained while interviewing the pool of youngsters for our longitudinal sample.

1976 Police Study

During 1976 selected police departments from across the state were studied by interviewing a number of police administrators and patrol officers. Questions were asked concerning the manner of dealing with youths, particularly DYS youths. In addition, respondents were asked to comment on the DYS reforms and how they affected their work. These data, like the court data, were used to describe more fully this stage of processing within the juvenile justice system —a stage that we touch on briefly with data from our longitudinal sample.

Cost Data

Cost data have been gathered, portions of which will be reported here. Cost data have been gathered by type of program to provide us with a basis for relative costs across different kinds of program settings.

Pretest of Instruments

The data-collection instruments used in the survey and observation work were pretested extensively in the field before administering them to the sample groups. Instruments used with the longitudinal sample were developed for a year and a half and underwent intensive pretesting for six months before being used in the sample. This process included drawing upon the experience of others by reviewing the literature, formulating and revising of questions by our staff, and most importantly, trying questions with youths and DYS staff, sharing with them what kinds of information we were trying to elicit, and letting them help us identify appropriate phrases and wording that made sense.

In 1972, for example, when attempting to adapt some questions from earlier studies and instruments, we found that some words such as "mess up" now had unexpected connotations for the youths we were interviewing. Such words drew stares and laughter. Through an exchange with a series of youngsters we were able to determine that "screw up" provided us with a better means of obtaining answers to the question of interest, and we trained our interviewers to adapt that particular phrase to the individual respondent, frequently using still stronger and more "adult" language [7].

Instrument construction and testing relied heavily on the competence of our staff, their ability to develop rapport with DYS staff and youths, and probing and exchange of ideas among and between our field staff and the project directors. Field staff and two of the project directors worked full time on the study, thus greatly enhancing the interaction among staff members and enabling the project directors to maintain control over what could have been an unwieldy process [8].

During pretesting we drew the basic structure and wording of many questions from delinquency literature. This effort had the side effect of providing a built-in degree of reliability and validity because many of the questions thus developed are the product of the various validity and reliability tests in previous studies. In addition, the previous studies themselves in their finished state provide tests of "construct validity" for the measures in question. We also took care to do much of our instrument development and pretesting in familiar territory so that we could triangulate our results as we obtained them with the results of both earlier and current observation and other interviewing.

There is one area of the longitudinal interviews where special procedures were used in the pretest, amounting to a small-scale statistical analysis. This was the semantic differential, which was administered as a paper and pencil test, and thus was not as tightly controlled by the interviewer. It was presented as a game to be done without trying to think out the meaning of things beyond the youth's immediate gut reaction. We plotted the results graphically to see if the profiles made sense and examined the results. On the basis of the results and guidelines in the literature, we selected a small number of items for the semantic differential out of a larger initial pool and calculated reliability measures for the items corresponding to each "concept" being responded to. These reliable sets of items were the ones we finally used in the interview.

STATISTICAL ANALYSIS

The statistics used in this study are a set of tools that enable us to interpret our findings. They were selected to insure the broadest use of all the information gathered on youths and programs in order to best predict the consequences of being processed through different kinds of programs and to gain a clearer understanding of what factors tend to impede or facilitate reintegration into the community. The analysis also permits us to infer what one could expect if program policies were altered in specific ways.

Because of the vast number of factors (e.g., background, social network, program experiences, and postprogram experiences) being considered in the analysis, we have had to rely extensively on complex statistical techniques. Unfortunately, results of these techniques cannot be presented in easily readable percentage tables. Such a presentation of two-variable or three-variable relationships would, for one thing, oversimplify what is actually a complex process of interacting factors that determine the outcomes under consideration and, furthermore, would require volumes to present.

Since some of these techniques will be unfamiliar to many readers, we will present a brief glossary of terms used in the analysis. This presentation should help the reader to understand the statistical procedures used. A more technical discussion of the underlying assumptions of these statistics can be found in Appendix A.

1. *Dependent variable*—the variable (such as recidivism) that is being influenced by other sets of factors (such as relationships with significant others and program experiences).

2. *Independent variable*—variables (such as relationships with significant others and program experiences) that interact to influence other variables (such as recidivism). A given variable such as self-image can be treated as a dependent variable or an independent variable depending on what is being explained. If we are trying to identify factors related to self-image, it is a dependent variable. If self-image is one of many variables being related to recidivism, it is treated as an independent variable.

3. *Variance explained*—the differences in the dependent variable explained by a difference in an independent variable. For example, the reduction in recidivism explained by an increase in a youngster's self-image.

4. *Zero-order correlation* (*r*)—indicates the relative strength of the relationship between any two variables. Value can range from −1. to +1. The relationship does not necessarily indicate causality. For example, one might expect to find a fairly strong relationship between the eating of ice cream cones and delinquency, but one would not suggest that eating ice cream cones causes delinquency.

5. *Statistical significance*—the number of times a particular relationship between two variables would probably be found by chance if one were to have repeated the measures in 100 independent samples. Thus if a relationship is significant at the .05 level, we would believe that such a finding would have been yielded by chance in only 5 percent of the repeated samples. Statistical significance should not be confused with theoretical significance. For example, the relationship between eating ice cream cones and delinquency may be statistically significant, but it is probably not of theoretical importance and it may be quite misleading. Thus statistics do not replace hardheaded interpretation of the findings.

6. *Controlling*—the addition of other variables to a zero-order relationship to further explain the original relationship. For example, if the relationship between eating ice cream cones and delinquency was controlled for age we would probably find that age explained most of the original relationship.

7. *Multiple correlation* (*R*)—indicates the strength of the combined relationship among two or more independent variables with a dependent variable.

8. *Multiple regression*—an equation that allows the simultaneous controlling of the effects of a number of variables that are related to the dependent variable while looking at the remaining effect of

an independent variable. The resulting equation allows one to predict the relationship of a set of factors with a dependent variable. For example, we may find that youths with positive ties to significant others, youths who are doing well in school, and youths who have positive self-images recidivate less.

9. *Multiple stepwise regression*—a process of generating the regression equation by allowing the variable that is most strongly related to the dependent variable to enter the equation first; its effect is then controlled as the next strongest variable enters, and so on.

Because multiple stepwise regression constitutes the backbone of our statistical analysis, we will document here the procedure used to generate those equations. Let us use placement into a DYS program as our dependent variable. All programs have received ratings on *social climate, extent of community linkages, quality of community linkages*, and an overall rating on the institutionalization-normalization continuum. In order to determine what kinds of youths enter what kinds of programs, we must run four separate regression equations, one with each of the four variables mentioned above as the dependent variable.

In the first equation, social climate is a dependent variable. First, a zero-order correlation matrix is run with all of the background and detention experience variables being related to social climate. The resulting matrix is then culled by singling out those individual relationships yielding statistically significant correlations and by also singling out other relationships that, while not statistically significant, are of particular theoretical interest. This new set of variables is then entered into a regression run with social climate as the dependent variable. A much smaller set of variables actually emerges in the regression equation. Many of the variables entered in the run fall out because their relationship with social climate becomes insignificant as other relationships are controlled. The resulting equation provides us with a parsimonious set of factors that predicts what kind of youths tend to be placed in a high social climate program and what kind tend to be placed in programs with harsher social climates.

It should be noted, however, that extraneous factors on which we did not gather data may also influence placement and that our attempt to measure accurately the factors that we did look at is necessarily crude. Thus we never reach a point of being able to say that x always produced y. For this reason, usually much of the variance in the dependent variable remains unexplained. Such is the nature of social research. The best that we can say is that youths with a given set of characteristics are likely to be placed in certain kinds of programs. These steps would then be repeated for each of the other dependent variables describing placement.

To make our analysis more readable, we have at times taken some liberties with our presentation by characterizing a value of the dependent variable in terms of the values of the independent variables from which the particular value of the dependent variable is predicted. This is not meant to imply anything other than the fact that the independent variables predict the dependent variable as indicated.

SUMMARY

While this chapter has sought to explain briefly some of the methodological issues confronting this book, we believe that those issues are certainly not unique to our work. It is our sense that the tri-level evaluation model can be useful to others in a variety of social service settings. It clearly has utility for the kind of research conducted here. It also can be a useful tool for agencies that are looking for a format for monitoring a large number of action programs; it can be used simply as a checklist, or it can be fleshed out more fully. As is the case in any monitoring system, policy-makers will have to place their own values on desired outcomes. The model can also be useful at the individual program level, providing staff members with a quick checklist to which they can add the specific needs of their own program.

✳ *Chapter 4*

Detention and Its Consequences

Detaining youngsters prior to a court adjudicatory hearing is a practice in this country that is frequently misused and abused [1]. Margaret Rosenheim points out that detention has traditionally been misused in three ways.

Detention is resorted to when another form of care would be more appropriate. Detention is used for the convenience or to satisfy the cautious instincts of officials when the child should not be separated from his family prior to his day in court (if then). And detention is used for punishment [2].

By law detention is usually required only for youths who present a clear and present danger to themselves or to the larger community and for youths for whom sufficient evidence exists to indicate that they would not otherwise appear for their court hearing. Yet detention is often applied much more widely, and the practices are often criticized as being punitive and discriminatory.

For many youngsters, detention is their first institutional experience with juvenile justice. The majority of the youths detained are not subsequently committed to the state correctional system, but in detention they get an inkling of what to expect if they continue to get in trouble. The socio-psychological effects of detention remain unclear but may have a substantial impact on a youth's self-image, confidence, or feelings of alienation. On the other hand, it is possible that many juveniles are able to neutralize the effects of this experience, particularly if the experience is not reinforced or repeated over and over [3].

61

As important or perhaps even more important than the social-psychological effects is the organizational labeling effect: detention is significant to others who must make decisions about a youth who in the judgment of the court must be separated from society while awaiting adjudication of his or her offense. At least to the casual observer—the neighbor, local store owner, or teacher—the youth has been labeled dangerous, threatening, and someone to be feared and avoided.

The reader may ask why a chapter on detention appears in a book primarily focused on community-based corrections. There are three reasons for its inclusion. First, detention facilities in Massachusetts are administered by the Department of Youth Services (DYS); therefore, reforms aimed at changing the department could be expected to affect detention practices as well. Second, detention became a major area of focus somewhat by accident. Because we wanted to obtain measures of youngsters' relationships, self-image, expectations, and aspirations as early as feasible in the juvenile justice process prior to entry into DYS programs, we interviewed youths who had stayed in detention for more than forty-eight hours. This feature of the design provided us with the opportunity to gather data on detention, specifically on youths detained for more than forty-eight hours, some of whom were later committed or referred to DYS and some not. In addition, many youths were committed or referred to DYS without first being detained, thus allowing us to look at the differences between committed or referred youths who had and had not been detained [4]. Third, and most importantly, detention became a primary consideration because preliminary analyses made clear the profound impact that detention decisions had on the continuing responses of DYS decision-makers to youths as they were processed through the system.

We have discovered a fairly classic example of organizational labeling. In this instance, the early detention decisions, which seem haphazard at best, serve to attach lasting labels to youths. These labels are regarded by persons in the corrections system as characteristics of the youth and are relied upon as a basis for making placement and treatment decisions. Not only does the fact of detention adversely affect future decisions, but also the place where one is detained. For example, youths detained in shelter care facilities received better placements when committed to DYS than did those detained in secure care. Yet, as we will show in this chapter, these detention decisions were considerably influenced by factors that were not characteristics of the youngsters themselves. Recognizing the influence of detention decisions on future decision-making underscores the importance of such early decisions and the need to exercise care and restraint in making them.

This chapter, then, will explore two kinds of detention decisions: the decision to detain and the decision where to detain. In doing so it will also consider the immediate consequences of detention. The next three chapters will trace out in some detail the longer run consequences. The full extent of labeling at the point of detention can only be realized as we follow the youths through the DYS programs and out into the community. We will make it clear, however, that decisions that appear innocent enough and expedient at the point of detention, even though not well founded, continue to haunt the youngsters as they move through the justice process.

The decision to detain has received relatively little research attention; this may be because the decision usually takes place in the course of a few minutes in a very informal setting. Typically, little information about the necessity of detention is available, and it is limited primarily to what the youngster, the arresting officer, and the probation officer can furnish. The influence of the police officer is seen as pivotal in this initial decision [5]. In Massachusetts, a youth may actually be detained by the police for twenty-four to forty-eight hours before a detention hearing occurs in the court. Although the brief court hearing is under the authority of the judge, it is frequently delegated to an intake clerk. The decision about where a youngster will be detained is the responsibility of DYS, which administers the detention facilities, and it is most frequently made by a combination of regional and detention staff.

Before 1972 almost all youths were detained in one of three sizable facilities with populations ranging from 40 to 200 youths. Each facility was jail-like in appearance although they varied considerably in their treatment of youths. Beginning in 1972, a network of shelter care facilities, making considerable use of YMCAs, was developed. Some of the seven administrative regions that make up the DYS have also developed detention foster home alternatives. Because individual regions developed detention alternatives independently of one another, some regions had a wider range of alternatives than others.

Detention was one of the last components of the DYS system to undergo extensive reform, and while our longitudinal sample was exposed to detention these reforms were still taking place. Consequently, the data reported here will unavoidably reflect detention facilities and procedures still in transition.

For purposes of analysis at the time our data were collected, we distinguish among three types of detention facilities available to DYS: custody, treatment, and shelter care [6]. Because each type of facility is entrusted with the responsibility of assuring that detained youths appear in court, a primary concern of each facility is to control youths and minimize runs. Each facility differs as to the mechanisms used to maintain control. The custodial units provide the least benign surroundings: the physical structure resembles a jail, and control is frequently maintained by force or threat of force. In the treatment units, control is exercised in a more therapeutic way with emphasis on positive peer pressure. In the shelter care units, control is maintained by keeping the youths busy with vocational, educational, and recreational activities. The physical environment of a shelter care unit is less like an adult jail than either a custodial or a treatment unit. At most this typology only indicates the central tendency of each type.

Seven hundred and sixty-nine youths were interviewed in detention. Of this group, 255 were eventually committed or referred to the department and completed the set of interviews for our longitudinal sample. In addition, 238 youths who had not been detained for at least forty-eight hours were committed or referred to the department and also completed the set of interviews. These last two groups comprise the sample of committed or referred youths, some of whom were detained and some not, which is our primary focus in this discussion. Thus we selected a sample consisting of what are generally considered to be the most serious youth offenders coming before the juvenile court. These youths would be more likely to require detention. One would expect to be able to determine, on the basis of youth characteristics, why half of these youths were detained prior to court and half were not. Yet after analyzing a large number of background variables, we can say very little about what factors significantly influenced the decision to detain.

In the course of the larger research project, we have interviewed court liaison staff, probation officers, judges, regional placement personnel, and intake workers employed in the various programs. It is evident that matching youths with detention and placement programs involves a considerable amount of intuition and trial and error as well as reliance on the more objectifiable youth characteristics. We cannot, of course, be certain that we have isolated all the most relevant variables affecting the decision to detain. Nonetheless, the kinds of variables considered below are typically referred to by decision-makers as variables that permit them to differentiate among youths for detention placement.

THE DECISION TO DETAIN

By looking at the characteristics of the cohort youths who were detained prior to court appearance and those who were not, we are able to sift out the factors that are most related to the decision to detain, at least for youths who are eventually committed to DYS. In looking at these youths, one would expect to find characteristics that would justify the decision to detain. Judges, police officers, and probation staff usually justify their decisions by claiming that the youngster is a threat to the community; one would therefore expect that youths committing serious offenses would be routinely detained. Detention decisions are also defended on the ground that the family environment has deteriorated to such a point that allowing the youngster to remain would be in itself debilitating. We would thus expect to find family-related factors explaining some of the differences between youths who were committed but not detained and youths who were detained before being committed.

Looking at Table 4—1, however, one is immediately struck by what does *not* seem to influence the decision to detain. Contrary to what many in the judicial branch say, current offense, offense history, and prior experience in youth corrections do not appear to be strongly related to the decision to detain. The only offense-related variable entering the regression equation is the number of prior court

Table 4—1. Multiple Regression of Detained on Background Variables

Background Variable	Coefficient	Standardized Coefficient
Ethnicity: Father Spanish-speaking	.24	.13**
Region IV	.25	.17***
Siblings charged with status offenses	−.26	−.14**
Number of court appearances before this commitment to DYS	.01	.11*
Police sometimes punish you for what others have done	−.17	−.16***
Kids don't judge you as good or bad	−.27	−.13**
Parents see you as a good kid	−.17	−.16***
Processed through a full-time juvenile court	.13	.12**
Regression Constant	.15	
Multiple R	.41	

appearances, and that is the weakest variable in terms of explanatory power in the equation. None of the current offenses or self-reported delinquency variables entered into the decision. Neither did prior commitment or referral to DYS. We can state, therefore, that under present practices youths detained prior to commitment are not significantly more dangerous than youths committed without detention. One must conclude that other factors must influence the decision-makers to detain or not detain.

The variable yielding the strongest coefficient is a regional variable [7]. Youths in region IV are more likely to be detained than youths in other regions. The importance of regional location is further confirmed if we look at the partial correlations of the variables that would have entered the regression equation next. Partial correlation readings indicate youths in regions II and III were less likely to be detained before commitments while youth in region VII were more likely to be detained. Given that youth characteristics across the regions are quite similar, we must look for another factor to explain why the region has such a strong effect on the decision to detain.

A plausible explanation can be linked to the distribution of detention resources across the state. Regions II and III had limited resources. Region II had only one treatment detention center, and region III had no detention facilities within its boundaries, having to rely on facilities in neighboring regions. On the other hand, regions IV and VII each had at least one shelter care unit within their region and were close enough to one of the large custody units to use it quite extensively. Thus it seems likely that one of the principal factors determining whether a youngster was detained or not was an availability of detention slots. Thus a youngster in one region might be detained while a similar youngster in another region would not be detained because of the lack of detention placements. A policy issue emerges from these data. One could take either the position that more detention slots were needed or the opposite position that because some regions have made do without such a large number of alternatives, other regions were detaining too many youths. We will return to this basic policy issue after we consider the impact of detention decisions on the youths themselves and on the people who will be making decisions about them in the future.

Other factors found to affect the decision to detain appeared in the data. Children of Spanish-speaking fathers were frequently detained. This finding may reflect a conscious or unconscious bias of police officers and court intake personnel. It suggests that the decision-makers believed Hispanic youngsters either posed a more significant threat to the community or themselves or else were less likely to appear in court if they were left free on their own recognizance.

Youths who lived in areas that maintain full-time courts were also more likely to be detained than youths living in areas that only maintain part-time juvenile courts. Again, given that the characteristics of youngsters going through both courts were not greatly dissimilar, one must wonder if the availability of detention resources to those courts did not influence the numbers of youths who could be detained.

Youths who believed that their parents considered them to be "good kids" were not likely to be detained. Youths who had brothers or sisters who had committed status offenses such as running away and truancy were also likely not to be detained. The first finding seems self-evident; it is quite likely that a positive relationship with one's parents would in most situations lead the court to believe that the youngster would not pose a substantial risk. The second statement is more difficult to explain. One might expect a youngster coming from a family that has already experienced some difficulties to be more likely to be detained. However, it may be that decision-makers feel frustrated by the family history of such youngsters and therefore respond with, "Oh, what else can you expect from that family?"

Other factors in the regression equation include the quality of interactions in the community with other youths and with police. Youngsters who believe that other youths do not judge them as "good kids" or "bad kids" are less likely to be detained. These youths may not feel under the same pressures to conform to the expectations of their peers as the youths who believe that they are constantly being judged.

The low multiple correlation for this equation suggests that the variables analyzed in this particular study do not significantly differentiate between youths detained prior to commitment and those not detained. It may be that the decision to detain is largely determined by interpersonal interactions at the time of the decision, or it may be that the decision is quite idiosyncratic. However, the equation does lead one to ask questions about the relation between the availability of detention placements and the decision to detain. One would hope that the decision would be based on the behavior of youths or on the characteristics of their situation and not simply on the availability of a slot. Because the fact of being detained has both immediate and long-run unfavorable consequences for youths, the justification for detaining youths should be clearly delineated and the actual decision-making process closely monitored. An act requiring only a few minutes becomes part of the youth's record and is relied upon by other decision-makers as a basis for making further judgments about the youth.

These findings are consistent with many studies that have focused solely on the detention decision. Pappenfort and Young suggest that it is quite possible "that prevailing judicial and administrative philosophy regarding the court's purpose and function may have a greater influence on the patterns of decisions than do the existence or use of explicit criteria to guide decision-making" [8].

It should be noted, however, that some studies of detention decisions using samples representing all the youths processed through the courts yield different results. For example, Bookin found in a study of selected Boston Metropolitan courts important associations between many background factors, both social and criminal, and the decision to detain. The findings in the larger populations admit considerable unexplained variance in the decision to detain [9]. We find that a substantial part of that variance in Massachusetts is among the youths committed and referred to DYS. Of this subsample of youths passing through the courts, half were detained and half not, and yet little good policy sense can be made of the distinction between who was detained and who was not.

WHERE DETAINED

Once the decision is made to detain a youngster, DYS personnel must decide where that youngster will be detained: in a shelter care unit, a treatment unit, or a custody unit. According to staff, the latter units are supposed to house only the most dangerous youngsters. The range of detention services was developed in part to provide more individualized detention services for youths.

It is therefore somewhat surprising, given the rhetoric of the staff, that delinquency history is relatively unrelated to where a youngster is detained. Youths who are charged with a crime against a person will most likely be detained in a custody unit, and youths who report themselves as frequently using drugs by themselves will not likely be detained in a treatment unit (Table 4–2). Other than these two connections, none of the offense-related variables explains where a youngster will or will not be detained. Once one has allowed for the detention of youths who commit crimes against persons and who indicated that they used drugs by themselves, youths with other charges are as likely to be placed in one type of facility, including custody, as another.

If delinquency history only sheds partial light on who is detained where, let us look at our equation again to identify other factors that may be influencing staff decisions. Where one resides has a direct influence on where one will be detained. Youths from region VII are most likely to be detained in shelter care units, while youths in region IV are predominantly detained in either shelter care units or custody units. Youths from regions I and II will almost always be detained in treatment units. As indicated earlier, the availability of detention slots and the type of detention slots are determined largely by the transitional state of DYS reform. A complete range of alternatives was not available within each region; thus placement possibilities were limited. However, the importance of placement in appropriate detention units becomes significant in later stages of the analysis, where we will show that the place where a youth was detained has a subsequent impact on future decisions made about the youth. It seems clear that whatever the fact of the matter, later decision-makers interpreted the place where a youth had been detained as reflective of youth characteristics rather than system characteristics.

Other characteristics of the youths' situation provide a picture of what kinds of youths were detained in what kinds of settings. Social class, for example, has a bearing. Youths whose fathers were better educated were likely to be detained in shelter care units. Youths whose fathers were employed in white-collar jobs were not likely to be detained in custodial units as were youths whose fathers were employed in unskilled jobs. This bimodal distribution suggests that youths of families with power to hold DYS accountable received better probation placements and that youths from poorer families may be in DYS in order to receive services for which they could not otherwise qualify. The notion that some youths have to be adjudicated to qualify for services is popular in this state. While we do not have conclusive evidence to substantiate this claim, our data suggest that this may very well be the case. This theme will be addressed more fully in our analysis of placement of committed and referred youths in Chapter 5 where we find similar placement patterns.

Youth perceptions of officials or people in authority is one of the factors that DYS staff people try to ferret out as they make decisions about detention placement. Youths with more positive attitudes toward officials are likely to be detained in shelter care units, while youths with negative attitudes are likely to be detained in custodial units. By looking additionally at the partial correlations of variables that are not included in the regression equation, we discover that

Table 4–2. Multiple Regression of Place of Detention on Background Variables

Background Variable	Shelter Care		Treatment		Custody	
	Coefficient	Standardized Coefficient	Coefficient	Standardized Coefficient	Coefficient	Standardized Coefficient
Ethnicity: Mother northern Europe					-.11	-.11**
Father's schooling	.02	.16***				
Father white-collar employed					-.21	-.21***
Father unskilled employed					-.13	-.10**
Sex female			.10	.12**		
Family is satisfied with income					.05	.10**
Region I	-.21	-.17***	.47	.44***		
Region II	-.17	-.15***	.41	.45***		
Region IV	.23	.20***			.18	.15***
Region VII	.22	.19***				
Self-reported past offenses: Drugs alone			-.10	-.10**		
Current offense: Offense against person					.17	.12***
Number of court appearances before this commitment to DYS					.02	.18***

Number of months at longest job	-.11				.01	.12**
Bosses never punish you for what others do					.11	.11**
Bosses never reward you for what others do		-.13**				
Significant other: Kid acquaintance illegal					.16	.13***
Parents usually punish you for what others have done			.12	.12***		
Kids don't view you as good or bad					-.23	-.14***
Kids you hang with want to become part of society					.13	.13**
Other kids sometimes punish you for what others do	-.19	-.13***			.16	.11**
Perception of officials	.07	.20***			-.07	-.19***
Ran from DYS prior to this commitment	-.08	-.11*				
Regression Constant	-.25		-.01		.21	
Multiple R	.50		.64		.61	

youngsters who are detained in shelter care units are more generally positive toward others, including their primary and secondary groups [10]. Youths detained in custody units think poorly not only of people in authority but also of members of their primary group.

Youths who identify as significant others youths who engage in illegal activity are also more likely to be detained in custodial units. It would appear that youngsters who have stronger ties with a delinquent group are considered to be higher risks than youngsters who have weaker linkages. Youths who apparently do not feel greatly pressured to conform to either deviant or nondeviant peer expectations (as measured by their sense that peers do not make judgments about them being "good or bad kids") are not usually detained in custody units. It is reasonable to expect that these youths are not as attached to deviant networks as are some of their comrades, who believe that they are constantly being judged.

Prior experience in DYS influences the detention placement decision. Youths who had run during prior DYS commitments were not likely to be detained in shelter care units. To assure appearance at the adjudication hearing, these youths were held in the more restrictive treatment and custody units.

Youths who believe that their parents punish them regularly for what others do are more frequently found in treatment units. Curiously in terms of work experience, the longer youths have worked on a job before getting into trouble, the more likely the youths are to be detained in a custody unit.

In our regression equations none of the school-related variables was found to be associated with place of detention. However, if we look at the partial correlations of variables that nearly were included in the equations, we note that youths who completed higher grade levels were less likely to be detained in custody units. Since age is not associated with place of detention, we can be rather certain that the above variable relationship is an indication that youths who fail or drop out of school are likely to be detained in custody units. Youngsters who believed that teachers thought of them as "bad kids" were most likely to be detained in the treatment units. Youths who believed that teachers did not make judgments about them were not likely to be found in custody units. These data tend to confirm the notion that teachers are important gatekeepers, not only through the decisions they make in their own classrooms, but also as developers of information on youths that is relied on by other decision-makers outside the school arena.

In summary, the decision to detain a youngster in a certain type of detention facility is largely determined by factors other than offense-related variables. It is determined to a great extent by the availability of detention slots. It is also influenced by social class and peer group relationships as well as by at least some past experiences with DYS. While one has the sense that the decision *where* to detain is less idiosyncratic than the original decision to detain, one is still hard pressed to find much logic behind the decisions. While such decisions may seem transitory and of little importance, it will become clear as we now turn to a discussion of their impact that they represent a pivotal block of decisions within the juvenile justice system.

IMMEDIATE CONSEQUENCES OF PLACE OF DETENTION

We have stated that detention decisions have long-run effects that shape youths' future life chances, particularly as they participate in the youth corrections system. However, one can also expect that detention, as an experience in itself, will have important immediate consequences for those who are exposed to it. For example, 50 percent of the youths detained in custodial units remain there for three weeks or more (Table 4—3). This is compared to 39 percent detained in shelter care and 32 percent in treatment units. Because length of stay is dependent upon the court's reaching a decision to adjudicate or to drop the case, the different lengths of stay are influenced by court liaison officers and probation officers as they prepare their cases and work out possible placements and by the judge's willingness to move quickly to resolve the case.

From our interviews with judges and other court personnel, it is clear that the process is sometimes intentionally slowed down in order to insure that the youth remains off the streets and in a secure setting. The judge who has little faith in the department's ability to hold a committed youngster in secure placement will choose to continue the case a few times, thereby "buying time for the community by keeping the kid off the streets." This is one way for the court to circumvent the community-based thrust of the reform. However, even this aberration has its limits because of the finite number of detention slots. Any increase in detention slots, particularly custodial slots, will increase the court's leverage.

The importance of the difference in length of stay is reinforced as we note the variation in quality of life across the types of detention. Sixty-five percent of the youths in custodial units claimed that some youths in the unit pushed others around, as contrasted with 49 percent claiming this in treatment units and 29 percent in shelter care units. Similarly, 64 percent of youths in treatment units, 54 percent

Table 4–3. Youth Reactions to Detention Experiences by Type of Detention

| | Youth Reactions | | | | | | | | | | | | |
| Type of Detention | Kids push other kids around | | Few kids run every- thing | | Staff and kids split into two groups | | Staff kept kids informed | | Staff let kids share in decisions | | Did you fit in | | Staff people see youth as good kid | |
	Percent Yes	(N)	Percent Yes	(N)	Percent Yes	(N)	Percent Yes	(N)	Percent Yes	(N)	Percent Yes	(N)	Percent Yes	(N)
Shelter care	29	(73)	36	(74)	44	(72)	57	(72)	62	(71)	67	(73)	44	(73)
Treatment	49	(55)	64	(55)	44	(55)	54	(56)	54	(56)	64	(55)	46	(56)
Custody	65	(80)	54	(81)	59	(80)	29	(78)	45	(80)	44	(81)	30	(79)

in custodial units, and 36 percent in shelter care units indicated that a few kids ran everything.

Staying informed about what to expect and about what is happening, particularly in a strange and sometimes harsh environment, is highly regarded by persons in general. Youths detained in shelter care facilities fared better at staying informed. Fifty-seven percent believed that they were kept informed, as compared to 54 percent in treatment units and only 29 percent in custodial units. It seems evident that the bulk of youngsters in custodial units were unenlightened.

Another attribute people share is the need to have some sense of power over their future. Youths were asked whether they believed that they shared in decisions being made about their futures. Again we discover that the shelter care units were most able to foster the kind of environment supportive of youth participation. Sixty-two percent of the youths indicated that they shared in decisions. This contrasts with 54 percent of the youths in treatment units and 45 percent of youths in custodial units.

Finally, respondents were asked whether they "fitted in" the environment of the detention facility. Sixty-seven percent of the shelter care youths stated that they did, compared to 64 percent of the treatment youths and 44 percent of the custodial youths.

It seems evident, therefore, that at least from the youngsters' perspective, clear-cut differences can be found in the quality of life experienced in the various detention settings. Custodial units provide the harshest and most restrictive settings. The fact that more youths in those settings stay for longer periods of time compounds the immediate effect of being detained there. Thus even if no other consequences for detained youths could be demonstrated, these immediate effects are varied and substantial enough to argue for more caution in exercising detention decisions.

Proponents of the labeling perspective argue that negative sanctions, such as detention, by social control agents produce alienation, a lowering of self-esteem, and the impetus to define oneself as a delinquent, thereby enmeshing the youngster more firmly in a delinquent career [11]. Detractors of the labeling perspective claim that these assumptions are not empirically founded [12]. A review of the literature shows that the empirical results are mixed [13].

With this controversy in mind and recognizing that Commissioner Miller was influenced at least in part by this perspective [14], we tried to determine whether the detention experience for the youths in this book had any short-run effect on self-image or perception of the primary group, the secondary group, or public officials. In our resulting regression equations, the best predictors of how these youths would view themselves and others after detention were their perceptions of themselves and others when entering detention. We did not discover dramatic shifts in perception; however, the quality of the detention experience does nevertheless remain somewhat determinative. For example, youngsters who believe that the detention staff considered them to be "good kids" had positive self-images; obversely, youths who believed that staff saw them as "bad kids" had poorer self-images. Longer periods spent in detention, especially in facilities where a few youths ran everything, are associated with negative perceptions of one's peer group. Youths leaving custodial units were less favorably disposed toward their primary group. Youths who believed that the detention staff did not consider them to be good or bad were less positive toward their secondary group. In addition, youths who did not feel that they fitted into the detention facility were more negative toward public officials.

The controversy remains unresolved. The data do not show radical alterations in self-perception or perception of others although detention did have some impact. From our point of view, identities and relationships are negotiated over time. Labels can be resisted or ignored by the individual. We would not therefore expect many youths to experience dramatic changes in their views of themselves or others because of one experience in detention.

More important to our analysis than direct or immediate social-psychological impact on an individual is the cumulative effect of decisions on other decision-makers, which in turn will have a restricting effect both inside and outside the justice system on the youngsters' future opportunities. We would expect that in time severe restrictions in opportunities would also alter and shape one's own identity.

The long-run consequences of detention will be traced further in later chapters as we analyze data about decisions to place a committed youngster within DYS, the impact of these placements, and the factors contributing to recidivism. However, even the immediate consequences we have noted thus far should be sufficient to caution decision-makers about making perfunctory detention judgments. Furthermore, when one realizes that most detained youths are not committed or referred to DYS, one must wonder whether the damage caused by severing any constructive ties that the youngster has in the community outweighs the need to detain the youngster in the first place. The fact that a youngster was detained will become part of the youngster's history, and it will be read and interpreted by others in the community for years to come.

✳ *Chapter 5*

Who Gets Placed Where?

Once a youngster is referred or committed to the Massachusetts Department of Youth Services (DYS), someone must determine where that youngster will be placed for services within the department. The central question to be addressed in this chapter is what kinds of factors influence the placement decision. We will begin by describing the range of programs in DYS, using the institutionalization-normalization continuum as an analytical framework. We will then see how a longitudinal sample was distributed across the programs, and finally we will analyze what factors determined placement.

THE RANGE OF PROGRAMS

In Chapter 1 we presented a conceptual framework for comparing and contrasting program settings along an institutionalization-normalization continuum. Here we will indicate how that framework was operationally defined for this book. We will then apply that framework along the range of programs, both private and public, operating within DYS. In doing so, we will show the analytical advantages of the continuum over the more standard typology for categorizing program settings.

Application of the continuum will show that while DYS has closed its training schools in a significant reform effort, many changes still remain to be made before the bulk of its client population are in settings than can be characterized as having high-quality linkages with the larger community environment.

Empirical documentation of the continuum was carried out by combining information from four data sources. A group of 586 youths were studied over a three-year period as they moved through the various programs of DYS. During that period the youths collectively had experiences in 132 programs, including nonresidential programs, foster care, forestry camps, group homes, boarding schools, secure care, and adult jails and houses of correction. These youths were routinely asked about their program experiences three months after they began the program, if they had not left prior to that point, and upon leaving the program if they had been in the program for at least one month. Seven hundred and twenty-one such interviews were completed. Questions asked of these youths provided an indication of the nature of the social climate and the quality of community linkages. The questions follow:

Social Climate

Communication

Do staff here try to make you understand why things happen and why they feel the way they do about it?

1. No.
2. Sometimes.
3. Yes.

Decision-Making

Do staff here usually let you share in decisions that they make about you?

1. No.
2. Yes, they ask me what I think before they decide.
3. Yes, they let me help make choices.

Control

If you screw up, will staff here punish you?

1. No.
2. Yes, they will separate me from the group.
3. Yes, they will take away my privileges.
4. Yes, they will hit me.
5. Yes, they will embarrass me in front of others.
6. Yes, they will make me feel guilty.

If you do well, will the staff reward you?

1. No.
2. Yes, they will include me in things.
3. Yes, they will give me additional privileges.
4. Yes, they will make me look good in front of others.
5. Yes, they will make me feel good about what I am doing.

Quality of Community Linkages

Access to Resources

Do staff here help you stay out of trouble?

1. No.
2. Yes, they encourage me by telling me that I can make it.
3. Yes, they help me get jobs, into youth groups, into new school programs and things like that.

Because of the expected wide dispersal of the longitudinal sample across the many available programs, the original research design also included a cross-sectional survey. We wanted a more concentrated picture of what was happening to youths in each of the programs that served the bulk of the longitudinal sample. Twenty-four programs were selected. In these programs all the youths or in large programs a sample of youths were asked a more extensive battery of questions that provide another assessment of the nature of the social climate and the extent and quality of community linkages. Two hundred fifty youths were interviewed in this survey. The questions are statements with which the respondents are asked to express their agreement or disagreement on a five-point scale. The questions follow:

Social Climate: [1]

Communication

The staff members try to keep you informed about what's happening with the general program here at _____ .

If a kid does well here, the staff will tell him so personally.

Kids in the general program usually tell someone when they think he's done something wrong.

If a kid does well here, the other kids will tell him so personally.

Decision-Making

The staff makes changes without consulting the kids.

If the kids really want to, they can share in decisions about how the general program is run.

Control

The staff is more concerned with keeping kids under control than with helping them with their problems.

If a kid screws up, the staff will punish him/her.

If a kid screws up, other kids here will punish him.

The staff will reward a kid for good behavior.

Other kids here will reward a kid for good behavior.

Fairness

Most of the rules here are fair.

The staff deals fairly and squarely with everyone.

All of the kids here try to take advantage of you.

There are a few kids here who run everything.

Kids around here usually get on your back for no reason.

Most kids here will beat you up to get what they want.

Extent of Community Linkages:

The kids in this general program spend a lot of time outside in the larger community.

Ratio of kids participating in programs outside the setting (based on a question asking what program strategies the youth participate in).

Quality of Community Linkages:

Communication

If a kid in this general program does well out in the community, people out there will tell him so personally.

Decision-Making

If a kid really wants to help plan his future out in the larger community he can.

Control

People in the larger community are more concerned with keeping kids from this general program under control than with helping them with their problems.

If a kid in this general program does well out in the community, people out there will punish him.

People in the outside community generally hassle kids in this program.

Access to Community Resources

Staff here help the kids get jobs outside, get into youth groups, into new school programs, and things like that.

People in the outside community don't help kids in this general program get jobs outside, get into youth groups, into new school programs, and things like that.

In addition to these two sources of information provided by youths, two other types of data are provided by staff. In eighteen of the twenty-four cross-sectional programs we were able to interview 88 staff members who provided their perspective on the three dimensions of the continuum. Throughout the time we followed youths in the longitudinal sample we were also able to interview informally 144 staff members and observe program functioning in seventy-two program settings. The questions used in the eighteen programs were similar to those used in the cross-sectional sample of youths and are shown below. Informal interviews and observations were coded on two dimensions. These are also shown below.

Social Climate:

Communication

If a kid does well here, the staff will tell him so personally.

Kids in the general program usually tell someone when they think he's done something wrong.

If a kid does well here, the other kids will tell him so personally.

Decision-Making

The staff makes changes without consulting the kids.

If the kids really want to, they can share in decisions about how the general program is run.

Control

The staff is more concerned with keeping kids under control than with helping them with their problems.

If a kid screws up, the staff will punish him/her.

If a kid screws up, other kids here will punish him.

The staff here will reward a kid for good behavior.

Other kids here will reward a kid for good behavior.

Fairness

Most of the rules here are fair.

All of the kids here try to take advantage of you.

Most kids here will beat each other up to get what they want.

Extent of Community Linkages:

The kids in this general program spend a lot of time outside in the larger community.

Quality of Community Linkages:

Communication

If a kid in this general program does well out in the community, people out there will tell him so personally.

Decision-Making

If a kid really wants to help plan his future out in the larger community he can.

Control

People in the larger community are more concerned with keeping kids from this general program under control than with helping them with their problems.

If a kid in this general program does well out in the community, people out there will punish him/her.

People in the outside community generally hassle kids in this program.

Access to Community Resources

Staff here help the kids get jobs outside, get into youth groups, into new school programs, and things like that.

People in the outside community don't help kids in this general
program get jobs outside, get into youth groups, into new school
programs, and things like that.

Informal Staff Interviews and Observations

Extent of Community Linkages:

1. None or little.
2. Some.
3. Frequent.
4. A lot with control.
5. Fluid.

Quality of Community Linkages:

1. No experience.
2. Tutoring/community participation in setting.
3. Recreational/cultural trips.
4. Encourage kids about jobs/schools and some participation in
   jobs and school.
5. Advocacy.

For those programs in which a few youths from the longitudinal
sample were placed but where we had no specific information on the
extent dimension, we were able to derive estimates based on either
what we knew about the programs from our informal sources or by
using the mode that other programs in the same program class (jail,
secure, boarding school, group home, forestry camp, foster care, or
nonresidential) had received. These programs typically had only one
or two youths in the sample, were beyond the New England region
(three programs), had closed before we were actually able to observe
them, or were jails. In any case we believe that we have been able to
provide reasonably sound estimates for the *extent* dimension, and we
have indicators for the other two dimensions in these programs on
the basis of questions asked of the youths in the longitudinal sample.

Information gathered from these four data sources was merged
in the following manner. Means and standard deviations for the
youth data were calculated for the twenty-four programs that were
in both the cross-sectional survey and the longitudinal sample. These
figures were used to compute standardized scores (z scores) for each
of the two youth data sets separately. Average weighted z scores
were calculated for each program by merging the z scores from the
two sets of data while weighting by the number of responses per pro-

gram per data set. These weighted z scores and the z scores for the remainder of the programs based on the longitudinal sample (normed on the twenty-four base programs) represent the summary measures of youth responses for the programs.

Next, the two staff data sources were normed on the average weighted z scores from the youths on the twenty-four base programs. Using the same means and standard deviations, standard scores were computed for the remaining programs having staff data. The two sets of staff data were then merged by averaging, weighting by the number of staff providing information for each program.

After obtaining average weighted z scores for youth data and also for staff data, we found it necessary to merge the two sets of data in order to arrive at a single score for each dimension for each program. Again, the standard scores were weighted and averaged on the basis of the number of persons responding per program. This time, however, the weights for the staff data were set on the average at 40 percent of the weight of the youth data. This weighting reflects our particular interest in how the consumer views or evaluates the program, while at the same time our concern is to have staff input to provide a tempered, balanced picture.

DYS programs can be classified in seven categories: nonresidential, foster care, forestry, group homes, boarding schools, DYS secure care, and jail. Table 5—1 displays the distribution of programs within the seven-category program classification variables by the z scores on the three-dimensional continua: *social climate*, *extent of linkages*, and *quality of linkages* with the community. Table 5—1 further displays the aggregate by the overall institutionalization-normalization continuum.

Results indicate considerable congruence between the distribution obtained by the more elaborate use of the continua and the distribution obtained by the more standard typology. However, it is also clear from this table that the continua yield further differentiation among correctional settings. It is evident that there are substantial differences *within* the category of nonresidential programs, *within* the category of group homes, and *within* other program categories. For example, looking at the overall continuum, one finds that the majority of the nonresidential programs are within two standard deviations above zero. However, a number of these programs are within three standard deviations below zero. The group homes are fairly evenly split on either side of zero. Even for DYS secure settings in which nearly all the programs fall below zero, they are rather evenly distributed across the first *three* standard deviations below zero. These differences within program class suggest substantial differences that are not part of the analysis if one simply relies on the basic seven-category program classification scheme. The nature of these differences becomes clearer as we consider the distributions of the dimensional continua within and across program classes.

As one would expect, all the nonresidential programs are above zero on the *extent of community linkage* dimension. However, a substantial number fall below zero on the *social climate* and *quality of community linkage* dimensions. The dispersion of these programs on the *social climate* dimension reflects in part the fact that the subcultures of these programs are permeated by the youth subculture in the community. If the youth subculture has negative components, they are likely to be reflected in the programs because the programs are attempting to deal with youths in their present environment, frequently by providing counseling or educational services and work experiences. Furthermore, because the youths come and go on widely differing schedules, staff may have to be more directive than in a residential program where staff can try to intervene more subtly through the group process. It may be easier in general to create a "we" feeling in a more isolated setting where all the residents have the time and are expected to deal with one another. There is more competition for a youth's time and interests in a nonresidential setting. This factor may have a substantial effect on establishing a positive social climate. Nearly a third of the nonresidential programs are below the mean on the *quality* dimension. This may be explained in part by the different program approaches, by the varying levels of acceptance of the youths and the program by different communities, and by the differing levels of resources available in the various communities.

Foster care also received high scores for the *extent of community linkage* dimension. While there is bound to be some variability across individual foster care placements in terms of frequency and duration of community contact, in general it is regarded as providing a relatively open setting permitting fairly fluid interaction for the youths in the community. On the *quality* dimension, programs group closely around zero. Factors affecting the *quality* dimension for foster care youths will largely be the same factors affecting any youths living in a community—the availability of community resources and the attitudes toward youths in general. Many of these youths are not identified as DYS youths in the foster home community, thus reducing the stigma of that association. Dispersion of the social climate ranges six standard deviations, indicating the differences in the quality of

Table 5–1. Distribution of Programs Across Program Types and the Institutionalization-Normalization Dimension Continua (Ns)

	Program Type						
Continua Standard Deviations[a]	Nonresidential	Foster Care	Forestry	Group Home	Boarding School	DYS Secure	Jail
Social Climate:							
(+3.00) — (+3.99)	2			1			
(+2.00) — (+2.99)	2	1	1	5			
(+1.00) — (+1.99)	3	1		6	3	3	1
(0.0) — (+.99)	6	2		14	3	3	
(−.01) — (−1.00)	7	1	3	14	3	2	
(−1.01) — (−2.00)		2	1	8	1	2	1
(−2.01) — (−3.00)	5	1	1	2	2	2	
(−3.01) — (−4.00)				3	1	1	
(−4.01) — (−5.00)				1			3
(−5.01) — (−6.00)				1	2	1	2
(−6.01) — (−7.00)							1
(−7.01) — (−8.00)							
Extent of Community Linkages:							
(+3.00) — (+3.99)							
(+2.00) — (+2.99)							
(+1.00) — (+1.99)	18	7		3	2		
(0.0) — (+.99)	7	1		23	3	1	
(−.01) — (−1.00)			4	13	7	4	
(−1.01) — (−2.00)			2	16	3	9	8
(−2.01) — (−3.00)							
(−3.01) — (−4.00)							
(−4.01) — (−5.00)							
(−5.01) — (−6.00)							
(−6.01) — (−7.00)							
(−7.01) — (−8.00)							

Quality of Community Linkages:

(+3.00) — (+3.99)							
(+2.00) — (+2.99)							
(+1.00) — (+1.99)	6	2		3	3	1	1
(0.0) — (+ .99)	11	3		19	3	7	1
(− .01) — (−1.00)	6	3		25	7	4	6
(−1.01) — (−2.00)	2		6	7	1	2	
(−2.01) — (−3.00)				1	1		
(−3.01) — (−4.00)							
(−4.01) — (−5.00)							
(−5.01) — (−6.00)							
(−6.01) — (−7.00)							
(−7.01) — (−8.00)							

Overall Continuum:

(+3.00) — (+3.99)							
(+2.00) — (+2.99)					2		
(+1.00) — (+1.99)	6			1	5	1	
(0.0) — (+ .99)	13	1	1	23	5	4	2
(− .01) — (−1.00)	4	5	3	23	1	4	6
(−1.01) — (−2.00)	1	2	1	7	1	4	
(−2.01) — (−3.00)	1		1	1	1	1	
(−3.01) — (−4.00)							
(−4.01) — (−5.00)							
(−5.01) — (−6.00)							
(−6.01) — (−7.00)							
(−7.01) — (−8.00)							

Total N	25	8	6	55	15	14	8

[a] The high standard deviations are result of the norming process.

life within the various foster home settings. One would expect to find as many different patterns of foster families as one would find in natural families.

Forestry programs fall below zero on the *extent of community linkages* dimension as well as the *quality* dimension. Almost by definition, many of the programs are relatively isolated from the community; some are quite remote. Thus it is not surprising that youths and staff perceive their linkages with the community to be somewhat poor. Still these programs receive a higher rating on quality than many group homes, boarding schools, DYS secure facilities, and jail categories. This factor may be a function of isolation; being isolated and engaged in intensive programming, the residents may not be subjected to as much hassling by the community as residents in some other programs. Possibly youths in forestry programs are not stigmatized by persons in the community to the same extent as youths in other programs because "going to camp" is something with which many people can identify. The New Deal CCC camps also provide a positive connotation for this type of activity. The *social climate* dimension yields scores that are more widely diverse although five of the six programs fall below the mean. One would expect that at least in those situations where survival in a strange setting is part of the program, less emphasis would be placed on group decision-making. The ruggedness of the program may also shape the perceptions of the respondents.

It is quite clear from our findings that all group homes are *not* alike. This may seem obvious, and yet much of the discussion in the field fails to draw such distinctions. On the *extent* dimension the programs are quite evenly divided on either side of zero. However, sixteen of the fifty-five group homes are as isolated as the jails and more isolated than five of the DYS secure facilities. The treatment modality is clearly related to the extent of community linkages in the group homes. The programs that are attempting to set up a fairly normalized family setting with residents participating in public schools, having jobs in the community, and making routine use of the recreational facilities in the community will score high. On the other hand, a group home relying on a self-help therapy model (particularly in its more extreme or pure form) may have little or no contact with the community. Instead, the emphasis is on building a strong positive social climate in which residents are able to deal with their feelings. Thus a positive social climate does not necessarily indicate that there will be extensive linkages with the community. Twenty-two of the group homes are above zero on *quality of community linkages*. In many of these cases, there is significant support from community residents for the program and its clients. Public schools will accept the youths, sometimes providing special services for those needing remedial assistance. Employers provide work opportunities in which youths can earn money. YMCAs and other community recreational facilities are open to the residents, and the police and neighbors do not regard the setting as posing any major threat. Staff members are usually actively engaged in involving the community in the program and in several instances work with other members of the community to generate additional resources for all youths in the community.

For the youths in the group homes falling below zero the relationship with the community is more guarded and in some instances openly antagonistic. For some of these programs it took a fight to establish the group home in the first place, and at the time of the survey a workable truce was still to be achieved. Staff in these programs frequently complained that they were not given a chance and that any youth crime problem in the community was attributed to the residents of the group home. Others complained that police hassled the residents and would pick them up on any minor violation in order to remove them from the community. In some of these programs, staff members were rather secretive about what went on in the house and what kinds of youths actually resided there. It is reasonable to assume that in some of these programs the staff members and youths were as antagonistic toward the community as community members were toward the program and its residents. In fact this antagonism was frequently used to strengthen the cohesion within the program setting. The conflict helped to foster a "we against them" feeling, having a positive effect on the social climate within the setting, but presenting numerous obstacles to the reintegration of the residents.

Group homes were widely dispersed across the *social climate* dimension with about half the programs falling on either side of zero. In some of these programs, staff members were trying to help clients develop their educational and work skills, take on increased responsibility for their own behavior, and come to a better understanding of themselves and others. Caring should not be equated, however, with permissiveness. Residents who were disruptive were punished, usually by removal of privileges. Other programs placed more emphasis on dealing with one's feelings and working through those feelings by verbal confrontation. The verbal confrontation approach did not necessarily yield poor ratings on social climate; in fact, in several instances it produced fairly favorable ratings. However, where the approach was not properly controlled by staff and deteriorated into one group of youths clashing with another (verbally or otherwise), the social climate ratings were typically negative.

A small minority of the group homes appeared quite institution-like in terms of social climate with tight controls on communications (at least one program did not permit any communication with any-one on the outside for the first month), high regimentation, and the threat of physical force if house rules were violated.

Boarding schools posed an interesting alternative for DYS. During the early seventies, boarding schools, which had traditionally catered to youths of the upper middle class, experienced a drop in enroll-ments and thus became interested in serving different kinds of youths, including DYS youth. However, many of the boarding schools had great difficulty dealing with the more abrasive DYS youngster, partly because the teaching staff had no prior experience or training in handling these youths. On the *extent* dimension, two-thirds of the boarding schools fall below the mean. Many of these facilities are quite large and fairly self-contained, requiring little other than tolerance from the community. They also tend to be isolated in the country or on the outskirts of small towns. On the *quality of community linkages* dimension, only slightly more than one-third of them are above zero. Boarding schools experience many of the same difficulties as group homes. Because they are relatively more isolated than some of the latter, it is probably more difficult to generate the kind of trust necessary to build supportive relation-ships.

The majority of the boarding schools received positive ratings on *social climate*. Some of the schools that did not were quite regi-mented. A number of these boarding schools no longer serve DYS youths, partly because their administrators came to believe that DYS youths posed too many problems for the schools.

Thirteen of the fourteen DYS secure facilities fall below zero on the *extent of community linkages* dimension. However, there is some dispersion that reflects in part the different kinds of secure measures employed. Some secure facilities can best be described as relatively humane jails—very isolated from the local community. A couple are self-help therapy models, in one of which residents have no contact with the community, while the other permits some interaction but runs a "tight house" when there have been incidents in either the community or the house. Other secure facilities have fairly routine contact with the community under stringent controls. In two such programs, a few youths have been permitted to work in the local community. The frequency of contact even in these programs varies depending on the pressures within the facility and from the community. Ratings on the *quality* dimension correspond to those on *extent*.

In terms of *social climate*, six of the secure settings fall within one standard deviation on either side of zero, suggesting that secure units can be developed without resorting to the extreme institutional social climates generally found in jail settings. These more humane programs typically rely on group-process models and minimize the level of regimentation within the setting. Although the threat of physical force is somewhat more prevalent than in most group homes, it is not the norm, even for handling acting-out youths. Other secure settings that received lower scores on the *social climate* dimension relied less on the group-process models and more on the threat of physical force by staff and among youths. The secure facility with the lowest score, as low as the jail with the lowest *social climate* rating, was outside the New England area and received much national notoriety. The three or four youngsters sent there were shortly brought back to Massachusetts by DYS.

While following the longitudinal sample of DYS youths, we found a few who had spent some time in jails for adult offenders [2]. On both the *extent* and *quality* dimensions, the jails received low ratings. In terms of *social climate*, the ratings by youths were again low, but at least two settings stand out as not as bad as the others.

The data above depict a correctional system with considerable diversity in the kinds of program settings available to youths. Not only does one find different kinds of program types in use, but also one discovers that within types there exists a considerable difference in terms of social climate and extent and quality of linkages with the community. Taken as a whole, DYS has a range of programs that represent considerable movement toward the community when contrasted with the traditional training-school model. However, from our observation of programs as well as the data gleaned from youths, it is apparent that although many of the private vendors are in the community, they remain quite isolated from the day-to-day life of the community. Many of these programs and their clients merely exist in the community—they do not participate in it.

DISTRIBUTION OF YOUTHS ACROSS RANGE OF PROGRAMS

The suspicion that DYS youth are not as involved in the larger community as originally intended is further confirmed when we look at the distribution of youths across the programs. Table 5−2 provides an overview of how youths are distributed across the dimensions and

Table 5–2. Frequency Distribution of Completed Youths from the Longitudinal Sample on Program Type and the Institutionalization-Normalization Dimension Continue

Continua Standard Deviations	Nonresidential	Foster Care	Forestry	Group Home	Boarding School	DYS Secure	Jail	N	Percent Total N
Social Climate:									
(+3.00) — (+3.99)	2			1				3	1
(+2.00) — (+2.99)	1	1		5	5			11	3
(+1.00) — (+1.99)	3	3		10	1			16	4
(0.0) — (+.99)	7	14		43	3	5		69	16
(−.01) — (−1.00)	32	4	103	46	2	34		217	48
(−1.01) — (−2.00)		27		15	5	12		56	13
(−2.01) — (−3.00)				4		2	1	8	2
(−3.01) — (−4.00)	4	3		10	1	14		26	6
(−4.01) — (−5.00)				3		24	4	24	6
(−5.01) — (−6.00)			1		2		2	8	2
(−6.01) — (−7.00)			1			1		2	.4
Extent of Community Linkage:									
(+3.00) — (+3.99)									
(+2.00) — (+2.99)									
(+1.00) — (+1.99)	24	44		2	2	2		72	16
(0.0) — (+.99)	25	8	101	65	4	6		108	23
(−.01) — (−1.00)			4	37	11	35		184	40
(−1.01) — (−2.00)				33	2	51	7	97	21
(−2.01) — (−3.00)									
(−3.01) — (−4.00)									
(−4.01) — (−5.00)									
(−5.01) — (−6.00)									
(−6.01) — (−7.00)									

Quality of Community Linkages:

Range								Total N	Percent
(+3.00) — (+3.99)									
(+2.00) — (+2.99)									
(+1.00) — (+1.99)	6	1		2	3		1	13	3
(0.0) — (+ .99)	20	36		51	3	8		118	26
(− .01) — (−1.00)	23	15	105	81	11	47		282	61
(−1.01) — (−2.00)				3	2	35		38	8
(−2.01) — (−3.00)						2	6	9	2
(−3.01) — (−4.00)									
(−4.01) — (−5.00)									
(−5.01) — (−6.00)									
(−6.01) — (−7.00)									

Overall Continuum:

Range								Total N	Percent
(+3.00) — (+3.99)									
(+2.00) — (+2.99)									
(+1.00) — (+1.99)	7	1			3			11	2
(0.0) — (+ .99)	29	42		48	4	2		125	27
(− .01) — (−1.00)	12	9	103	65	9	48		247	54
(−1.01) — (−2.00)	1		1	24	2	15		42	9
(−2.01) — (−3.00)			1		1	27	6	29	6
(−3.01) — (−4.00)								7	1
(−4.01) — (−5.00)									
(−5.01) — (−6.00)									
(−6.01) — (−7.00)									

N	49	52	105	137	19	92	7	461[a]	
Percent Total N	11	11	23	30	4	20	1		

[a] Total N of completed youths is 493. Thirty-one youths were either placed directly on parole or did not stay in a single program for at least a month—these youths are classified as having "no program" and are not included in this table [3]. One respondent was in a program that did not receive any ratings on the dimension.

program types at initial placement in the system [3]. Thirty-nine percent of the youths in the sample are in programs that fall above zero on the *extent* dimension. Twenty-one percent are in programs located more than one standard unit below zero at the low end of the continuum. These results suggest that while on the whole the new system is more community based than the old training-school system (in a 1971 to 1972 sample of youth from training schools only six percent had routine involvement with the community), the current system still limits considerably the contact between youths and the community. In terms of social climate, 24 percent of the youths in the sample are in programs that score above zero. Another 48 percent, however, are in programs that fall one standard unit below zero. About 12 percent of the youths in the sample are in programs that fall near the lower end of the continuum. The bulk of the latter group of youths are in the secure care facilities. Less than a third of the youths in the sample are in the programs scoring above zero on the *quality* dimension, and the same is true for the overall continuum.

We should parenthetically note that the initial placement of youths was sometimes quite slow. Occasionally youths were held in detention centers after commitment technically "awaiting placement." Departmental spokesman indicated that these temporary placements did not constitute actual program placements. Youths were held there because appropriate placements were not available. We took a fairly conservative posture about this issue. If a committed youngster stayed in a detention facility awaiting placement for more than a month, we designated that facility as the youth's initial placement. Certainly from the youngster's point of view, he or she was functionally being held and acted upon by DYS staff. We also believed that such a designation was appropriate because particularly the custodial and treatment detention facilities were seemingly being informally used for secure care purposes [4].

Again, we are forced to recognize that while the replacement of the training school with the vast array of programs operated primarily by the private sector has brought about significant change in the social climate of program settings and has routinely exposed more youths to the larger community, the new system does not exhibit the extent and *quality* of linkages with the community that one would expect in a truly community-based system. We should not be surprised, then, to discover in Chapter 7 that this less than thorough change in the nature of relationships with the community has not produced the desired reduction in recidivism.

THE PLACEMENT DECISION

The decision to place a youngster in a specific program was usually made by a regional worker in charge of placement. These decisions were reviewed and monitored by the regional administrator. Other actors were also involved in some of the decisions. Judges would frequently request a secure setting for selected youths. While they did not have the power to demand a specific placement, their desires could not be routinely ignored. At other times, the private vendor would place constraints upon the decision by indicating that the vendor would not accept certain kinds of youngsters. However, the competitive nature of the private vending process held this kind of influence to a minimum. In some cases youths could play an active role in choosing where they would be placed. It was believed that if the youngsters participated in their own placement decision they would have more stake in the program and would therefore be less likely to abscond. In many instances, the youth and the program staff agreed to a three- or four-day trial period, providing both parties time to determine if the program was appropriate. The extent of youth participation, while uneven in practice across the state, had limits even where it was the norm. For example, if the youngster was given perhaps five programs to choose from and rejected each of them, the staff would then autonomously make the decision.

In order to address the question of program impact on youths, we must first find out what kinds of selectivity were operating in the placement decisions. Were youths being "creamed" for some programs—that is, were some programs only dealing with the less seriously acting-out youngsters, thereby enhancing their probability of success? Or were placement decisions made primarily on the basis of what kinds of youths were expected to do best in what kinds of programs? Or were placement decisions made as a response to crisis with the available slots dictating where youths would be placed?

Given that we have been studying a changing system in the natural setting without having the luxury of being able to control the object of study or randomize the flow of clients into the various programs, we have had to obtain as much background information on youths as feasible in order to sift out the factors that tend to determine where a committed youngster will be placed. We shall first consider each of the institutionalization-normalization dimensions—*social climate, extent of community linkages, quality of community linkages*, and the overall continuum—to determine what kinds of youths are placed in the more normalized settings.

Social Climate

What kinds of youths are placed in programs with the more supportive relationships between staff and youths and among youths? As was the case in the detention analysis, we proceed by first looking at a correlation matrix of all background variables, comparing family characteristics, offense history, prior DYS history, and detention and court experiences with the social climate dimension. The variables that appear to be significantly associated, plus any additional theoretically significant variables, are submitted to regression programs, thus permitting us to sort out which variables remain significantly related when all others in the regression equation are taken into account.

Certain features of a youth's offense history seem to influence the probability of the youth being placed in a program setting with a positive social climate (Table 5−3). Youths who were charged with car theft, who indicated that they frequently committed crimes against persons with others, and who said that the youths they hung around with regularly used heroin were likely to be held in programs characterized by poor social climates. Conversely, youths who indicated that they regularly committed status offenses by themselves were more likely to be placed in programs with positive social climates.

Proclivity toward violence was another factor that tended to influence the placement decision. Youths who disagreed with the statement that it was all right to beat up people to get what you want were more likely to be placed in programs with positive social climates.

The influence of detention is also quite apparent in this equation. Youths who stayed longer in detention and youths who believed that the detention staff viewed them as "bad kids" were most frequently placed in programs with poor social climates. We also know from Chapter 4 that custody detention was the type of detention most strongly related to these two variables. It seems clear that placement decision-makers have interpreted the prior detention decisions as having a sound logical base that confirms their notions that the youngsters need a relatively restricting environment. Given the idiosyncratic nature of the detention decisions, one must question whether this organizational labeling effect is well founded.

Other factors related to placement at this juncture include a social class variable: youths whose fathers are white-collar workers are more likely to be placed in program settings with positive social climates. One might expect that middle-class parents are inclined to oversee what happens to their youngsters in DYS and have more power to hold DYS accountable for its decisions.

Table 5–3. Multiple Regression of Initial Placement Within DYS on Prior Experiences

Prior Experience Variable	Social Climate		Extent of Linkage with Community		Quality of Linkage with Community		Overall Continuum	
	Coefficient	Standardized Coefficient	Coefficient	Standardized Coefficient	Coefficient	Standardized Coefficient	Coefficient	Standardized Coefficient
Ethnicity: Father Mediterranean			−.34	−.13**				
Religion Protestant	−.45	−.12**						
Sex female	.44	.10*						
Father white-collar employed	.54	.14**						
Father skill employed			−.30	−.16***			−.28	−.14**
Don't know whether mother has a job			.30	.12**				
Mother's schooling			−.06	−.14***	−.04	−.13**		
Region II			.33	.13**				
Region IV			−.33	−.13**				
Region VI			.41	.21***			.36	.17***
Number of times moved state to state					.04	.14**		

(Table 5–3. continued overleaf)

Table 5-3. continued

Prior Experience Variable	Social Climate		Extent of Linkage with Community		Quality of Linkage with Community		Overall Continuum	
	Coefficient	Standardized Coefficient	Coefficient	Standardized Coefficient	Coefficient	Standardized Coefficient	Coefficient	Standardized Coefficient
Self-reported past offense:								
Status offenses alone	1.02	.11**					.55	.11**
Person offenses with others	-1.24	-.10*						
Drugs alone			.28	.10*				
Car stealing with others					-.16	-.12**		
Current offense:								
Car stealing	-.47	-.11**					-.31	-.14**
Number of court appearances prior to this commitment			-.03	-.14**			-.04	-.17***
Friends use heroin	-.96	-.12**						
Friends both older and younger than self					.15	.11*		
Beating others up to get what you want not OK	.64	.22***					.34	.22***

	b	β	b	β	b	β	b	β
Judge committed you so you would learn skills	.58	.13**						
Judge sometimes punishes you for what others do	-.56	-.13**						
Probation officers sometimes reward you for what others do					-.23	-.11*		
Kids never reward you for what others do			-.19	-.11*				
Number of days in detention	-.01	-.12**			-.01	-.17***	-.01	-.17***
Detention staff members view you as bad kid	-1.05	-.14**						
Few kids did not run everything in detention					-.17	-.11*		
Prior commitment/referral to DYS			-.27	-.14***	-.13	-.09*	-.24	-.12**
Regression Constant	-2.53		.95		.49		-.86	
Multiple R	.48		.46		.36		.41	

That females are more likely to be placed in relatively more supportive social climates is somewhat surprising, particularly because it is commonly believed that the quality of services for girls lags behind that for boys. This may be partially explained by noting that forestry is used rather extensively for boys, and the nature of the program works against a strong positive climate.

Youths who indicated that judges had committed them to DYS to help them learn skills were placed in settings with a more positive social climate. This seems to confirm the belief that judges do influence placement outcomes even if informally.

Extent of Linkages with the Community

The *extent of linkages with the community* is the most clear-cut indicator of the youngsters' freedom to move about without extensive external controls. Once again we find some evidence to suggest that decision-makers are making placements based in part on the youth's offense history. Youths with greater numbers of prior court appearances and youths who had previously been committed or referred to the department were more likely to be placed in programs with fewer and less frequent linkages with the community. However, it is noteworthy that neither current charges nor self-reported delinquency (with the exception of youths who indicated they used drugs by themselves) were related to extent of linkage. Thus for the most part, one is just as likely to find one offense type in a high linkage program as another.

As was the case with the detention decisions, the place where one lives influences the kind of program in which one is placed within DYS. Youths living in regions II and VI are more likely to be placed in programs with higher levels of interaction with the larger community than youths in region IV. On the basis of our program surveys and observations, we know that region II uses foster care extensively and that region VI has had difficulty setting up group homes and uses nonresidential and secure programs heavily. At the time of the study, region IV used group homes and secure care almost exclusively.

Again we discover the unevenness of the reform across the state has had immediate consequences for youth—similar youths may be placed in very dissimilar programs. These differences can be attributed to factors such as staff orientation, availability of resources, and community resistance. An inadequate range of services within one region as contrasted with another promoted injustice. This may be one of the unintended consequences of a reform administered through a regionalized structure. At the time of this writing, it appears that some of the program inequities across the regions have been reduced. The leveling has been accomplished by the setting of uniform standards, budget allocations, and tighter central office management of the regions.

When the family variables in this equation and the variables whose partial correlations indicate that they were almost included in the equation are taken together, they leave us with a tentative indication that the department may be relied upon as a last resort social service agency for certain kinds of families, particularly for families that cannot qualify for welfare services. Youths who do not know whether their mothers work (an indication that the youths have not lived with their mothers for some time), youths whose fathers are engaged in unskilled employment, youths whose families feel that they can do nothing about their sense of powerlessness, and youths whose families have moved because of urban renewal are likely to be in the programs with the greatest *extent of linkages with the community.* We know from the first section of this chapter that such programs are nonresidential and foster care programs. On the other hand, youths whose fathers are engaged in skilled labor and whose mothers have higher levels of education are not likely to be in programs with a high extent of linkage. For youths in such programs, this may be seen as one alternative for providing the families with services. These data and this speculation tend to support some of the popular notions espoused by line staff and judges—that is, for some of these youngsters to receive services they must first commit a crime to qualify for help. If this is the case, we may want to devise methods for provision of such services outside the justice system.

Quality of Linkages with the Community

The only specific offense variable that seems to influence chances of a youth being placed in a program with good quality linkages is self-reported car stealing with others. Such youths not only frequently steal cars, but they are part of a network that supports such behavior. They are not likely to be placed in programs with quality linkages with the community. Offense history, as measured by prior commitment or referral to the department, is also related: youths who have been in DYS previously are less likely to be in a program with high-quality linkages.

We again find the influence of detention is a factor in DYS placement. The longer a youth is detained, the less likely it is that this youth will be placed in a program that has quality linkages. Even youths who were detained in the better detention facilities (as evidenced by youths saying "no" to the statement that a few kids run

everything) are likely not to be placed in programs with quality linkages. It therefore appears that even youths detained in shelter care
facilities are not likely to be placed in quality linkage programs. Prior
detention, then, seems to be a negative factor in the decision on
where a youth will be placed within DYS. Yet in Chapter 4 we found
little difference between committed youths who had been detained
and those who had not. Again we are led to believe that the detention effect on placement is at least in part a consequence of organizational labeling.

We find that youths whose mothers have higher levels of education
are not found in quality linkage programs. It should be remembered
that children from the more well-to-do families will probably not be
processed through DYS except in more extreme circumstances.
Those who are in DYS either present a substantial risk to the community or come from families that present a substantial threat to
their welfare. It is not too surprising, therefore, to find that these
youths are not in the more open programs.

Youths who indicated that probation officers had frequently rewarded them for what others did were also less likely to be placed
in the quality linkage programs. We have frequently found in our
interviews with probation officers and judges that they feel they
have already tried every community-based option available before a
youngster is committed to the department and therefore expect that
the youth will be held in a secure setting. This expectation may be
partially influencing the decision made by DYS regional placement
personnel.

From our regression equation we know that the type of youths
most likely to be placed in the programs with high levels of quality
linkages were youths who had not been detained and who had not
been previously committed to the department. They also tended to
be youths who had moved frequently from state to state and youths
who had friends of all ages.

Overall Institutionalization-Normalization Continuum

We will now consider the aggregated or overall institutionalization-
normalization continuum to summarize what kinds of youths are
most likely to be placed in the more institutionalized versus the more
normalized settings. Having already looked at the underlying dimensions, we can expect to find some selection in terms of offense history. Youths with more prior court appearances are likely to be in
the settings toward the institutional end of the continuum. A similar
pattern is found for youths who had previously been committed or
referred to the department. Youths who were charged with car steal-

ing are also more likely to be placed in settings toward the institutional end of the continuum. It is noteworthy that no distinction can be made in terms of placement among youths charged with other kinds of offenses, including crimes against persons.

Youths who indicated that they frequently committed status offenses by themselves were more likely to be in the normalized settings. It seems clear that an attempt is being made to sort out youths who are more committed to a delinquent career, as documented by the number of past court appearances and prior commitment or referral to DYS, and that these youngsters tend to be placed in the more restrictive settings. It should be noted that these factors are a combination of youth actions and actions previously taken by system decision-makers. Car thieves may be singled out for harsher treatment because of the nuisance factor that they raise in the community. It is also likely that if a car thief were to escape or run from a placement, such a youth would immediately use his or her delinquent skills, get into further trouble, and perhaps embarrass the department. It may not be surprising that such youths are singled out for the tightest control. It is evident that a proclivity to violence is also a characteristic for sorting youths. Youngsters who indicated that it was not all right to beat up other people to get what they wanted were more likely to be found in the normalized settings than youths who took a contrary view.

The long-run impact of detention is once again documented. Youths who had been detained for long periods were most likely to be placed in settings toward the institutional end of the continuum. On the other hand, youths who had not been detained at all were most likely to be placed in a setting more closely approximating the normalized end of the continuum.

Region VI, the Boston area, is the only region variable to enter this final equation. Youths from that region are more likely to be in programs on the normalized end of the continuum. It should be pointed out again that this region encountered great difficulty in setting up group home and foster care alternatives and therefore made extensive use of nonresidential programs. The region also sent a lot of youths outside the region to boarding schools. The lack of middle-range alternatives may have brought about inappropriate placements at both ends of the continuum.

The only family variable entering this last equation indicated that youths whose fathers were employed in skilled labor were less likely to be in normalized settings.

In sum, these regression equations concerning placement within DYS reflect some selectivity in terms of delinquent history. While specific offenses, with the exception of car theft, are not good predictors of where one will be placed, prior exposure to the courts and to DYS are. Youngsters who have been formally identified as engaged in delinquent careers over time are less likely to receive quality placements. However, other factors also predict where youths will be placed. It seems clear that family variables are related as are prior experiences in detention. The range of resources within regions also influences the placement decision. One is left with the sense that a kind of reverse creaming does occur in this process—the most serious offenders or hard to handle youngsters *tend* to be in programs on the institutionalization end of our continuum. But the bulk of the youths in the sample are distributed across the *entire* continuum, not just in the high-quality programs. One must wonder if the pressures to place quickly rather than making an attempt to meet specific needs of youths may not explain much of the dispersion across these programs, thereby reducing the extent of selectivity in program placement decisions.

THE RUNNER

A corollary question to the question of asking where a youth is placed is—does the youth stay? A frequent criticism of community-based programs is that they offer too little security to prevent youths from simply running or walking away from the program.

Official records reporting runs are remiss at best; one certainly expects underreporting because a high run rate generally casts a poor light on the program and system administrators. However, there are occasions when one suspects an inflated rate, that is, when administrators are trying to make a case for more appropriations for secure facilities. Allowing for the possibility of these inconsistent biases in order to get a fragmentary estimate of the rates of running in institution-based and community-based systems, we were able to calculate the average percentage of the population who ran from the Industrial School for Boys at Shirley during fiscal 1968. This rate—25 percent —was then compared with the information that we had gathered in 1973 and 1974 while tracking deinstitutionalized youth for interviewing. An identical 25 percent rate was found. While these data and their comparability remain suspect, they suggest that neither the institutional system nor the community-based system was prepared to amass the kind of security necessary to keep the run rate at a bare minimum. A concentration camp was not in the offing. This comparison is particularly important when we nostalgically recall the training-school era as if it provided ironclad protection for the community.

For a more detailed analysis of the running phenomenon within the community-based system we must turn to the information from our longitudinal sample. Each youth was asked whether he or she had run from a program during his or her current stay in DYS. The results (Table 5—4) show that youths in nonresidential programs were least likely to run. Youths in nonresidential programs tend to be under less constraint than youths in other program types. When nonresidential youths drop out of a program they are generally not defined by staff or others as runners, and frequently no further action is taken against the youth unless he or she commits another crime.

Youths who were in more programs during their stay in DYS were more likely to have run than those who were in fewer programs. This

Table 5—4. Multiple Regression of Run from DYS on Preprogram and Program Experience

Preprogram and Program Experience Variable	Coefficient	Standardized Coefficient
Ethnicity: Mother Spanish	−.26	−.13***
Last school grade in	−.04	−.11**
Judge committed to DYS so you would understand yourself	−.11	−.11**
Commit or referral	−.15	−.14***
Ran during prior commitment to DYS	.27	.27***
Estimate of other kids getting into further trouble at entry to program	.06	.13***
Extent to which others act on youth's behalf at entry to program	.13	.14***
Self-image at entry to program	−.13	−.18***
Perception of secondary group at entry to program	.09	.14***
Number of programs experienced in DYS	.05	.10**
Initial placement group home with low ratings on institutionalization-normalization continuum	.17	.13***
Final DYS program—nonresidential	−.30	−.19***
Nothing that you or others can do will keep you out of trouble	.14	.09*
Regression Constant	.64	
Multiple *R*	.60	

is probably a function of running in the first place. Frequently, if a youth runs from one program this youth will be placed in another program.

There is no apparent distinction among running rates in the remaining programs. However, when we add the continuum to the program type we discover another program factor related to running. Group homes with low scores on the overall continuum yield a higher rate of runs. This suggests that the pattern of running is not simply dependent on the characteristics of the youths but that youths are responding, at least in part, to the characteristics of the program. Programs with poor services will experience the most runs, making it critical that considerable thought and effort be given to providing constructive experiences for youths in order to hold on to them.

Having considered the nature of programs from which youths most frequently run, what can we say about the youths themselves? Youths who indicated that they had run at some point during their current stay in DYS also indicated that they had run from DYS during prior commitments. Thus many of these youths were in fact chronic runners. They had had prior experience at running, and we might expect that they possessed the skill to "make it" at least for a while on the run and were not particularly afraid of the consequences of running.

Runners not only have a low opinion of the program from which they run, but also a low opinion of other significant actors around them prior to entry into DYS. Runners are frequently unfavorably disposed to the way teachers and other DYS youths interact with them. They also believe that chances of other DYS youths in the program for getting into further trouble are great. They do not believe that efforts by DYS and others in the community, even added to their own determination and fears, will keep them out of further trouble. This profile is further substantiated as we note that in the initial interview runners tended to indicate that others had taken responsibility for trying to help them. Runners apparently feel locked into a delinquent life-style and powerless to change.

Youths who were unlikely to be runners were referred to the department rather than being formally committed and youths who entered DYS with more positive self-images. They also believed that significant others had not given up on them. Typical nonrunners also had attained a higher level of education before being committed or referred to the department. It can be argued that these youngsters had more things going for them in the community, and as suggested by our placement data, they tended to receive the better quality placements.

Only one family variable entered the equation. Youths whose mothers spoke Spanish did not run as frequently as others. This may in part reflect the tendency for Hispanic youths to be placed in the more secure settings in the first place.

Taken *in toto* runners appear to be the system's failures. They are frustrated by the DYS system and by the larger network, particularly of authority figures, in the community. Nonrunners, on the other hand, are more responsive to both themselves and others around them. They see hope while runners despair; they at least have the elements of a supportive network and are willing to work through the problems of these relationships whereas runners are isolates.

What is the staff response to runners? We found that it was often colored by the political stirrings of the moment. When security becomes a public issue, staff will respond accordingly. However, regional staff will admit that running is not necessarily a bad thing for some youths. Some take the position that runners are trying to make it on the run and staff will actually stay in close contact with them to see if they are capable of making it on the streets without getting involved in crime. If they can, they leave them there; if they cannot, they return them to yet another program. It should also be noted that some program staff members are reticent to report runs because a high incidence of running means a cut in their purchase-of-service revenue and may not look good to DYS administrators.

Two program strategies have been devised to deal specifically with runners. First, because running frequently occurs during the initial introduction to the program—that is, within the first week or two— many facilities operate a fairly closed program during that initial period, enabling the youths to adapt to the environment before allowing them the privilege of moving easily back and forth across the boundaries of the facility. Second, other programs take the position that runners should be placed in the nonresidential settings, thus removing the challenge of "breaking out." These special nonresidential alternatives, frequently referred to as tracking programs, offer a substantial amount of service and security. One staff member may work with as few as two youths, thus gaining time to learn how each youth is handling himself or herself.

SUMMARY

In this chapter we have used the institutionalization-normalization continuum as an analytical framework for describing the range of programs operating within DYS. The continuum has provided a richer set of descriptive data than the traditional program typology. It clearly shows the existence of sharp differences in terms of social climate and extent and quality of linkages with the community within program categories.

The distribution of programs and youths across the continuum strongly suggests while DYS made significant strides in improving the quality of services for its youths during the study period, it still did not manage to provide services in normalized settings for many youths. This may be due in part to the uneven implementation of the reform effort across the state. The unevenness was due in turn to differences in staff orientation toward the youths, variations in appropriate treatment models, fluctuating availability of resources across regions, different levels of community resistance, and variation in the ability to develop strategies not only to neutralize that resistance but also to involve communities in the delivery of services to their own youths.

❋ *Chapter 6*

Short- and Long-Run Consequences of Program Settings

A major objective of youth correctional programs is to bring about immediate and lasting change. Analysis in this chapter will show that for the most part short-run gains tend to be lost as the youths return to their own homes. It is evident that the programs under study were neither broad enough in scope nor sufficiently thorough in their follow-through with youths to assure lasting constructive effects.

In previous chapters we have described the nature of the various treatment settings across the institutionalization-normalization continuum and have seen how different kinds of youngsters are distributed across the continuum. We have shown that, while the traditional expectation is that the current charge in court will strongly determine where a youth is placed, for our sample this was not the case. We did find, however, that those youngsters with a longer offense history and with prior placement within the department would be more likely to be placed in the less open programs. In our description of the program settings in Chapter 5, we were in part looking at some of the immediate consequences of being placed in programs. That is, we were sorting out the variations in the quality of life in terms of relationships among youths, among staff, and between youths and staff, as well as considering the extent and quality of linkages with the community, in order to locate programs on the institutionalization-normalization continuum.

In this chapter, we move on to a discussion of the short-run and long-run consequences of having been placed in certain kinds of programs. We consider to what extent the programs brought about changes in a youngster's self-perception, perception of others, and aspirations and expectations, and we ask whether any such changes were long-lasting. It is expected that program efforts should increase a youngster's ability to cope with his or her life situation.

Analysis of factors related to short-run consequences indicates that the Massachusetts Department of Youth Services (DYS) programs were having a modest success in increasing youngsters' coping abilities or their ability to deal with their environment. However, background experiences prior to DYS also seem to have contributed much to these short-run consequences. When aspirations and perceptions were measured after the youths had returned to the community, much of the program impact was found to be diminished. At this point, situational factors in the community contribute a great deal to the way one views oneself and others, and life experiences prior to DYS continue to play an important part. It is quite apparent that the modest advances achieved within the department's programs were not sufficient to counter the influences to which the youths returned. As we analyze recidivism data in Chapter 7, we shall show that many of these program efforts apparently did not go far enough to reach directly into the youths' experience with networks that supported nondeviant behavior. Data in that chapter will provide some insights that may help to refine program efforts aimed at reintegrating youths into the community.

For now, however, let us look in more detail at the factors that seem to impede or facilitate a youngster's ability to deal effectively with the environment. The emphasis in this chapter will be on the effect or lack of effect of programs although we will touch on other factors that also enter our analysis.

The majority of youngsters (58 percent) in our sample remained in the program in which they were originally placed for the duration of their stay in DYS. While we have information on each program experience that lasted for more than one month, for purposes of discussing short- and long-run consequences we will treat the last program exposure as our primary indicator, showing where to place the youngster's experience on our institutionalization-normalization continuum. In order not to lose entirely the cumulative effect of moving from program to program, we will include in our matrix of variables all measures taken on the initial placement and a sequence variable reflecting movement on our continuum over as many program placements as the individual youth experienced.

SHORT-RUN CONSEQUENCES

The short-run consequences that we will look at as youths leave their final placement include: (1) their estimation of their own chances for staying out of trouble in the future; (2) their estimation of the chances of other youths in the program for staying out of trouble in the future; (3) their aspirations and expectations; (4) their self-image; (5) their perception of their primary group; (6) their perception of their secondary group; and (7) their perception of public officials. These factors represent for many staff the kinds of outcomes that they are trying to shape and on which—in contrast to the sole criterion of recidivism—they feel more comfortable being measured or evaluated. Theoretically one would expect that positive changes in these factors would be related to a reduction in recidivism. Aspirations, expectations, self-image, and perception of others are commonly regarded as indications of a youngster's readiness for realistically coping with his or her life situation.

In a later section of this chapter, we will look at these measures six months after completion of the final program. This will determine whether any observed changes were in fact lasting or whether they were washed out by exposure to the situational influences of the community. We will consider these indicators as well as background experiences as we seek to explain different recidivism outcomes in Chapter 7.

Because one of our principal theoretical interests is to determine any relationships between these outcome variables and the institutionalization-normalization continuum and its underlying continua, we will vary our reporting procedures somewhat. Zero-order correlations for the dimensions and the continuum will be reported to provide the reader with a description of the immediately observable relationships between programs at various places along the continuum and the outcome under discussion. It should not be expected that these dimensions will always show up when using the controlling regression technique because of the powerful influence background variables have on these outcomes. Perhaps one should not expect that a brief four-month or even one-year stay will somehow outweigh years of exposure to family, schools, and neighborhoods. In any case we will show the descriptive relationships between the programs and outcomes as well as provide a detailed picture of the variables that are most influential in shaping such outcomes as self-image and perception of others.

Youths' Estimation of Their Own Chances for Staying Out of Trouble

None of the *social climate*, *extent*, or *quality* dimensions, nor the overall continuum, enters this regression equation (Table 6–1); however, each factor has a low positive correlation with youths' estimation that their chances for staying out of trouble are good. The only program variable that enters the equation directly is that youngsters who are moved from one normalized setting to another are less likely to believe that their chances are good. Having looked at the actual sequence patterns we know that the bulk of this movement consists of youths being moved from one foster home to another. It therefore seems evident that this removal reinforces the youngsters' sense of

Table 6–1. Multiple Regression of Chances Respondent Will Stay Out of Trouble After Program or Preprogram and Program Experiences

Preprogram and Program Experience Variable	Coefficient	Standardized Coefficient
Father's schooling	.03	.15**
Siblings charged with status offenses	−.40	−.16***
Self-reported past offenses: Public misbehavior alone	.39	.11*
Don't use drugs	.17	.13**
Police view you as neither bad nor good	−.21	−.13**
Police regularly punish you for what others do	.17	.13**
Probation officers sometimes punish you for what others do	−.39	−.17***
Bosses never punish you for what others do	.28	.16***
Estimate of chances of staying out of trouble at entry to program	.30	.30***
Sequence of programs normalization to normalization	−.37	−.11*
Perception of primary group during program	.15	.18***
Regression Constant	−.18	
Multiple *R*	.55	

failure. The effect of such movement makes explicit the need for careful foster home placement as well as training to teach foster parents what to expect from delinquent youths and how to tap the resources of DYS to better serve each youngster.

The single best predictor of whether youths will feel their chances for staying out of trouble are good is how they felt about their chances after court. Youths who were optimistic at that point continue to be optimistic at the conclusion of their program experience.

The offense history of a particular youth does not seem to be strongly related to the youth's sense of whether he or she will stay out of trouble in the future. The only offense-related variable entering the equation was self-reported misbehavior that the youths did by themselves; those youths are optimistic about their chances.

Ties to supportive networks seem to explain much of the difference in perceptions of chances. Youths who felt good about their chances for staying out of trouble were youths who were favorably disposed toward their primary group and who claimed that they did not use drugs. Their fathers also tend to have attained higher levels of education, a fact suggesting that they may have had more material resources available to them than some of the other youths in the sample. One can infer that these youths still had some strong ties to people who generally supported nondeviant behavior. On the other hand, youths who indicated that a sibling had also been charged with a status offense were more pessimistic about their chances and less favorably disposed toward their primary group. Not only did these youths have available role models supporting deviant roles, but their relationships with parents and other primary group members were more strained.

While youths at the point of departure from the programs had different perceptions of their chances for staying out of trouble in the future, the programs seemingly had minimal impact on those perceptions. The differences are more appropriately traced to the youths' family and community experiences prior to DYS.

Chances of Other Youths in the Program
for Staying Out of Trouble

Youths tend to be less optimistic in general about other youths in the same facility than they are about themselves. Forty-six percent believed that their own chances of staying out of trouble were excellent. However, 59 percent indicated that at least half of the remaining youths in the program would not stay out of trouble. Youths in programs with more positive social climates, higher levels of contact with the community, and higher quality of contacts are more likely to expect that other youths in these programs will stay out of trouble. Thus while youths in programs across the continuum remain fairly optimistic about their own chances, the youths in the most supportive environments believe when looking around them that others in the same environments will also do well after leaving the department.

Table 6−2 indicates that the best predictor of the other residents' chances of staying out of trouble after completing a program was the estimate made at point of entry into the program. Thus actual program content played a secondary role in predicting chances of staying out of trouble. Program settings, however, emerge in the regression equation as related to estimates of other youths' chances. Youngsters in DYS secure units and in jail are most pessimistic about the chances of other youths staying out of trouble in the future. On the other hand, youths in nonresidential programs that received low scores for departing considerably from normalization on the institutionalization-normalization continuum were more optimistic about the chances of other youths in the same program. Since all nonresidential programs received high scores on the *extent* dimension, it seems likely that a low *social climate* score in these programs was the major reason for a low overall score. (It was necessary for these youths to deal with community actors in order to receive the kinds of support other youths received in programs with more positive social climates.) Here we can begin to see that positive social climates by themselves are not necessarily associated with positive consequences in the short run.

Another program-related variable that entered as a predictor was an indication by youths that the thing that would keep them out of trouble in the future was actions taken by DYS. These youths were also optimistic about the chances of other youths. It seems reasonable that these youths believed that DYS was helping them and their comrades in the specific program in which they participated.

Youths who believed that it was harder for DYS youths to take part in schools, work, and other opportunities in the community were less optimistic about other youths' chances of staying out of trouble. It seems evident that youths involved in the system are aware of some of the implications of being labeled as unable to continue functioning in the open community.

Youngsters whose fathers are employed in white-collar jobs and youths whose families had to move because of urban renewal were also pessimistic about the chances of other youths in the program for staying out of trouble in the future.

Table 6-2. Multiple Regression of Chances of Other Youths in Program Getting into More Trouble with the Law After Departure from Program on Preprogram and Program Experience

Preprogram and Program Experience Variable	Coefficient	Standardized Coefficient
Father white-collar employed	.47	.17***
Self-reported past offense: Property and person with others	−.37	−.11*
Moved because of urban renewal	.75	.17***
Harder for DYS youth to stay out of trouble	.39	.17***
Bosses don't view you as either bad or good	−.75	−.19***
Teachers never reward you for what others do	−.40	−.16***
Judge was fair	.30	.12**
Chances respondent won't get into trouble at entry into program	−.21	−.12**
Estimate of other youths' chances at entry to program	.25	.27***
Final DYS Program: Secure care	.47	.15**
Final Program: Adult jail	1.25	.13**
Final DYS Program: Nonresidential with low rating on institutionalization-normalization continuum	−.77	−.11*
Most important factor for staying out of trouble is action taken by DYS	−.32	−.10*
Regression Constant	1.06	
Multiple *R*	.60	

Aspirations and Expectations

There is almost no zero-order relationship between the institutionalization-normalization dimensions and youth aspirations and expectations at the end of the program. Social climate is slightly positively related while extent and quality of linkages are slightly negatively related.

The resulting regression equation (Table 6−3) indicates that youths who had high levels of aspirations and expectations in terms of education, occupation, and income at entry into the program also tended to have higher levels of aspirations and expectations at the

Table 6−3. Multiple Regression of Expectations and Aspirations on Preprogram and Program Experience

Preprogram and Program Experience Variable	Coefficient	Standardized Coefficient
Ethnicity: Mother French-Canadian	−.44	−.14***
Father white-collar employed	.24	.12**
Don't know whether mother has a job	−.36	−.15***
Region VI	.22	.12**
Self-reported past offenses: Drugs with others	.28	.14***
Current offense: Property and person	.31	.11**
No contact with police	.49	.11**
Police don't make judgments as to your being good or bad	.46	.14***
Probation officers never reward you for what others do	.22	.12**
Court liaison officer views you as neither bad nor good	.44	.16***
Expectations and aspirations at entry to program	.44	.44***
Initial DYS placement: Foster care with low ratings on institutionalization-normalization continuum	1.62	.26***
Sequence of programs irregular ending in program with high institutionalization scores	−.74	−.15***
Final DYS placement: Foster care with low ratings on institutionalization-normalization continuum	−1.90	−.36***
Final placement: Adult jail	.78	.11**
Regression Constant	2.02	
Multiple R	.70	

end of the program, suggesting once again that life experiences before the youths enter DYS are more influential than any particular set of experiences within DYS.

Some program variables do appear to be related to aspirations and expectations although the implications of those relationships are not immediately clear. Youths who were *initially* placed in foster care programs that rated low on the institutionalization-normalization continuum have higher levels of aspirations and expectations. However, youths whose *final* placements were foster care programs with low or less normalized ratings were associated with lower levels of aspirations and expectations. This contradiction leads one to question whether the sequencing of program experiences might influence perceptions, and we do find in the equation that youths who were moved erratically from normalized settings to institutionalized settings and back to normalized settings (or vice versa) were less likely to have high levels of aspirations and expectations. We also find that youths who were placed in jails tended to have higher levels of aspirations and expectations. One should note that these aspirations and expectations may not be realistic, and it may be that unrealistic expectations contributed to the acting-out behavior initially.

Two offense variables appear in this equation. Youths who were charged with property and person offenses and youths who indicated that they used drugs with others were likely to have higher levels of aspirations and expectations.

Youths whose fathers were employed in white-collar jobs had higher aspirations and expectations, as did youths who had favorable experiences or no contact with police. On the other hand, youths indicating that they did not know whether their mothers had a job (an indication of mother absence) had lower aspirations and expectations.

Self-Image

Social climate, quality of community linkages, and the overall continuum are related significantly to positive self-image. The more normalized the setting, the more likely one will be to find youngsters with a positive self-image once the program is completed. Once again we find that *extent of linkages* yields only a low positive correlation, which is not significant, suggesting that simply placing youngsters in the community may have only marginal value. What does have a positive impact, at least in helping youngsters feel more positive about themselves, is a stress on quality of contact with the community as well as supportive relationships within the program. Perhaps it should be reiterated that "high-quality contacts" refer to a situation in which staff members encourage youths to participate in jobs and schools, where at least some youths are doing so, and where in general a strategy of advocacy in the community on behalf of youngsters is adopted by staff instead of limiting community contact to such transitory experiences as recreational and cultural trips.

Although eighty variables were selected for a regression run, only six actually entered the regression equation (Table 6–4), yielding a rather high multiple of .67. That is, on the basis of knowing the direction of these six variables, one is in a fairly good position to predict the nature of the self-image of a particular youngster in DYS. The strength of one's self-image upon entering a program is the best single predictor of self-image at exit from the program. This fact suggests that whatever happens in juvenile corrections will probably have a minimal impact on the self-image for most youths. The fact is particularly noteworthy because many staff members indicate that improving self-image is a major objective of their programs.

Other factors that are associated with positive self-image include the number of people whom the youths admire and the youths' perception of secondary group members. Thus it seems reasonable to expect that youths who believe that they have some supportive relationships, particularly with adults outside the family, are able to view themselves as persons of value. Youths who are fortunate enough to have a positive social climate in their final DYS program are also likely to have a positive self-image, which reinforces the notion that

Table 6–4. Multiple Regression of Self-Image on Preprogram and Program Experience

Preprogram and Program Experience Variable	Coefficient	Standardized Coefficient
Self-reported past offenses: Offense against person alone	–.54	–.11**
Went to school regularly prior to entry to DYS	–.04	–.10*
Number of people look up to, trust, and admire	.04	.16***
Self-image at entry to program	.56	.55***
Perception of secondary group at entry to program	.12	.14**
Final program social climate	.05	.12**
Regression Constant	1.57	
Multiple R	.67	

supportive relationships are important for developing and reinforcing a positive self-image. Given the rather sharp differences in social climate between the current community-based system with the baseline measures that we obtained on the training-school populations, one must conclude that in terms of creating an environment that is better able to foster positive self-image the reforms at DYS have moved in the right direction.

Two variables entered the regression equation that indicate an association with poor self-images. Youths who said that they had acted alone in committing offenses against persons were less likely to have positive self-images. Surprisingly, youths who had been attending school regularly before entering DYS were also less likely to have a positive self-image. This last relationship is particularly disturbing. Two alternative explanations seem plausible. First, although these youths attended school regularly before commitment or referral to the department, school nevertheless may have been a devastating experience in shaping their own evaluations of themselves. This interpretation would certainly feed into the notion that these youths, although in school, saw themselves as either social or academic failures. Perhaps this is a partial explanation for their involvement in delinquent behavior. Another explanation is that youths who were attending school regularly prior to being committed to DYS suffered a loss of face and belief in themselves because of removal from part of their environment that they believed to be supportive and helpful. This may be an indication that commitment resulted in breaking ties with one of the few things that these youths had going for them and would further suggest that placement in DYS may yield far-ranging negative consequences for their future reintegration.

Other variables whose partial correlations indicate they nearly entered the regression equation provide further indication of factors that tend to shape self-image for youths in this sample. Youths who indicated that they did not hang around with former DYS youths before entering DYS tended to show positive self-images after completing the DYS program. Youths who had as their final placement boarding schools that were rated high on the normalization continuum also showed positive self-images. On the other hand, youths who were in DYS on drug charges tended to have poorer self-images. Youths whose mothers are employed in skilled work, who said that they spent a lot of time hanging around on the street corner before being committed to DYS, and who had friends who frequently used alcohol also tended to have poorer self-images. Youths who had been employed for relatively long periods of time before DYS also had poor self-images; here again we may be seeing effects of the experience of failure, for while they were employed for a significant period of time something clearly went wrong because they later became involved in delinquent behavior and ultimately were committed to DYS. A sense of failure may have been compounded because they had already tried the world of work and found it wanting and now wondered about the future and their ability to cope or their chances to have meaningful work experiences.

A further program relationship is also apparent from the partial correlations. Youths who are initially placed in boarding schools that score high on the *institutionalization* end of the continuum are likely to have poor self-images upon completion of their DYS experience.

Perception of Primary Group

Zero-order correlations show that youth perception of the primary group is related to the underlying dimensions of the *institutionalization-normalization* continuum. Significant positive correlations are found for *social climate*, *quality of community linkages*, and the overall continuum: that is, the more normalized the setting the more favorable the perception of primary group members. The *extent* dimension yields a low negative correlation, perhaps reflecting the difficulty of working on primary relationships in an open setting. This result should not necessarily lead one to the conclusion that one must isolate youths, for we can see that where quality linkages exist youths are positively disposed toward their primary group.

Again, the regression equation (Table 6–5) shows that the single best predictor of a youth's perception of the primary group is the measure taken at entry into the program: youths who were more favorably disposed toward their primary group at entry continue to be so at the exit point. Two program variables emerge as predictors. Youths whose final program received high *social climate* scores were likely to view their primary group favorably. However, the more programs a youth has been in, the less likely the youth will be favorably disposed. Thus while sequencing programs may be desirable for some youths (if the sequencing is reasonably designed), the haphazard moving of youths about from program to program would seem to have some short-run negative consequences.

We also find that youths who think positively about themselves at time of entry into the program will be more positively inclined toward their primary group at the end of the program. Similarly, family variables appear to be important determining factors. Youths whose families were satisfied with their level of income and youths whose mothers attained higher levels of education were positive. This is not surprising since one would expect that these youths have more

Table 6–5. Multiple Regression of Perception of Primary Group
on Preprogram and Program Experience

Preprogram and Program Experience Variable	Coefficient	Standardized Coefficient
Ethnicity: Mother Mediterranean	.37	.15***
Family is satisfied with its income	.12	.12**
Mother's schooling	.04	.11**
Don't know if community residents feel that they can control what happens to them	.21	.10**
Region IV	−.24	−.10**
Self-report past offenses: Offense against persons alone	−.69	−.13***
Teachers judged you as neither bad nor good	−.25	−.15***
Bosses judged you as neither bad nor good	.31	.12**
Friends use alcohol regularly	−.18	−.10**
Persons you admire or trust generally do break the law	.24	.13**
Perception of primary group at point of entry into program	.39	.39***
Self-image at point of entry into program	.21	.18***
Processed through full-time court	−.23	−.13***
Number of programs processed through in DYS	−.11	−.14***
Social climate of final DYS placement	.11	.23***
Regression Constant	1.72	
Multiple R	.71	

material resources available. On the other hand, youths who did not
know whether their families and neighbors believed that they could
do anything about their sense of powerlessness were also positively
disposed toward their primary group.

Youths who indicated that they hung around with other youths
who used alcohol regularly were not favorably disposed toward the
primary group. This suggests that the choice of their friends probably
created tension for them with their parents.

Youths who were processed through full-time courts were less positive toward their primary group than were youths processed through the part-time courts.

Perception of Secondary Group Members

As used here, the term "secondary group" includes school teachers and other youths in the DYS programs. In terms of zero-order correlations, social climate and the overall continuum are positively and significantly correlated with positive perceptions of secondary group members. The *extent* dimension is positively related, but with a low coefficient. Quality of community linkages is more strongly related, but still not significantly.

Looking at the regression equation (Table 6−6) for "perception of

Table 6−6. Multiple Regression of Perception of Secondary Group on Preprogram and Program Experience

Preprogram and Program Experience Variable	Coefficient	Standardized Coefficient
Ethnicity: Mother northern Europe	−.27	−.14**
Number of people look up to, admire, and trust	.03	.09*
Significant other: Kid acquaintance illegal	.30	.13**
Friends use alcohol regularly	−.26	−.14**
Hang on street corner	−.07	−.13**
Self-image at entry to program	.28	.24***
Perception of secondary group at point of entry to program	.24	.24***
Detention staff sometimes reward you for what others do	.25	.12**
Probation officer viewed you as a good kid	.23	.13**
Number of programs processed through in DYS	.12	.15***
Social climate of the final DYS placement	.06	.13**
Final DYS program: Nonresidential with low rating on institutionalization-normalization continuum	.63	.14**
Regression Constant	2.33	
Multiple *R*	.61	

secondary group," one sees that the measures of perception of secondary group and self-image taken prior to entry into DYS are most strongly related to the dependent variable, the secondary group. It is interesting to note that even when controlling for other related variables, the way one sees oneself continues to have a strong influence on the way one views others. Thus it certainly seems appropriate for youth workers inside and outside the juvenile justice system to devote attention to helping youngsters understand themselves and their relationships with others in order to strengthen their self-perceptions and sense of self-worth. Two other variables positively related to perception of the secondary group seem to fit into the same pattern. Both the number of persons one admires and the belief that probation officers perceive them as "good kids" characterize youths who feel most positively toward secondary group members. Of those persons one admires, if the significant other is a youth acquaintance who engages in illegal activity, this will tend to enhance the respondent's opinion of secondary group members. This may be an artifact of having DYS youths in our secondary group.

Youths who indicated that they were sometimes punished for what others did while in detention were likely to think highly of secondary group members—probably suggesting a bonding among DYS youths as a result of a common plight, particularly if they believe they were being unfairly punished. Positive social climate in the final program is also related to positive perceptions of the secondary group, as is the increasing number of programs through which a youth is processed during a youth's DYS experience. In addition, youths who complete their DYS experience in a nonresidential program with a low overall score on our continuum are more positively inclined toward the secondary group.

Variables that are related to negative perception of the secondary group are youth relationship variables. First, youngsters who indicated that they spent a lot of time hanging around on the street corner prior to entry into DYS were unfavorably disposed toward the secondary group members. Second, respondents who claimed that their friends frequently used alcohol were also unfavorably disposed.

Perception of Public Officials
Zero-order correlations show that each of the dimensions of the *institutionalization-normalization* continuum and the overall continuum is significantly and positively related to a favorable perception of public officials. That is, the more normalized the treatment setting, the more likely youths will be favorably disposed toward police

and the DYS. Thus a fairly consistent pattern has evolved through this discussion of short-run consequences—the more normalized the setting, the more likely one is to find a positive impact on short-run consequences.

The regression equation (Table 6−7) shows that youths who emerge from programs that receive high ratings for *extent of contact with the community* are more favorably disposed toward public officials than youths in the less open settings. One might expect that youths in open program settings would feel more positively toward DYS. However, youths in these programs are also more apt to be exposed to routine contact with the police. On the other hand, prior to entry into DYS these youths did not spend a lot of time hanging around on the street and therefore probably had less contact with the police.

Table 6−7. Multiple Regression of Perception of Public Officials on Preprogram and Program Experience

Preprogram and Program Experience Variable	Coefficient	Standardized Coefficient
Family is satisfied with its income	.16	.12**
Mother employed in unskilled labor	.33	.11**
Community residents feel that they do not control what happens to them	.36	.14***
Self-reported past offense: Car stealing alone	−.37	−.14***
Months at longest job	.02	.14***
Teachers sometimes punish you for what others do	−.41	−.16***
Don't hang around with DYS kids	.38	.16***
Self-image at point of entry into DYS program	.23	.15***
Perception of officials at point of entry into DYS program	.35	.39***
Perception of secondary group at point of entry into DYS program	.18	.14**
No contact with parents	−.75	−.13**
Extent of linkages with community of final DYS placement	.13	.11**
Regression Constant	.15	
Multiple *R*	.70	

Youths who were less critical of public officials at the end of the program tended to be youths who were less critical of them upon entry into DYS. They were also favorably disposed toward their secondary group, and they tended to have more positive self-images than youths who were critical. If youths feel good about themselves and have reasonably good relationships with secondary group members, then youths are likely to feel positively toward police and the DYS as well.

These youths also had worked longest and came from families that were apparently satisfied with their income. Interestingly, youths who came from families that did not feel that they could do anything about their sense of powerlessness and youths whose mothers were employed in unskilled jobs were also favorably disposed toward public officials. One might expect that these youths would strongly resent police and the DYS. It may be the case that they felt that they were gaining something from being in the department. They were not being tightly confined, and they were in a position to receive counseling help. Some of them may have found a staff person who was willing to be their advocate. These last two factors may further support the notion that DYS is being used as a last-resort welfare system for these kinds of families; it may be that some of these youths welcome and are responsive to that support.

Youths who were critical of the police and DYS were youths who had had no recent contact with their parents and who stole cars by themselves. One might expect that the lack of parent contact and support would be pivotal in shaping youths' view of officials as well as their assessment of their own personal worth. These youths also believed that teachers frequently punished them for what others did.

Looking at the short-run consequences as a whole, it seems reasonable to say that the program setting is at least moderately related to youths' perception of themselves, their aspirations and expectations, and their perceptions of others. However, it must also be recognized that factors that seem most strongly related to outcomes are the experiences that youths had prior to entry into DYS. It seems clear that for most youths DYS is only providing an opportunity for "slowing down" and some help in understanding their situation. We will now consider how long any of these effects actually last as the youths return to their own community setting.

LONG-RUN CONSEQUENCES

One of the major research questions in this book is what factors facilitate or impede reintegration of delinquent youths into the community. We have sought answers to this question by following the cohort youths beyond the DYS program into the community. Youths in forestry programs, group homes, boarding schools, and secure facilities were interviewed six months after they were released or at the time of recommitment if they failed to make it in the community for the initial six months. Youths in nonresidential and foster care programs were given a final interview nine months after entry into those programs. Because these programs incurred relatively small costs to the department, youths could remain in them for long periods of time, a fact that makes research comparisons difficult at best. Functionally, however, nonresidential and foster care youths are exposed to the same influences as are other youths living in the communities. It therefore seems reasonable to interview them about their networks and relationships, their difficulties and harassments. It should be noted that while these youths continued in the program for long periods of time, if a youngster decided that he or she had had enough and terminated participation in the program, the justice system generally did not return the youth to that program or any other program. Only a new crime would bring the youth back into the system.

This section will look at background experiences, program effects, and relationships with the community after release and examine the impact of these things on aspirations, self-image, and perception of significant others. It is expected that these latter variables will be related to recidivism, which will be explored in Chapter 7. Taken together, Chapters 6 and 7 should give us a basis for dealing with the question of reintegration.

Our procedure for analysis will change slightly. We will first consider an equation that includes the possibility for background experiences prior to DYS, and we shall allow detention, court, and DYS experiences to enter but hold out experiences in the community after program completion. A second equation will also be run to include the possibility for these later community experiences to enter. This two-stage analysis is used because the postprogram community experiences and the long-run consequences are measured at the same time. One may consider the postcommunity experiences partly as intervening or interpretive variables and partly as additional factors that work out program influences. The simultaneous measurement also introduces the possibility that these factors may be in part caused by the dependent variable.

The Extent to Which Youths Take
Responsibility for Themselves

Positive social climate of the program setting, quality of community linkage, and the more normalized settings are positively and significantly related to the extent to which youths take responsibility for themselves. "Taking responsibility" means sharing in decisions or actions affecting the youth's own situation. Extent of community contact is positively associated, but it does not yield a significant zero-order correlation.

The regression equation (Table 6—8) shows that youths who felt more positively about themselves at the end of their program experience tended to take more responsibility for their actions six months later. It should be remembered that these youths tended to have had DYS experiences in the programs with the more positive social climates. Postprogram community experiences continued to support this relationship. Youths who indicated that they had more people whom they looked up to, trusted, and related well with and youths who believed that program staff thought of then as "good kids" were also likely to take more responsibility for themselves. It seems very clear that the kind of support system surrounding a youth will in large part determine how the youth will control his or her own situation.

We also find that a youth's perception of public officials is related to the extent to which the youth takes responsibility for his or her own behavior: that is, youths who are favorably disposed toward public officials are more apt to take responsibility. Again we should remember that youths in program settings with a higher extent of linkages with the community were most likely to feel favorably disposed toward public officials. It may be the case that youths in the more open settir.gs were encouraged in those settings to take more responsibility for their actions.

A pattern around rewarding and punishing of youths emerges in these equations. In general, youths who are punished or rewarded regularly for what others do are less likely to take responsibility for themselves. The only exceptions to this pattern are youths who report that they were sometimes rewarded for what others did in detention. It is likely that these youths are finding that being rewarded or punished for what others do does not seem fair or logical. The resentment that builds up over time may increase the possibility that these youths will further withdraw to the point where they are simply being acted upon by others, increasing the sense that they have little control over their own destiny. This may further corroborate their notions that they also have little control over their delinquent activity.

Even in this discussion of long-run consequences we find that a youth's detention in custody has explanatory power. Youths who were initially held in custody detention were not as likely to take responsibility for themselves. We know that these youths were also

Table 6–8. Multiple Regression of the Extent to Which Youths Take Responsibility for Themselves on Preprogram, Program, and Postprogram Experience

Preprogram, Program, and Postprogram Experience Variable	Equation with Preprogram and Program Experience Only		Equation Including Postprogram Experience	
	Coefficient	Standardized Coefficient	Coefficient	Standardized Coefficient
Preprogram and Program Experience:				
Mother was in trouble with law	-.23	-.14***	-.18	-.11**
Region VI	.12	.13***		
Self-reported past offense: Drugs alone	.21	.17***		
Kids hang with are afraid of DYS	.06	.18***		
Staying out of trouble is not more difficult for DYS kids than for others	.17	.16***	.15	.13***
Perception of officials during program			.04	.11**
Self-image at departure from program	.13	.24***	.07	.13***
Extent to which youths take responsibility for themselves upon entry to DYS	.20	.20***	.11	.11***
Respondent's estimation of own chances of not getting into further trouble reviewed at entry into program	.06	.10**		
Detention staff sometimes reward you for what others do	.30	.20***	.15	.10**
Detained in custody detention	-.13	-.14***		
Processed through full-time court	.09	.11**	.10	.12***

Postprogram Experience:		
Number of people look up to	.02	.13***
Friends admire DYS kids	.07	.13***
Want a steady job	.08	.16***
Program staff view you as good kid	.11	.14***
Parents view you as bad kid	−.19	−.18***
Program staff regularly punished you for what others did	−.12	−.12***
Parole staff viewed you as bad kid	−.19	−.13***
Bosses never punish you for what others do	.10	.10**
Police don't judge you as good or bad	.17	.15***
Kids hang with want to be part of society	.09	.10**
Parole staff never reward you for what others do	.10	.12***
Regression Constant	.82	.85
Multiple R	.57	.71

placed in the harsher program settings; therefore neither in detention nor in placement were they likely to be considered responsible or encouraged to take responsibility. Given the idiosyncratic nature of the detention decisions in the first place, this result simply seems to be a self-fulfilling prophecy produced to a great extent by the decision-makers.

Generally, youths who take responsibility for themselves are youths who want to be part of legitimate and law-abiding society. Some of them also indicated that they would like a steady job. It has been interesting to note in our observations of programs that youth employment has emerged as a pivotal concern for many of these youngsters. Nonresidential programs that offer a rather nominal weekly stipend ($10 to $20) have had at least moderate success in slowing down youths' delinquent activity. Being able to spend money for things that they want gives the youths a sense of dignity. Many of these youths could make considerably more money on the streets participating in delinquent acts. Some readers may wonder why delinquent youths should be paid, but we should remember that most of us provide our own youngsters with spending money and that being able to impress their peers is important for most youths. In sum, it appears that youths are more likely to take responsibility for themselves if they believe that there is a constructive place for them in society.

The Extent to Which Others Act on Behalf of Youths

Zero-order correlations indicate that youths in more normalized program settings with positive social climates and quality linkages with the community are more likely to perceive that others are acting on their behalf. The *extent* of linkages is negatively related. The implication is, therefore, that merely placing youths in a program that permit them to interact freely in the community will not necessarily enhance their perception that others are working on their behalf.

This implication is further supported as we look at the initial regression equation (Table 6—9). There we find that youths in nonresidential programs with low scores on the institutionalization-normalization continuum are also less likely to believe that parents, staff, parole officers, teachers, employers, and others are acting on their behalf. Conversely, youths with positive self-images are more likely to perceive others as helping, and we know that these youths tend to come from programs with positive social climates. Thus it appears that the type of program setting does influence a youth's perception that others are helping.

The best single predictor of such perceptions is the perception that youths had when entering the system. The nature of the youths' network is quite important in determining how they will perceive the extent to which others act on their behalf. Youths leaving the programs favorably disposed toward their primary group were more likely to believe that others were helping. Youths who indicated that the people whom they admired and trusted did not do things that would get them in trouble with the law were also likely to perceive others as acting on their behalf. Surprisingly, however, the more individuals a youth indicated that he or she admired or trusted, the less likely this youth was to see others as helping. This seems to suggest that a few close relationships are more beneficial than a large number.

Intervening variables from postprogram experience reinforce the notion that relationship variables strongly influence the way youths perceive others helping them. Youths who believed that parents, program staff, police, and parole officers regarded them as "bad kids" were less likely to perceive others as helping them. In addition, youths who believed that other youths, employers, program staff, and significant others did not routinely punish them for what other youths did were more likely to believe that some persons were acting on their behalf. For the most part, youths who believed that they were frequently rewarded for what others did also were more likely to believe that people helped them. It seems quite clear that the way youths see themselves perceived and reacted to influences their perceptions of how helpful others are to them.

It is of interest to note again the influence of exposure to the school system. Youths who indicated in their initial interview that they attended school regularly were less likely to believe six months after program contact that other persons actually acted on their behalf.

The postprogram experiences tend to wash out the program effects that were apparent in the initial equation. To the extent that these experiences are not caused by the program, the lasting effect of program experience, at least in terms of youths perceiving that others act on their behalf, is dissipated by the effect of the youngsters' new set of experiences with those community actors.

Aspirations and Expectations

Zero-order correlations of the continuum dimensions are each positively associated with higher levels of aspirations and expecta-

Table 6—9. Multiple Regression of the Extent to Which Others Act on Behalf of Youths on Preprogram, Program, and Postprogram Experience

Preprogram, Program, and Postprogram Experience Variable	Equations with Preprogram and Program Experience Only		Equations Including Postprogram Experience	
	Coefficient	Standardized Coefficient	Coefficient	Standardized Coefficient
Preprogram and Program Experience:				
Father's religion other			−.21	−.11**
Ethnicity color: Father Irish	.22	.15**		
Mother unskilled labor	.18	.11**		
Region IV	−.19	−.11**		
Number of people you look up to	−.03	−.12**		
People you admire and trust do not break the law	.14	.11**		
Friends of all ages	.14	.12**		
Go to school regularly			−.04	−.11**
Self-image during program	.11	.14**		
Extent to which others act on behalf of youth at entry into DYS	.22	.22***		
Extent to which others act on behalf of youth at end of program	.10	.13**	.17	.17***
Perception of primary group at end of program	.09	.12*		
Final program: Nonresidential with low score on continuum	−.46	−.13**		

Postprogram Experience:

Kids never punish you for what others do	.28	.18***
Parents see you as bad kid	-.22	-.14***
Parole staff never reward you for what others do	.20	.17***
Police see you as bad kid	-.22	-.19***
Program staff see you as bad kid	-.22	-.11**
Parole staff see you as bad kid	-.23	-.11**
Bosses never punish you for what others do	.25	.17***
Best community program sometimes rewards you for what others do	.38	.14***
Parole staff sometimes reward you for what others do	.29	.13***
Program staff never punish you for what others do	.15	.13***
Bosses regularly reward you for what others do	.41	.14***
Parents never reward you for what others do	.16	.14***
Regression Constant	2.29	.97
Multiple R	.65	.46

tions. However, none was statistically significant. The level of aspirations and expectations after youths had been in the community for six months is best predicted within our regression (Table 6—10) by the level of aspiration that they had at the end of the program. This fact suggests that program impact has some carry-over effect. Youths with higher levels of aspirations were also youths who at the point of exit from the program were favorably disposed toward members of their secondary group. An intervening variable from the postprogram community experience further substantiates this experience. Youths who indicated that they had good, supportive experiences in school on their return from the program also expressed higher levels of aspirations and expectations.

The importance of constructive involvement in the educational arena is underscored by these data. Be it public education or some kind of alternative school, a favorable school experience provides not only basic survival skills but also hope for the future. For many youths in this sample, the school has been a source of disappointment and failure, a place where people in authority reject them and want nothing more than to be rid of them. Either way, the school experience continues to influence greatly the way youths think about themselves and their place in society. It seems clear that delinquents cannot simply ignore or forget the signals that they receive in the school setting; those signals will either sustain them or haunt them.

Youths whose current charge was a crime against persons or who indicated that they had by themselves committed crimes against property and persons also share an optimistic attitude about their futures in education, work, and income. It is possible that the crime against persons was a direct result of interpersonal conflict; the delinquent act itself may have worked out or alleviated the problem. It is also likely that these youngsters are not as committed to a delinquent life-style as the car thief or the burglar. Or it may be that some of these youths are simply not being realistic about their futures. Ironically, these unrealistic expectations may in turn lead to more delinquent activity that will afford them opportunities for wealth and prestige.

Youths who believe that the major factor that will keep them out of trouble in the future is fear are youths who have the lowest levels of aspirations and expectations. If, as many believe, the setting of goals enhances commitment to conforming values and life-styles, it is ironical that producing fear in our youths is one way to delimit their goal setting and commitment. One must wonder what will happen to

Table 6–10. Multiple Regression of Expectations and Aspirations on Preprogram, Program, and Postprogram Experience

Preprogram, Program, and Postprogram Experience Variable	Equation with Preprogram and Program Experience Only		Equation Including Postprogram Experience	
	Coefficient	Standardized Coefficient	Coefficient	Standardized Coefficient
Preprogram and Program Experience:				
Number of times traveled to other states	.26	.11**		
Self-reported past offenses:				
Drugs with others	−.29	−.14***	.37	.11***
Property and person alone	.34	.11**	.32	.11**
Current offense: Offense against person				
Expectations and aspirations at entry to program	.20	.19***	.17	.17***
Expectations and aspirations at end of program	.48	.46***	.45	.43***
Perception of secondary group at end of program	.13	.12***		
Fear major deterrent at end of program			−.25	−.10**
Postprogram Experience:				
Assessment of school experience after return to community			.17	.21***
Regression Constant	.57		1.05	
Multiple R	.65		.67	

youths who feel that fear of the system is an important way of keeping them out of it, and yet who have neither the initiative nor the skills required for many legitimate roles in society.

Self-Image

None of the program variables enters directly into the self-image equations. However, the zero-order correlations for *social climate*, *quality of linkages*, and the overall continuum are positive, and social climate is significant. The *extent of linkage* correlation is negative but not significant. We know from earlier in this chapter that self-image measured at the end of the program was determined in part by exposure to programs with positive social climates. Another program-related feature enters as an intervening variable. Youths who have left the program and believe that program staff continue to view them as "good kids" feel more positively about themselves (Table 6−11). Thus we must conclude that programs do have a continuing effect on self-image once a youngster leaves, although this effect may not be as strong or as direct as some program administrators hope.

The support system surrounding the youngsters continues to have direct effect on self-image. Youths who indicated in their initial interview that they admired, trusted, and related well to an adult relative who did not routinely break the law reflected positive self-images, as did youths who reported that their peers would regularly reward them for what other youths did. Surprisingly, youths who indicated that they had good relationships with supervisors or teachers had poorer self-images. These may be youngsters who are accepting the models of their teachers and are struggling to succeed, but at least in their own eyes are failing to measure up. This factor may be related to our earlier finding that youths in our sample who went to school regularly prior to entry into DYS have poorer self-images than youths who did not go to school regularly. Although they attend school more regularly than others in the sample, the school experience is still not self-enhancing for them. One is left with the impression that public school for these youngsters exacerbates their internal struggles over whether they can "make it" rather than providing supports for alternative routes to successful learning.

Perception of Primary Group

Primary group relationships should be an indication of the degree to which youths have close relationships and the extent to which members of this group influence the youngsters in question. Looking at the factors influencing youths' perceptions of their primary group after they have been in the community for some time, one discovers

Table 6–11. Multiple Regression of Self-image on Preprogram, Program, and Postprogram Experience

Preprogram, Program, and Postprogram Experience Variable	Equations with Preprogram and Program Experience Only		Equations Including Postprogram Experience	
	Coefficient	Standardized Coefficient	Coefficient	Standardized Coefficient
Preprogram and Program Experience:				
Father white-collar employed	.28	.17***	.23	.14***
Significant other:				
Adult relative legal	.15	.10**		
Supervisors, teachers legal	-.18	-.10**	-.20	-.11***
Self-image at point of entry to program	.19	.19***	.15	.15***
Self-image at end of program	.50	.51***	.49	.50***
Postprogram Experience:				
Kids regularly reward you for what others do			.37	.11***
Parents view you as a good kid			.19	.14***
Staff view you as a good kid			.13	.09**
Police view you as a bad kid			-.16	-.11***
Parole staff view you as a bad kid			-.35	-.13***
Regression Constant	1.32		1.65	
Multiple R	.69		.73	

once more that direct program impact is washed out by preconditions and the postprogram experiences of youths. *Positive social climates* are significantly correlated with *favorable perception of primary group members* such as parents, friends, and program staff. *Extent of linkages with the community* is negatively related while *good quality linkages* are positively related, as is the overall continuum. But none of these descriptive variables enters the regression equation (Table 6−12) when we control for other factors.

As was the case before, the previous perceptions of primary group members at the points of entry and exit from the program are the best predictors of perceptions at this point: youths who indicated positive images earlier are more likely to continue to do so.

Other factors that youths with favorable perceptions have in common include the sense that other youths in the community think of them as "good kids" and the fact that these youths admire or look up to more persons. These youngsters, therefore, not only feel comfortable with their peers but also have a number of significant others to interact with and to use as role models. They are part of a network; their counterparts tend to be more isolated.

Youths with positive connections with the primary group tend to be older than youths without those connections. These older youths may have worked out some of the difficulties with parents, or they may on the threshold of adulthood have outgrown the period of turbulence and rebellion that is not uncommon for many adolescents. Perhaps these youths are finding a place for themselves, and this factor more than any specific program experience may provide them with a stake in society and foster generally conforming behavior. In contrast, it is noteworthy that youths who used "pot" regularly at the time of the final interview indicated a tension with the primary group. Their continued expression of "doing their own thing" probably generated some conflict with their parents as well as with some of their peers. Given that they had already been in DYS, the use of pot may have reflected to some parents that more troubles lay ahead.

The importance of interaction with parents is emphasized by our data. Note that youths who believed their parents thought of them as "bad kids" also demonstrated unfavorable reactions to the primary group in a significant proportion of cases. It is clear that perception of the primary group is an interactive matter—people generally like those persons who provide positive feedback. If that feedback is negative, it is not uncommon to find a hostile assessment of the source. These data continue to support the notion that while the specific makeup of the family (intact or broken) is not related to outcomes, the nature of the interactive pattern within the family yields considerable influence.

Perceptions of Secondary Group

None of the continuum dimensions is significantly related to perceptions of the secondary group at the zero-order level. With the exception of *social climate*, all dimensions and the overall continuum are in the positive direction.

In the regression equation (Table 6–13) the best predictors of the sample's perception of the secondary group are the prior measures at the beginning and the end of the program experience. The measure at the beginning of the program falls out as we add the intervening variables from the final interview. Again we discover a class differential: children of white-collar working fathers are more favorably disposed toward members of the secondary group. In contrast, youths whose fathers are employed in skilled labor are less positive.

The supportive network of a youngster is also related to the youngster's perceptions of the secondary group. Some youths indicate that they admire, trust, and relate well to an adult relative who does not routinely do things that could get him or her in trouble with the law. These youths are more positive toward their secondary groups. Youths who believe that other youngsters view them as "good kids" also tend to be more positive.

Another factor that is apparently indicative of how youths perceive their secondary group is their belief that others reward or punish them for what other youths do. There is a strong pattern suggesting that youths are not receptive to being either rewarded or punished for what others do. This may reflect a significant individualistic sense of fairness. That is, it is not fair, in the youths' view, to punish or reward one youth for what other youths have done.

Perception of Officials

Each of the dimensions and the overall continuum yield a positive zero-order correlation with perception of officials. Social climate, quality of linkages, and the overall continuum are significant.

In the regression equation (Table 6–14), the single best predictor of youths' perception of officials six months after exposure to the community is their perception of officials at the end of the program. That is, youths who were favorably disposed at that time are likely to remain so. The reader will recall that the extent of contact with the community was positively related to that earlier perception. Social climate also has an indirect effect in this equation through self-image. Youths who feel better about themselves are more favorably inclined toward public officials, and we know that a program's

Table 6–12.   Multiple Regression of Perception of Primary Group on Preprogram, Program, and Postprogram Experience

Preprogram, Program, and Postprogram Experience Variable	Equation with Preprogram and Program Experience Only		Equation Including Postprogram Experience	
	Coefficient	Standardized Coefficient	Coefficient	Standardized Coefficient
Preprogram and Program Experience:				
Age at initial interview			.07	.12***
Previously committed or referred to DYS	.18	.11**		
Police sometimes reward you for what others do	-.48	-.13***		
Police view you as neither bad nor good	.20	.10**		
Self-image during program	.17	.16***		
Perception of primary group at entry to program	.24	.24***	.25	.26***
Perception of primary group at end of program	.38	.38***	.40	.41***
Postprogram Experience:				
Number of people look up to and admire			.04	.12***
Kids in community afraid of DYS			.09	.12***
You use marijuana regularly			-.17	-.11***

Parents view you as bad kid		-.29	-.13***
Other kids view you as a good kid		.16	.11**
Staff at the worst community program in which you participate don't judge you		-.81	-.13***
Kids sometimes punish you for what others do		-.32	-.13***
Regression Constant	.78	.43	
Multiple *R*	.67	.72	

Table 6–13. Multiple Regression of Perception of Secondary Group on Preprogram, Program, and Postprogram Experience

Preprogram, Program, and Postprogram Experience Variable	Equation with Preprogram and Program Experience Only		Equation Including Postprogram Experience	
	Coefficient	Standardized Coefficient	Coefficient	Standardized Coefficient
Preprogram and Program Experience:				
Father white-collar employed	.20	.10*	.32	.16***
Father employed in skilled labor	-.22	.10**		
Self-reported past offenses: Property and person alone	.31	.10*		
Kids hang with regularly use a combination of drugs	-.38	-.12**		
Significant other: Adult relative legal	.25	.14***	.35	.19***
Perception of secondary group at entry to program	.16	.16***		
Expectations and aspirations during program			.18	.19**
Perception of secondary group at end of program	.35	.34***	.32	.31***
Expectations and aspirations at end of program			-.27	-.27***

Postprogram Experience:		
Assessment of school experience	.20	.25***
Teachers sometimes punish you for what others do	-.25	-.10***
Bosses view you as neither bad nor good	-.42	-.13***
Staff at the best community program in which you participate regularly punish you for what others do	-.68	-.15***
Other kids never reward you for what others do	.17	.10*
Other kids view you as a good kid	.25	.15***
Regression Constant	2.14	2.45
Multiple R	.52	.63

Table 6–14.   Multiple Regression of Perception of Officials on Preprogram, Program, and Postprogram Experience

Preprogram, Program, and Postprogram Experience Variable	Equations with Preprogram and Program Experience Only		Equations Including Postprogram Experience	
	Coefficient	Standardized Coefficient	Coefficient	Standardized Coefficient
Preprogram and Program Experience:				
Father's schooling	.06	.18***	.06	.17***
Self-reported past offenses:				
Public misbehavior with others Offenses against persons with others	.80	.10**	−.32	−.10**
Harder for DYS kid to stay out of trouble	−.27	−.12***	−.23	−.11**
Judge sent you to DYS in order for you to learn some skills	.43	.13***	.49	.15***
Perception of officials at entry to program	.13	.13***		
Not placed in program	−.53	−.12***		
Perception of officials at end of program	.53	.51***	.58	.57***
Self-image at end of program	.18	.12**		
Postprogram Experience:				
Police view you as a bad kid			−.47	−.22***
Police never reward you for what others do			.40	.13***
Regression Constant	−.29		1.05	
Multiple *R*	.71		.73	

social climate does influence self-image. An additional program-related variable entering the equation is the fact that youths who were not initially placed in a program or who did not stay in a program for at least a month are more critical of public officials. These youths were apparently unsatisfied with their placement decisions and apparently were not particularly happy to be left alone. This may suggest that these youths actually wanted some kind of help but did not see it as forthcoming.

Youths whose fathers had higher levels of education were more likely to be less critical toward the police and DYS. On the other hand, youths who believed that the police thought of them as "bad kids" were more likely to be critical. Youths who said they had been placed in DYS by judges in order to learn skills were more favorably inclined, while youths who believed it was harder for DYS youths to make it in school and the world of work harbored more resentment toward DYS and the police.

SUMMARY

It seems evident from the data presented in this chapter that DYS program experience had a positive impact on some youths in ways which, one would expect, increased their ability to cope with their life situations. These ways are measured in terms of short- and long-range consequences. However, it is also abundantly clear that a youth's life experience prior to entry into DYS was the more potent force. After a youth left DYS, many of the positive effects of a program were either enhanced or washed out by the relationships that the youth reestablished in the community.

※ *Chapter 7*

Recidivism

For many people recidivism remains the "bottom line," the final measure of the effectiveness of any correctional program. It is a measure that is frequently overused and abused; nonetheless, it has value when interpreted cautiously. Most importantly, recidivism is more aptly conceived as a summary measure of society's efforts at reintegrating a youth rather than merely a measure of actions taken by a correctional system. This point will become clearer as we consider the factors that contribute to recidivism.

In this chapter, we will analyze two criteria generally used in relation to recidivism. First, we consider as recidivists youths who have reappeared in juvenile or adult court for any offense other than traffic offenses in the year following their Massachusetts Department of Youth Services (DYS) exposure. Second, we consider as recidivists youths who have reappeared in court on a new charge that results in their being placed on probation, recommitted to DYS, or committed to the adult correctional system in the year following their exposure to DYS. The first criterion is very conservative since it ignores the disposition of the case—some of the charges are simply dropped. The second, while more restrictive, is also rather inclusive given the general nature of recidivism studies in juvenile corrections because it takes into consideration youths who graduate to the adult criminal justice system.

It is difficult to sort out the extent to which recidivism represents the behavior of a particular youth, the impact of having been in a specific program setting, the interplay of the youth with family, schools, and other social institutions, or the decisions of other juvenile justice decision-makers such as policemen, probation officers, and judges. The court appearance criterion most accurately reflects decisions of police officers and court intake officers. The disposition criterion reflects the decision of the judge. In order to reflect the interplay of the youth in the community, we have also looked at the characteristics of youths who self-reported delinquent activity during their final interview, and we have examined the kind of relationships they had. The impact of program experience will be looked at as it concerns these activities and relationships.

We are able to include the recidivism data for these youths because the state has a centralized record-keeping system within the probation office. While the data presented here are the best that we can obtain, we remind the reader that official records are sometimes missing, out-of-date, or simply inaccurate. Given that we will be comparing rates over two time periods, separated by some eight years, any systematic improvement or deterioration in record maintenance over this time could influence the comparisons. It should be noted that the probation office, like any responsible department, has been engaged in a fairly continuous effort to improve its record-keeping ability over the years.

In this chapter recidivism will be viewed from a variety of perspectives. First, we compare overall rates between the current system and the institutional system represented by a sample of youths paroled from the institutions in 1968. We will show a slight increase in recidivism over time. Some regions are doing better than they did in the past while others are not doing so well. We will also show that youths in different kinds of settings recidivate at different rates. These differences cannot be entirely explained by the initial selection process by which youths were assigned. Self-reported delinquency, reappearance in court, and kinds of dispositions will be examined through regression techniques to identify the different kinds of factors that influence these different measures of recidivism. It will become apparent that while the reform attempts within DYS have improved the relationships between youths and staff and among youths within the program settings, the attempt to penetrate the community relationships has not gone far enough. It will also become clear that reforms inside DYS can be expected to have only modest effects on reintegration of youths if corresponding changes in other social institutions responsible for the care and nurturance of youths are not also made.

SYSTEM COMPARISONS

We will first consider system recidivism rates over time, looking at
comparisons between the longitudinal sample of youths from the
community-based system who entered between 1973 and 1974 and
a sample of youths paroled from the institutions prior to the major
reform efforts.

The 1968 institutional sample constitutes a representative sample
of 308 youths paroled from DYS institutions between July 1, 1967,
and June 30, 1968. The sample includes 72 girls from the Lancaster
School for Girls, 25 boys from the forestry program, 27 boys from
Oakdale (an institution for young boys), 39 boys from the Lyman
School for Boys, 102 boys from the Shirley Industrial School for
Boys, and 43 boys from the Bridgewater Institute for Juvenile Guidance (the most secure facility in that system). Table 7–1 shows the
distribution of this sample for boys by paroling institution and
region to which they were paroled.

Youths for this sample were selected from parole release lists
maintained by the former Massachusetts Youth Service Board institutions for fiscal 1968. It should be noted that these numbers are not
necessarily proportioned to the average daily population of youths in
each institution. The sample is a close approximation of the propor-
tions of youths released on parole in a given year and is accordingly
affected by department policies related to parole criteria, institutional transfers, length of stay, and so on. Such a sample should
provide the closest possible comparison to the 1974 sample. Again,
however, because we had to rely on records maintained over a period
of years (records that had been moved from place to place), one may

Table 7–1. Distribution of 1968 Sample of Boys by Region and Institution
(Ns)

| Institution | Regions | | | | | | | |
	I	*II*	*III*	*IV*	*V*	*VI*	*VII*	*Total*
Oakdale	5	4	5	5	0	5	3	27
Forestry	3	6	3	2	4	4	3	25
Lyman	6	8	4	6	3	8	4	39
Shirley	18	16	15	17	6	21	9	102
Bridgewater	5	5	6	3	3	15	6	43
	37	39	33	33	16	53	25	236

question the representativeness of the sample. Nevertheless, it remains the best baseline sample that we could construct.

Table 7−2 records the number of boys recidivating by institution in the 1968 sample. Using the criterion of reappearance in court during the twelve months following release, the Oakdale youths recidivated at a slower rate than did youths from the other institutions. Bridgewater has the highest rate. When we examine the disposition index—that is, the numbers of youths placed on probation or recommitted to either DYS or adult institutions—we find that Oakdale and forestry youths were somewhat less likely to receive severe dispositions; Bridgewater youths were most likely to receive such dispositions.

Official recidivism rates for boys are shown in Table 7−3 for both the 1968 and 1974 samples across the DYS regions. For both recidivism criteria, we find that overall system comparisons show an 8 percentage point rise in recidivism over this period. This difference is statistically significant at the .001 level using a chi-square test of significance. The question remains—what does this mean? Was the reform effort a failure in terms of recidivism? We think not. In the rest of this chapter, we will explore further what this simple comparison means and what factors seem to contribute to increased recidivism.

As we break the overall comparisons down by region, we discover some fascinating differences. In both samples and on both recidivism criteria, region III had the lowest recidivism rates even though the rate increased over the years. Region VII, which had the worst court appearance rate in 1968, moved to the third best in the 1974 sample while region V's rank dropped considerably. Regions II and VII had the worst rates on the disposition criterion in 1968 but ran second and third in 1974 with lower absolute rates. Again region V dropped considerably. The increase of absolute recidivism rates in five of seven regions is not statistically significant; that is, one would expect this outcome or more extreme differences by chance as often as 45 percent of the time.

These data strongly suggest that the reform efforts produced uneven results across the regions. One plausible explanation is that the reforms were unevenly implemented. Some regions were able to establish more diverse program arrangements than others, which resulted in lower recidivism rates. Regions II, III, and VII had considerable diversity of program types. Region IV had few nonresidential alternatives when the 1974 sample was gathered. In contrast, in region I a number of group homes were being closed because of financial crises, thereby reducing the placement alternatives. Region

Table 7–2. Recidivism Rates for Boys in the 1968 Sample by Institution

Recidivism Criteria	Oakdale	Forestry	Lyman	Shirley	Bridgewater	Total
				Institution		
			(Percent)			
1. Reappearance in court						
12 months	44	60	66	64	77	66
2. Probation or recommitment						
12 months	33	36	49	47	65	47
N	(27)	(25)	(39)	(102)	(43)	(236)

152 Diversity in a Youth Correctional System

Table 7–3. Recidivism Rates for Boys in the 1968 and 1974 Samples by Region

Recidivism Criteria	Regions							
	I	II	III	IV	V	VI	VII	Total
				(Percent)				
1. Reappearance in court								
12 months								
1968	73 (37)	69 (39)	48 (33)	58 (33)	62 (16)	75 (53)	80 (25)	66 (236)
1974[a]	73 (41)	75 (53)	54 (48)	68 (44)	80 (46)	85 (105)	69 (58)	74 (395)
2. Probation or commitment								
12 months								
1968	40 (37)	67 (39)	24 (33)	36 (33)	44 (16)	57 (53)	60 (25)	47 (236)
1974[a]	58 (41)	45 (53)	40 (48)	52 (44)	65 (46)	64 (105)	50 (58)	55 (395)

[a] The 1974 sample includes eighteen boys who did not receive a complete set of interviews.

VI was unable to develop a viable foster care network and was having considerable difficulty establishing viable group homes, forcing placement personnel to rely heavily on nonresidential and secure care programs and on sending youths to other regions for placement. Region V remained the most traditional in approach, using few foster homes and hardly any nonresidential alternatives. With these kinds of program differences across regions, it is not surprising to find variability among recidivism rates. Regions with a diverse range of programs yielded lower recidivism rates. One could argue that stronger central office control should have been exercised over program development across the regions. In some regions, such control may have reduced the level of creativity, but it may have strengthened it in other regions. It seems apparent that by the late seventies this type of control was being instituted.

The 1968 and 1974 populations are different in two respects, which may also contribute to the overall comparison. First, the youths being served in 1974 were considerably older than youths being served in 1968. Fifty-eight percent of the youths in the 1974 sample were 16 or older, compared to 33 percent entering DYS in 1968. Oakdale, in the earlier period, was designated for young boys aged 8 to 10, and they had a low recidivism rate. This may suggest that more of the youths in the 1974 sample had been involved in delinquent careers for longer periods of time. It should be noted, parenthetically, that in subsequent detailed analyses within the 1974 sample age did not emerge as a significant predictor of recidivism. However, youths in that sample were more similar in terms of age than were youths in the 1968 group.

While the actual number of youths in either sample who were committed for serious offenses (i.e., crimes against persons) is low, 10 percent of the population served in 1974 were charged with crimes against persons compared to 2 percent in 1968. Coupled with the increase in the number of serious offenders has been a movement to remove status offenders from DYS. It seems likely that the differences in terms of age and offense characteristics would mean that the 1974 population was a more difficult population with which to work. We will show later in our regression analysis that status offenders were less likely to reappear in court; thus as the proportion of this group diminishes in our second sample we would expect an increase in the absolute recidivism rate of the more narrowly defined population of delinquent youths.

A comparison of Tables 7-3 and 7-4 indicates that girls are less likely to reappear in court, be placed on probation, or be recommitted than boys. However, girls in the 1974 sample were recidivating at

Table 7—4. Recidivism Rates for Girls in the 1968 and 1974 Samples[a]

	Total Sample	
Recidivism Criteria	1968 Percent N	1974 Percent N
1. Reappearance in court		
12 months	24 (72)	37 (99)
2. Probation or recommitment		
12 months	10 (72)	25 (98)

[a] The 1974 sample includes seventeen girls who did not receive a complete set of interviews.

higher rates than girls in the 1968 sample. The earlier discussion of different program mixes by region, age, and serious offenses should apply for girls as well as boys. It is also quite possible that as attitudes toward the status of women have changed in recent years, police, judges, and other criminal justice decision-makers may be less likely to view girls as requiring protection from exposure to the correctional system. If such a change in attitude is in fact taking place, one would expect the recidivism rate for girls to increase.

It is difficult at best to compare recidivism rates over a significant period of time. We do have a comparison sample drawn at the same time as our 1973–1974 sample: that of youths who were detained but not committed to DYS. Of that sample 72 percent of 283 boys had reappeared in court within one year of being released from detention, and 64 percent of 219 boys, on whom disposition data were available, had been either placed on probation or committed to DYS or an adult institution. These comparisons suggest that youths who were committed or referred to the department did better than youths who were simply detained without the follow-up services of the department.

PROGRAM COMPARISONS

Regional differences within the comparative recidivism rates suggest that the mix of program settings within a region may influence recidivism outcomes. Here we will examine differences in rates across program settings. First, we will look at rates by program types. Second, we will consider rates according to the underlying dimensions of the institutionalization-normalization continuum.

One-year court reappearance and disposition data are presented in Table 7—5 for each of the program types. Youths in foster care are less likely to reappear in court and less likely to receive severe dispo-

Table 7-5. Recidivism Criteria by Final Program Type

Final Program Type	Reappearance in Court Percent	Probation or Recommitment Percent	N
Nonresidential	70	45	(56)
Foster care	49	41	(63)
Forestry	70	50	(93)
Group homes	62	46	(125)
Boarding schools	59	53	(17)
DYS secure care	82	67	(67)
Jail	86	71	(7)
No initial program	84	55	(31)

sitions. While youths in nonresidential programs frequently reappear in court, they are not as likely to receive severe dispositions as youths in some of the other settings. Youngsters in DYS secure care programs are very likely to reappear in court and are also quite likely to receive harsher dispositions. It is worth noting that youths in our "no program" category reappear in court at a very high rate and receive moderately severe dispositions relatively speaking. Thus it seems clear that leaving these youngsters alone did not result in their staying out of trouble and in fact seemed to make matters worse. It seems likely that these youths could have done better if they had been in programs that could have captured their imagination and gotten them involved.

Table 7-6 displays the recidivism outcomes according to the underlying dimensions of the institutionalization-normalization continuum. The data generally support the notion that the more the quality of the program is enhanced by improving social climate, linkages with the community, and quality of those linkages, the less likely youngsters will be either to reappear in court or to receive a severe disposition if they do reappear. In other words, the more normalized the setting the better are the youngsters' chances of not recidivating. It should be remembered that in our analysis of program placement decisions some selectivity did occur—youths with more prior court appearances and youths who had previously been in DYS were more likely to be placed in programs yielding lower scores on the continuum. However, the seriousness of the current charge did not determine where a youngster would be placed. It seems probable that the availability of program slots and the program mix within specific regions played such an important part in determining where

Table 7—6. Recidivism Criteria by Institutionalization-Normalization Dimension and Overall Continuum

Dimension Standard Deviation	Reappearance in Court Percent	Disposition Percent	N
Social Climate:			
(1.00 + over)	47	32	38
(0.00) — (0.99)	63	47	78
(− 0.01) — (− 1.00)	72	52	194
(− 1.01 + under)	65	54	118
x^2 significance	.02	.09	
Gamma significance	.18	.04	
Extent of Community Linkage:			
(1.00 + over)	53	40	94
(0.00) — (0.99)	67	48	100
(− 0.01) — (− 1.00)	73	54	150
(− 1.01 + under)	68	56	84
x^2 significance	.01	.12	
Gamma significance	.02	.02	
Quality of Community Linkage:			
(1.00 + over)	45	40	20
(0.00) — (0.99)	57	41	118
(− 0.01) — (− 1.00)	72	54	257
(− 1.01 + under)	70	58	33
x^2 significance	.006	.10	
Gamma significance	.002	.01	
Overall Continuum:			
(1.00 + over)	27	20	15
(0.00) — (0.99)	61	43	129
(− 0.01) — (− 1.00)	71	54	230
(− 1.01 + under)	68	57	54
x^2 significance	.003	.02	
Gamma significance	.01	.004	

these youths were placed that the kind of selectivity referred to above does not entirely explain the differences in recidivism that we find across the continuum.

Once more, it seems reasonable to suggest that the department's reform efforts were going in the proper direction. But too few youths were appropriately placed in the more normalized settings to greatly affect the overall system recidivism rate.

REGRESSION ANALYSIS

In order to learn what kinds of factors tend to influence a youth's chances for recidivating, we ran multiple stepwise regression equations using as dependent variables (1) self-reported delinquency at the time the last interview was administered; (2) appearance in court within one year; and (3) being placed under control of the juvenile or criminal justice system within one year. For each of these indices, we first analyzed an equation that included the possibility for all variables to enter the equation, measured to the point of completion of the program. Second, we analyzed an equation permitting the addition of possible intervening variables from the final interview given after youths were in the community for six months or had reappeared in the juvenile justice system. The first analytical procedure is the most conservative; the second runs the risk of having variable measures for some youths at the time they formally recidivated, thus making causal inference suspect. However, we analyzed the data both ways in order to exhaust the available information in our attempt to learn what influences a youth's chances of reintegration.

It should be noted again that interpreting the meaning of recidivism is a very complex problem, particularly in trying to sort out the extent to which it reflects a youngster's behavior, the impact of program experiences, or the decisions of other juvenile justice decision-makers such as policemen, probation officers, and judges. With this caveat in mind, we will first look at the factors related to self-reported delinquency.

Self-Reported Delinquency

During the final interview, six months after leaving DYS, youths were asked if they were doing things presently that would get them into trouble if they got caught. This question was also asked of them in their initial interview. (Interviewers were trained to identify *patterns* of behavior. We were not simply interested in learning whether youths had ever done something that would get them into trouble.) In both cases, as one might expect, the sample as a whole tended to underreport this delinquent activity. In the first instance, 87 percent indicated that they were doing such things. Of course, all were in the sample in the first place by virtue of their being in trouble with the law. It may be that some of the respondents did not believe that they were doing anything wrong. It may be that they were simply not telling us the truth. It seems more likely that they simply did not consider their delinquency to be routine behavior. In the last interview, administered six months after being exposed to the community, 40 percent indicated that they were regularly doing things that could get them into trouble. Again this represents at least a moderate amount of underreporting because we know that 55 percent of the sample had reappeared in court by this time and that 35 percent were back under control of the juvenile or adult systems. Bearing in mind the differences between these percentages and official delinquency, it seems worthwhile to sort out the kinds of relationships that exist between background characteristics, experiences of youths, and self-reported delinquency.

Looking at the equations related to self-reported delinquency (Table 7−7), one is immediately struck by the absence of any official delinquency history variables such as the charge for which the youths were committed to DYS, the total number of prior court appearances, or the age at which the youths first appeared in juvenile court. While many people believe that these factors are good predictors of delinquency, they do not seem to be so for self-reported delinquency. Later, when we look at the equations for (a) court appearance within a year of program completion and (b) being placed under control of the juvenile or adult system during the initial postprogram year, we will find that official delinquent history emerges as a better predictor of those occurrences. In fact, self-reported delinquency is more related to actual youth behaviors or relationships within the community; court appearance is more closely tied to past official delinquency history and social class; and being placed under some form of control is more closely related to prior experiences of youths in the juvenile justice system. This is probably not too surprising because the youth is in the best position to know about his or her own situation; police and intake officers are responding to their experience or the record of official experience with the youngster's acting-out behavior. The judge, in making disposition decisions, is frequently the most removed from the youngster's actual situation and is forced to rely on the judgments and recommendations of staff and others based on their prior experience with the youngster in the system.

Our analysis strongly confirms the notions that repeated or chronic delinquency is typically a group phenomenon. That is, it flourishes where there is a network that provides emotional support for deviant actions, technical skills and knowledge, and general access to delinquent opportunities. Youths who are most likely to report delinquency are youths who during the initial interview said that they regularly used drugs, stole cars, were truants, or ran away with other youths. Before entering DYS, then, these youths were in at least loosely defined associations that provided supports for their deviant actions. These youngsters also indicated that the people they looked up to or admired, trusted, and talked to freely were people who themselves regularly broke the law. This fact further confirms the notion that those youngsters had a variety of supports for their illegal actions.

If repeated delinquency is influenced by a youth's associational network, we could assume that staying out of trouble would also be influenced by a network. Again the initial equation supports this position. Youths who at the end of their program experience looked favorably upon their primary group are less likely to report further delinquency than youths who seem more alienated from their primary group. Furthermore, youths reporting in the initial interview that they did not "hang around" with kids who regularly used drugs were less likely to report delinquency after they left the program.

Taken alone, these network-related variables are quite suggestive. Where networks supporting delinquency exist, working on the youngster alone will probably have a marginal effect at most on his or her chances of staying out of trouble. The pressures and the opportunities to conform to deviant expectations are probably too great.

As we add variables reflecting postprogram community experiences, the argument is simply made stronger. Factors such as using drugs, being a truant, or running away with other youths prior to entry to DYS remain in the equation, as does the importance of primary group relations. In addition, we discover that following the program the youths once again most likely to report delinquency look up to, trust, and relate well with people who themselves break the law. Another factor related to this supportive deviant network is that youths reporting delinquency also indicate that their friends use alcohol regularly. In contrast, to go along with the favorable perception of primary group members as a basis for forming a supportive network to impede delinquency, youths staying out of trouble indicated that they did not use drugs.

An oddity in this analysis is that youths using marijuana were also less likely to report delinquency. This may reflect the growing view in the country that marijuana use should not in itself be viewed as a criminal or deviant activity. Furthermore, it may suggest that networks supporting marijuana use do not support the more traditional forms of delinquent or criminal activity. This is a somewhat surprising finding and requires further research, but it may be that using marijuana provides a rather unobtrusive means for young people to

Table 7–7. Multiple Regression of Self-Reported Delinquency on Preprogram, Program, and Postprogram Experience

Preprogram, Program, and Postprogram Experience Variable	Equation with Preprogram and Program Experience Only		Equation Including Postprogram Experience	
	Coefficient	Standardized Coefficient	Coefficient	Standardized Coefficient
Preprogram and Program Experience:				
Race Black	−.17	−.14**		
Self-reported past offenses:				
Drugs with others	.17	.14***	.23	.20***
Status offense with others	.36	.10**	.47	.14***
Car stealing with others	.12	.13***		
Kids you hang with don't use drugs	−.11	−.10*		
People you admire and trust break the law	.11	.09*		
Teachers view you as neither bad nor good	.13	.12**		
Bosses view you as a bad kid	.30	.10**		
Police don't make judgments about you	−.16	−.14***	−.15	−.11**
Judge viewed you as neither bad nor good	−.16	−.14***		
Judge said he tried to punish you	−.17	−.12**		
Perception of primary group at end of program	−.12	−.19***	−.14	−.23***
Expectations and aspirations during program	−.16	−.27***		
Expectations and aspirations at end of program	.19	.33***		

Fear is major deterrent at end of program to keep you out of trouble	.13	.15**
Self-image at end of program	.11	.10**
Postprogram Experience:		
Use marijuana regularly	−.23	−.23***
You don't use drugs	−.43	−.42***
Kids hang with use alcohol regularly	.14	.14***
Persons you admire and trust break the law	.23	.16***
Bosses view you as bad kid	.54	.13***
Boss views you as neither bad nor good	.23	.12**
Fear is major deterrent to keep you out of trouble	.16	.11**
Other kids sometimes punish you for what others do	−.20	−.13***
Regression Constant	.83	.69
Multiple R	.54	.62

express their need to be different. Or it may reflect a youngster's means for coping with family and school environments that the youngster finds intolerable.

The apparent importance of the kind of support system for a youngster provides us with a key to explaining why the initial positive effects of the DYS programs disappear by the time we look at recidivism. The community experience both before and after the program simply overwhelms even the more constructive elements of the programs. It seems clear that the programs are having little positive effect on the networks to which a youngster will return. Our earlier suspicions are then borne out: many, if not most, of the programs are still not successfully working with people and resources of the community. In Chapter 5 we pointed out that it is more difficult to promote a positive social climate in a nonresidential community that is daily exposed to the cross-pressures that youths experience. It seems quite evident that these cross-pressures are precisely what must be dealt with. More needs to be done to strengthen the constructive ties within families, the schools, and the world of work; and more needs to be done to blunt the influence of the deviant support system. Isolating the youngster to provide a less hectic atmosphere for treatment is ignoring the battlefield to which the youngster will return and where the youngster must ultimately learn to survive without constantly being at odds with law enforcement officials.

These equations also suggest a second key for understanding why the programs are not as effective at reducing crime as they might be. In the first equation, the reader will notice that youths with higher levels of aspirations and expectations at the end of the program are more likely to report delinquent activity. While this variable falls out in the second equation when other intervening variables are added, in that equation we discover that youths with more positive self-images are more likely to report delinquent activity. On the surface these seem like very strange findings. After all, many programs are established on the principle that delinquent youths need to be shown that they are "OK kids" and that if properly motivated they can achieve much in legitimate roles within society. These findings do not necessarily contradict that principle, but they do suggest how one might go about enhancing self-image and aspirations. In earlier equations we found that both variables were determined in part by the nature of programs, that is, programs that were viewed as having more positive social climates tended to increase the self-image and aspirations of the youngsters. Typically, many of these programs were among the most isolated from the community.

We have commented in earlier chapters on the fact that it was easier to develop a positive social climate with youths taking responsibilities in relatively closed environments. This isolation, coupled with a positive social climate, may work to produce an unrealistic view of society and what youths can immediately expect to achieve in the open society. In the closed program, the youths are given responsibility and are often respected for their leadership abilities. Many youths have gained more in stature and responsibility in the program than they ever will in the larger community—and most certainly they will find it difficult to gain the same rewards from legitimate actions as soon as they return to the community. We are *not* suggesting that youths should be denied the opportunity to take responsibility for themselves, but we are pointing out that if this opportunity is provided in a situation divorced from real world pressures, youths may be badly deceived and will reenter the community with unrealistic expectations that may very well widen the gulf between them and legitimate society. In order to achieve the kinds of rewards they had been accustomed to receiving, they may be forced to opt for leadership roles within a deviant subculture. The tendency to inflate expectations would necessarily be kept in balance in program settings that work closely with youngsters in their own living situations.

Court Reappearance

Whether or not a juvenile will reappear in court is largely a decision of police and court intake officers. Thus as we try to interpret the equations with court appearance as a dependent variable, we should remember that while many of the youngsters have been charged with some sort of delinquent act, how far a youth penetrates the formal juvenile justice system is critically determined by the decision-makers who act as screeners in the early stages of the process.

The resulting equations for reappearance in court (Table 7-8) yield a different distribution of independent variables than did the equations for self-reported delinquency. We find more variables reflecting the official offense history of the youngster and no variables reflecting self-reported acts that the youth detailed in our initial interview.

The younger youths are when they appear in court initially and the more times they appear, the more likely they will be to recidivate. The median age at first appearance is 13.75. It seems clear that the earlier youngsters are exposed to the formal court processing procedures the more difficult it will be to break the cycle of delinquency. At least three factors may affect this phenomenon. First, early exposure may result in earlier development of a delinquent self-image, ideology, and skill level. Second, early exposure enhances the possibility that the youngsters will be tracked or set aside from the

Table 7–8. Multiple Regression of Reappearance in Court on Preprogram, Program, and Postprogram Experience

Preprogram, Program, and Postprogram Experience Variable	Equation with Preprogram and Program Experience Only		Equation Including Postprogram Experience	
	Coefficient	Standardized Coefficient	Coefficient	Standardized Coefficient
Preprogram and Program Experience:				
Father's schooling	-.03	-.19***	-.03	-.23***
Mother's schooling	.05	.21***	.04	.16***
Sex female	-.16	-.13**	-.15	-.12**
Region III	-.23	-.15***	-.23	-.15***
Number of court appearances before this commitment or referral to DYS	.02	.11*		
Age first juvenile court appearance	-.01	-.10*	-.01	-.13**
Current charge: Status offense	-.29	-.24***	-.20	-.16***
Significant other: Kid relative legal	.15	.11**		
Judge committed you as punishment	.13	.11**		
Probation officers regularly punish you for what others have done	.16	.10**		
Processed through a full-time court			.11	.11**
Expectations and aspirations during program	-.08	-.15***		

Postprogram Experience:		
Most of your friends are younger than yourself	−.33	−.12**
Hang with same kids as before	.10	.11**
Beating others up to get what you want is not OK	−.12	−.16***
Significant other adult acquaintances legal	−.25	−.16***
Police view you as a bad kid	.10	.11**
Bosses sometimes punish you for what others do	−.26	−.10**
Regression Constant	1.07	1.39
Multiple R	.56	.61

normal experiences of youngsters in schools and other community activities. And third, early exposure may identify the youngsters as delinquent to other decision-makers, making it easier for them to redefine their past and future experiences with the youths to coincide with this delinquency label, thereby reducing the alternatives for coping with the youngsters and their acting-out behavior outside the juvenile justice system.

If we couple these findings with the fact that status offenders in the sample were less likely to recidivate than youngsters charged with other offenses, we can begin to see some empirical justification for diversion of less seriously acting-out youths from the formal juvenile justice system and for decriminalization of status offenders. In addition, if our suspicion is true that DYS was being used to a certain extent as an alternative to the welfare system—that is, as a means of providing some crisis-oriented services to youths and families—we must conclude that the risk of stigmatization involved in the formal juvenile system is simply too great for this situation to continue. Other more direct, nonstigmatizing mechanisms must be developed. Early exposure and exposure for less serious offenses to a formal judicial system reduce the chances of these youngsters ever joining the mainstream of our society.

Decision-makers who screen youngsters for appearance in court are at least somewhat cognizant of each youth's network of deviant and nondeviant persons. Those relationships appear to play a part in the decisions made about the youngsters. Youths who indicated at entry into DYS that they admired and trusted a relative, also a juvenile and someone who did not regularly break the law, were more likely to reappear in court. This variable drops out of the second equation, which includes the intervening variables from the final interview. In that equation we find that youths who continued to hang out with the same youths that they had been with before entry to DYS would be more likely to appear in court again. In contrast, youths who indicated that most of their friends were younger than themselves and who believed that it was not OK to beat up someone to get what they wanted were less likely to appear in court. Thus police officers are apparently making some of their judgments based on their knowledge of the youngsters' involvement with peers. The inability to effect change in the youths' network in the community is observed by the police and probably confirms their suspicion that the youngsters have not changed and are simply becoming more committed to a delinquent career.

It is worth noting that youths returning to the community who say that they have an adult acquaintance whom they admire, trust, and relate well to are less likely to appear in court. The fact that they have an adult to relate to may keep them out of trouble in the first place, but if they do get into touble, having such a person to advocate or stand by them is apparently an asset when dealing with the police or court intake officers. This finding has some straightforward program implications. If we can link youngsters who have been in trouble with adults who provide legitimate role models, we have enhanced those youngsters' chances for successful reintegration. Many of these youths have been very isolated and alienated from the adult world. For many, the bridge may not require a lot of sophisticated treatment, but rather an adult who will care as well as set limits.

Social class, as reflected by father's schooling, is also related to reappearance in court. Consistent with much of the literature is the finding that youths of the middle class are treated differently from those from the lower strata. Police officers are generally more hopeful that youths from the more stable middle class will have parents who will intervene and handle the matter informally in order to keep their youngsters from getting a juvenile record. Whether well founded or not, police share very different perceptions of the lower-class and middle-class parent, perceptions that shape their reaction to juveniles. Of course the middle-class parent also has more power to exert influence over the police officer should the officer overstep his authority.

Curiously, the mother's schooling has just the opposite relationship with reappearance in court—the more schooling the mother has achieved the more likely her youngsters will be to reappear in court. This may, as some suggest, reflect a mother actively engaged in pursuing a career where youths are not receiving quality parenting. Or (if we continue to assume more schooling means greater likelihood of outside employment) it may simply reflect situations where police officers attempt to take a youngster home and, finding no one there, transport the youth to a detention facility, thus making a court appearance almost certain.

Reappearance in court is also determined to a degree by where youths live. Youths in region III are less likely to reappear than youths in other regions. This finding may be somewhat tied to social class because this region is one of the wealthier regions of the state. And as noted earlier, region III does not have the detention resources available in other regions.

Variables reflecting the nature of the juvenile justice system response also help to explain reappearance in court. Youths who indicated in their initial interview that the judge committed them to DYS in order to punish them and that probation officers regularly punished them for what others did were more likely to reappear in court. While these variables dropped out of the second equation when intervening variables were added, two more system variables entered the equation: youths who believed that police saw them as "bad kids" and youths who had initially been processed through full-time courts were more likely to reappear in court.

Placed on Probation, Recommitted to DYS, or Committed to Adult System

The last criterion of recidivism that we will examine is the judge's decision regarding the disposition of the case. Basically we ask, in what ways do youths receiving more severe dispositions differ from youths whose cases are treated less severely or who do not come to court at all? Perhaps another way of saying this is, what kinds of factors seem to be taken into account by judges when rendering disposition decisions?

Somewhat surprisingly, neither official delinquency history nor self-reported delinquency history are good predictors of who will or will not receive severe penalties (Table 7-9). The single exception is that the younger youths are when first appearing in juvenile court the more likely they are to be given a more severe disposition. One might expect that these youngsters would have been before the court more than others, but the total number of court appearances does not make it into our equations. The importance of early exposure to court does underscore, however, the imperative of keeping youths out of the juvenile courts until every alternative is exhausted.

Four of the factors entering our initial equation reflect experiences that the youths have had in the justice system. Youths who have run from DYS are more likely to receive severe dispositions upon return to court. It would appear that the fact of running has reinforced the view that these youngsters pose a serious threat to the system and the community. As we discovered in Chapter 5, absconding from a program is itself influenced by a number of situational factors, including program conditions as well as the youths' own characteristics. Thus the failure of the system to cope with youngsters who run is ultimately important in determining what will happen to them in the future. It is clear that programs can have long-run negative as well as positive effects.

Other system-related factors entering the equation include how probation officers and judges punish or reward youths for what others do and the fact that detention staff view the youngsters as neither good nor bad. The largest group of variables in the equation involved the prior experience of the system with the youngsters rather than youth behavior in the community. One must wonder if at this point in the process decisions are not being made on the basis of a paper trail rather than the youngsters' social situation.

Type of disposition is related to family relationships. Youths whose mothers work are more likely to receive severe dispositions. Apparently judges are indicating that they have less faith in youngsters' being able to go straight if their mothers are not at home. Whether this supposition is accurate is another matter. One would expect, for instance, that in many cases the additional income may be used to provide extra resources for the family—and one cannot simply assume that children of working mothers are left to roam the streets. Nonetheless this factor does seem to shape the judge's decision about the future of these youngsters. When intervening variables are added to the equation the new equation includes another family variable—namely, that children who indicate that they no longer have contact with their parents are more likely to receive stiffer dispositions.

Some kinds of youth behavior do apparently shape the judge's decision. Youths who indicated during their initial interview that they used alcohol regularly receive heavier penalties when they reappear in court. This factor is probably somewhat indicative of participation in a deviant subculture, although not one that is necessarily crime oriented. Youths who scored well on taking responsibility for themselves also receive more severe dispositions. It may be that youths who take responsibility are not receiving enough support from legitimate networks and are therefore making their way into more accepting deviant networks. Zero-order correlation confirms the notion that youths who really take responsibility for themselves are often the same youngsters who are frequently in conflict with adult authority figures. These youths are continually questioning why things are the way they are, why the rules cannot be changed, and why teenagers are treated like small children.

We frequently place our teenagers in a curious dilemma. On the one hand, we want them to be responsible, mature, miniature adults—on the other hand, when they do think for themselves and act independently, we find the experiences very threatening. The youngsters in this sample who have taken major responsibility for their lives may not have received adult support to channel that youth initiative into constructive directions. It may very well be that they have become the defiant ones and are now in part being punished for having taken charge.

Table 7—9. Multiple Regression of Dispositions on Preprogram, Program, and Postprogram Experience

Preprogram, Program, and Postprogram Experience Variable	Equation with Preprogram and Program Experience Only		Equation Including Postprogram Experience	
	Coefficient	Standardized Coefficient	Coefficient	Standardized Coefficient
Preprogram and Program Experience:				
Ethnicity: Father northern Europe	-.18	-.16***	-.16	-.14**
Sex female	-.24	-.18***	-.22	-.17***
Mother is employed	.12	.11**	.13	.13**
Region III			-.16	-.10*
Use alcohol regularly	.11	.11*		
Age first court appearance	-.01	-.13***	-.01	-.12**
Ran from DYS during last commitment or referral	.12	.12**	.12	.12**
Extent to which you take responsibility at end of program	.11	.11**		
Judges never reward you for what others do	-.18	-.14***	-.14	-.12**
Probation officers sometimes punish you for what others do	.23	.13**	.22	.13**
Detention staff view you as neither good nor bad	.14	.10**		

Postprogram Experience:			
Beating others up to get what you want is not OK		-.11	-.14***
Significant other: Adult acquaintance legal		-.21	-.13**
No contact with parents		.25	.10*
Regression Constant	.65	1.24	
Multiple R	.45	.47	

The additional intervening variables include two more network-related factors. Youths reporting that it is not OK to beat up someone to get what you want and youths who admire, trust, and relate well to an adult acquaintance who does not routinely break the law are less likely to receive severe dispositions.

SUMMARY

We began with the premise that recidivism, however measured, is but one of many indicators that can be used to provide evidence of the viability of correctional programs and reforms. While it is clear that recidivism is not the sole responsibility of correctional programs (certainly families, schools, welfare, and employment policies must share part of the responsibility), neither should correctional programs be allowed to duck the recidivism issue entirely.

Second, when looking at indicators of recidivism over time, representing the training-school system of the late sixties and the community-based system of the middle seventies, we saw that the absolute rate had increased slightly. Numerous explanations are possible for this increase, reflecting changes in the makeup of the DYS population over time, broader societal trends in youth crime, changing attitudes toward females, and changes in police and court resources. Nonetheless, it is clear that the reforms in DYS did not bring about a decrease in the recidivism rate, and it is equally clear that the reforms did not generate an explosive youth crime wave. In fact, two of the seven DYS regions experienced a decrease in rates over the eight-year comparison period.

Third, zero-order correlations alone would suggest that the move toward community-based programming has considerable value in successfully reintegrating delinquent youths. However, as we add background variables and data from postprogram experiences within the community, it becomes apparent that the links with the youngsters' communities are crucial. Recidivism rates and our earlier analysis of program placement show that the programs have simply not gone far enough in setting up these linkages. It is also clear that only a fairly substantial minority of the youths sampled were in programs falling on the normalization side of our institutionalization-normalization continuum.

Fourth, with the aid of regression equations, we have been able to point out factors that explain these recidivism rates or, to put it another way, permit us to talk about factors that impede or facilitate reintegration. One must be in a position to affect both the deviant and the legitimate networks of which the youths are a part. This

means day-to-day work with families, developing plausible work opportunities, and negotiating with school authorities as youths experience difficulties. It may mean helping volunteer groups such as
churches reach out and support youths. It may mean having programs advocate changes in the distribution of resources for a community's youth population. What is being done, for example, to provide
constructive recreational alternatives for youths aged 13 to 18? It
will mean working with youths while they are being pulled back and
forth between deviant and legitimate roles—to help them sort out
what is going on in their lives at that moment and what the consequences of various courses of action may be.

It is clear that moving from training-school models does not necessarily mean that programs will be readily tied to local community
networks. Instead of having "institution kids" we now have a new
group of "agency kids." They are generally treated better, but their
experience in these agencies is still quite foreign to the worlds in
which they live. If these private agencies are to prevent recidivism
better than the training-school model, they must take the risk of
becoming involved in the community to a more significant degree
than simply retaining a "community board."

In our hurry to help, we have often adversely affected some
youngsters' chances of staying out of further trouble with the law.
Friends, family members, decision-makers in the justice system, decision-makers in schools, bosses on the job, staff in volunteer programs,
and the youths themselves are affected when they are formally processed through the juvenile justice system. It is easy to move from
this first justice system experience to categorizing the youths as dangerous or as losers. It is quite likely that most people unfamiliar with
the justice process make the same distinctions among offenders as
the courts do. The relationships between age at first court detention
experience and DYS placement, or between the runner, the juvenile
offender, and the recidivist suggest we should use the justice system
as an alternative to help acting-out youths as the *very last resort*. We
do respond to labels. Placing a youth prematurely in the justice system is like placing him or her in a vise—the youth is at the mercy of
the people who turn the handle.

Last, the phenomenon of delinquency is complex. It is situational,
social, psychological, and emotional. And it is abundantly evident
that reforming the youth corrections system will have, at best, minimal impact if there are not comparable reforms in our schools, in our
employment and welfare practices, in our voluntary organizations,
and perhaps even in our most sacred of institutions, the family.

✳ *Chapter 8*

Conclusions and Policy Implications

The Massachusetts experience with deinstitutionalization and community-based services provides the broadest empirical base to date for examining the efficacy of the community-based model for delivering services to delinquent youths. The extensive research design employed here, coupled with the uniqueness of the reform efforts under study, provides a rare opportunity for drawing policy implications to facilitate further advances in the conceptual and practical development of community-based services.

Earlier analysis has presented data describing the impact of reform efforts on youths being served. In trying to interpret the data, we have frequently posed alternative explanations of the results. We have generally referred to policy implications indirectly. Here we will directly address the implications of the findings for further policy development by drawing on the preceding analysis and on our observations of program operations and discussions with staff. This chapter will consist of two major sections. The first will address the overall issues of the reform effort and the general conclusions of the study. The second will address specific policy issues concerning the operations of a community-based system of diverse programs for youths.

GENERAL REFORM ISSUES

1. *A community-based system is a viable alternative to a training-school system.* The Massachusetts experience with deinstitutionalization has brought about change throughout the youth corrections

system—altering the type of youngster being admitted, particularly in terms of age, expanding the corrections area to include extensive involvement of private agencies, and setting up a massive array of programs that are considerably more community based than the traditional training schools used in decades past. The reform was not an attempt to augment a training-school system with a few model community-based programs handling a carefully screened population. While the overall results are not perhaps as outstanding as the proponents of reform had hoped, the results do suggest strongly that the vast majority of committed delinquents can be handled in relatively noninstitutional settings. Even youths requiring secure facilities can be handled in smaller, more humane settings than the traditional large training school.

When we compare responses of a sample of youths from the traditional training-school cottages with a sample from the community-based system, it is evident that youths in the community-based system are more likely to believe that they are exposed to more humane care. These youngsters are more likely to have better relationships with staff and their peers than did youths in the training schools. One does not find the existence of negative peer subcultures to the same extent in the new system as in the old. In addition, youths in the community programs are more favorably disposed toward the reward and punishment measures being employed than youths in the training schools. Observations also support the belief that the use and threat of physical force have diminished during the transition from training schools to community-based programs. While abuses still do remain, and the programs need to be closely monitored to control such abuses, generally the relationships between staff and youths and among youths show sharp improvement.

Linkages between the youths and the community have been greatly expanded in the newly constructed system. In the training-school sample, only 6 percent of the respondents indicated that they had routine contact with the community. In the new system over 50 percent of the youths indicated that they had such contact. However, from the distribution of youths and programs across the institutionalization-normalization continuum, it seems clear that most of the youths are in programs that, while more closely linked to local communities than the training schools of the past, are still not adequately interacting with the youths' network of family, peers, school officials, and vocational opportunities. This deficiency may be due in part to the community's apathy or its fear of these youths, or it may reflect the private agency's distrust of the community or its need to hold on to youths in order to continue functioning. These issues will be dealt with more fully below.

Short-term outcomes such as improved self-image, improved perception of others, and enhanced expectations and aspirations increase in settings that can be described as more normalized within the programs and the community. Again, the data support the notion that the department, in replacing the training-school system with a community-based system, made a move in the right direction.

Long-term gains in self-image, perception of others, and expectations and aspirations were generally not realized. Both pre- and postprogram experience in the community tended to affect these outcomes more dramatically than did program experiences. Frequently, short-run gains were diminished as the youths returned to their community networks. Follow-up work with youths in their normal living situations appears to be a badly needed missing link in the delivery of services by the department.

Recidivism, another long-term measure of the youngsters' reintegration into the community without further delinquent behavior, proved a complex indicator. Comparisons between a training-school sample and the community-based sample showed an increase in recidivism for the latter group. While numerous possible explanations of this difference are plausible, such as the older age of the community-based sample, it seems clear that the new system did not systematically produce the desired decreases in recidivism. Regions that most adequately implemented the reform measures with a diversity of programs did produce decreases in recidivism over time, as did those programs receiving ratings reflecting a higher degree of normalization on the institutionalization-normalization continuum. Regression analyses strongly support the notion that for youths who recidivated the department was unable to penetrate the networks to which the youngsters would return. We are left again with the conclusion that while the department has moved in the right direction, the quality of linkages between youths and the networks in the community must be improved to bring about any substantial reduction in recidivism rates.

In economic costs, the community-based system compares quite favorably with the training-school system. The average cost per day (including parole) for the training-school system was $29; for the community-based system the comparable cost was $30. Thus the new model has not placed a substantially higher cost burden on the taxpayer.

As one might expect, the level of costs across program types is quite variable. The breakdown of total costs per day is as follows: nonresidential, $23; foster care, $13; forestry, $40; group care, $31; boarding schools, $28; secure facilities, $57. These figures clearly show that programs that are most community based, such as foster

care and nonresidential facilities, were the most economical to operate. Boarding schools, group homes, and forestry programs were
more expensive. The most expensive programs were the secure care
facilities. Total costs for a system are largely determined by how
many youths require group residential and secure care. The more
youths who can be adequately supported in nonresidential programs
and foster care, the less expensive are the total costs. We have evidence, then, that what seems to be most desirable for a large portion
of the treatment population costs the least.

In summary, the findings strongly favor the community-based
approach as a viable alternative to the training-school model for
facilitating the reintegration of troubled youths into constructive,
legitimate roles within their local community settings. Analysis of
this experience has yielded numerous suggestions for further sharpen-
ing our understanding of community-based service and for forging
practical innovations in the delivery of services within community-
based settings. Let us now turn to some of the more general policy
implications of this analysis.

2. *In order to be more effective in reintegrating youths into the
community, juvenile corrections must enlarge its vision of its own
arena.* Working on a youth as the sole object of treatment ignores to
a large extent the youths' actual life situation—that is, the situation
to which most youths return. Formal treatment takes place in a relatively brief span of time in the context of a youth's whole life up to
that point. If programs are to have any lasting effect, they must
effectively relate to groups with which the youths will continue to
interact. We have observed that short-run gains in the Massachusetts
programs have been determined to a great extent by the experiences
of youths prior to entry, and short-run gains are frequently erased as
the youngster returns to his former networks.

To ignore the youths' family, peer group, school and work opportunities represents an admission of defeat even before the youth has
had an opportunity to prove himself or herself. To ignore these networks is to abdicate genuine responsibility; we may be able to prevent a youth from committing more crime while in a secure setting,
but we attempt no lasting redirection of his or her career patterns.
The youngster is obviously a major actor in determining his or her
own destiny, but well-intentioned efforts can easily be blocked without the support of significant others and constructive responses from
our basic social institutions. If we are not prepared to interact with
the youngsters' real world, the likely result for many of them, already officially labeled delinquents, is further alienation, despair, and

criminal activity. Their choices, over time, become severely limited when help is provided only in a fragmented and frequently irrelevant manner.

Expansion of the correctional arena to include the youths' community networks may require a more "proactive" (concerned and involved) approach to youths and their problems than was generally maintained by correctional staff in the past. It will require an advocacy posture by the staff at all levels of the correctional system. By "advocacy" we do not mean that staff will always be playing out adversarial roles on behalf of youths although this may be important at times. Rather we mean taking risks to act on behalf of youths in establishing constructive relationships with community networks. Three levels of advocacy may be conceived. A given staff member may focus on one level or may participate in two or all three levels.

The first level is individual advocacy. Here a staff member focuses on the individual and the individual's relationships. The staff member may, for example, play the role of a parent by finding out what kinds of problems a youth is having in school. The staff member may want to meet the youth and the vice principal or teacher to attempt to sort out and straighten out behavioral or academic problems. If this staff member helps a parent in doing these tasks that is even better, but if faced with a disinterested parent, the staff member would act on behalf of the youngster in that specific situation. There is a tension between this advocacy approach and the commonly understood role of developing a viable one-to-one relationship with a youth. The latter requires only working with the youth, frequently becoming the youth's friend. Individual advocacy goes beyond that notion: the trust relationship requires getting involved in the youngster's total situation. It may very well require a critical posture toward the way in which the youth is managing his or her situation. Advocacy as envisioned here does not remove responsibility from the youth, but provides the youth with a support system that helps the youth learn to manage that responsibility more effectively. The staff person becomes a resource who the youth can call upon in any situation; the actual action taken by staff would be negotiated between the youth and the staff person and would ultimately be negotiated with other significant persons.

A second level of advocacy is what we call "community advocacy." Here, the focus is on making existing resources available to all youths in a particular community or, if such resources do not exist, participating in processes that will generate them. For example, if adequate recreational resources exist for youths aged 8 to 14, but do not exist for older youths, then steps should be taken to draw attention to this lack and remedy the situation. The same could be said, of course, for alternative educational or vocational opportunities. Again a tension exists in this approach for community-based agencies. There is much fear that if programs operate on a high plane of visibility they will be destroyed by political pressure. On the other hand, if these programs can be seen as providing services and acting on behalf of youths in general in the community, they may in fact receive greater support and ultimately cooperation in their efforts to provide quality services.

The third level of advocacy is "public policy advocacy." Again one may find workers at all levels using this approach to a certain extent, but one would probably expect the top level administrators in the public and private agencies to be most directly involved. By public policy advocacy we mean efforts taken to modify guidelines for dealing with youths across the state. This may involve lobbying for administrative changes or for specific legislation. For example, public policy advocacy includes the removal of CHINS youngsters from juvenile corrections, enacting legislation supporting special educational needs, or taking action to make other departments, such as mental health, more responsive to the needs of youths. This level is not without its own kind of tension. Top administrators frequently desire to take a low profile approach in order to reduce their own visibility and to diminish the likelihood of public attack. Meddling in the affairs of other agencies or systems is frequently frowned upon by other bureaucrats and can be politically risky. On the other hand, youth problems cannot be so nicely untangled. Policies of other agencies and systems to a large extent do influence what can be accomplished by a juvenile corrections department. To ignore that fact and not take a proactive stance places one in the position of working under a grave handicap—an additional handicap that the youths involved, and therefore the society of which they are a part, can ill afford.

Such an expansion of the juvenile corrections arena need not mean continual embroilment in needless conflict. Many parents would like to be more involved with their own children. Many schools would like to better understand and serve these youths. Many public administrators in a variety of agencies would like to improve their coordination of services for youths. We are not proposing a system of chaos or conflict where the youngster is always right or always wins. We are proposing instead an approach that takes into consideration all the actors including the youths. This approach may place actors in a state of creative tension with one another from time to time, but we are convinced that such a state will provide an environment in which the good intentions of the various actors can be sorted out to serve the youngster best and thereby provide more long-run protection for society.

3. *Because youths pass through several overlapping service systems, decision-makers should be keenly aware of the consequences of organizational labeling.* We have shown with the data on the cohort sample that decisions made at the point of detention influence decisions made once a youngster is committed to the Massachusetts Department of Youth Services (DYS). This example only serves to illustrate the consequence of many decisions made about a youth, decisions that become part of the youth's personal biography. Teachers who categorize youths as slow learners in one grade are attaching a label to the youngsters that will often follow them for the remainder of their educational career. Such a label may become a self-fulfilling prophecy that no one can easily change—because any constructive change might not be expected, therefore, the effort might not even be considered. Likewise, decisions by DYS personnel to place youngsters in a secure facility may pose more difficulties for the youths in reentering the community when it comes to finding an alternative school placement, a new job, or friends who are in legitimate roles. Such a decision not only sets the youngsters apart within the correctional system, but it may very well set them apart in the community to such an extent that the probability increases that delinquency or criminality will be one of their few career options.

The fact that code words or labels have long-run consequences for youths does not mean that they should not necessarily be used; it should suggest, however, that youths should be categorized very cautiously. Decisions like those made at detention hearings or placement conferences should be monitored carefully. The persons who make such decisions should be held accountable for the power that they wield over youngsters' lives. Criteria justifying decisions should be clearly defined and defensible. Youths should not be held in secure care because "no other alternative is available." Such a placement is a disservice to the youths and in the long run to society as well. We as a society cannot afford to waste our young by inappropriately labeling them. Yet such labels continue because of the system's inadequate ability to respond effectively to the youths' needs.

Expanding our conception of the corrections arena should reinforce the importance of organizational labeling. Information is shared across the youth service systems. Correctional agencies are not only a repository of people; they are also a repository of paper— paper that dictates to a great extent how people and agencies respond toward an individual. The results of past decisions made by teachers, police, probation officers, judges, detention staff, and correctional staff during any prior commitments describe for the indefinite future the youngsters, their situation, and what has been done to and for them. The reliability of such records becomes critical as we come to recognize fully the extent to which they are relied upon for formulating new directions and actions about youngsters. Recorded information may fail to make even gross distinctions among youths. For example, two youths are charged with assault and battery with a weapon—one used a shoe and the other a butcher knife. Both are held in secure detention because of the charge, and both are likely to be placed in secure care because of where they were detained.

Having sketched in broad strokes the general conclusions and policy implications of the reform effort in Massachusetts, let us direct our attention to specific implications—first for program development and second for managing a community-based corrections system.

IMPLICATIONS FOR PROGRAM DEVELOPMENT

Advocacy in the Community. Throughout the analysis of the institutionalization-normalization continuum, we discovered that while the extent of linkages of programs with the community is often considerable, the quality of those linkages is often inadequate. Yet analysis of recidivism data has shown that linkages with significant others such as teachers, employers, parents, and peers can play an important role in facilitating youngsters' successful reintegration. Youngsters who were able to point to some adult figure with whom they had a trusting relationship and whom they could talk to and admire were more likely to stay out of further trouble than were youths who had no such relationship.

These findings imply that program staff should look at the youngsters' total situation carefully to identify any constructive relationships they may already have. If found, those relationships can then be augmented by the efforts of staff. Not only is this more helpful for the youths, but it also makes clear to program staff that they are not the only people who care and that they need not try to save the world by themselves. The significant other may be a parent, teacher, neighbor, employer, clergyman, coach, or whatever—the important thing is that whatever trusting relationships youths have with a legitimate adult role model should be supported and not severed because the youths are now being served by the department. It may be that these persons can only provide moral support, or it may be that they can intervene with others in the community on behalf of the youngsters if they are shown how and can see that their assistance is needed and desired. As the youths leave the program, these relationships will very likely determine whether or not they receive the kind of support that will enable them to find their own legitimate role in the community.

Particularly when youths are moved to a residential program, any prior supportive relationships with people in their home community will be difficult to maintain. To insure that those relationships are nurtured, program staff will have to take a proactive, advocacy stance—making it clear that continued support for the youngsters are needed and wanted by staff as well as by the youngsters. To bring this about, staff will have to admit that their own relationships with the youths, no matter how positive, are not enough. A supportive network requires more actors than program staff alone.

Systematic Work with Families. One of the saddest experiences associated with this research was, on the one hand, discovering the lack of attention paid to families by programs and, on the other hand, when interviewing youths in homes, discovering many parents who sought information about their youngsters and the treatment programs from our research staff because these parents were not receiving this information either from program staff or from the department. At the very least, parents should be adequately informed of the processes involved in the juvenile justice system, including the correctional agency. Who makes decisions? What are they based on? When will the youths be able to return? What progress, if any, are they making? What can parents do?

It also seems reasonable that someone, perhaps detention staff, inform parents of their rights and the rights of their children. Interviews with court staff indicate that many court-appointed lawyers are not really carrying out this function. Their role is described as "interpreting the court process to parents and youths so they will go along with decisions being made." When one realizes how baffling the juvenile justice system is to an outsider, it is not surprising that more parents are not involved with their children in the various steps through that system. One wonders if a shroud of mystery is not cast around these processes to assure that outside involvement is kept at a minimum.

Program staff who were interviewed about conditions that contribute to youngsters' delinquency cited family problems as the primary cause. Much is generally said about broken and destructive families or both. The classic horror story of the drunken father rap- ing his daughter is usually volunteered as documenting the problem. That such rapes happen is certainly tragic; it is unlikely, however, that they happen as often as the story is told. Our own data do not support the notion that most of the youths in DYS come from single-parent families. In fact, research on single-parent families strongly supports the contention that such families, like two-parent families, can yield high-quality relationships with youths. It is diffi- cult to sort out to what extent family problems are simply used as a "cop-out" by staff—for example, "The family caused the problems and we are expected to make the kid right."

Given the belief that family problems contribute so much to delin- quency, it is surprising that parents are so frequently ignored in the treatment process. Foster parent training programs are available that teach foster parents how to work with youngsters in trouble. Partici- pants are trained in communication, decision-making, rewarding and punishing, advocating—in general how to develop good relationships with these youths. Why are not such training programs made avail- able to natural parents on a voluntary basis?

Systematic Work with Schools. The school is the crucible com- mon to all our young. There, most youngsters experience some suc- cesses, and most experience some failures. For the youths studied here there have been more failures than successes. Yet if one is to succeed in our technological society, the importance of an adequate education cannot be overstated. In the analysis of factors influencing reintegration, we found that youths who favorably described their school experiences were more likely to stay out of trouble than youths who recounted poor experiences. If corrections to be con- cerned with the youths' total situation, as we posit here, then atten- tion to relationships with schools must receive a high priority.

We have noted earlier that for youths in residential or nonresiden- tial programs who are also enrolled in school, individual advocacy would require staff to become fully aware of the youngsters' progress and interactions at the school. The staff person would be charged with not only understanding the pressures of the situation but also intervening where needed to insure that the youths were receiving the best possible education. We are expecting the staff person to do no more or less than a concerned parent.

If youngsters are returning to their home community, having spent some time in a program outside that community, program staff should be able to inform school administrators and individual teachers of the youngsters' progress and perhaps to provide insights into what poses problems for the youngsters' learning and what seems to enliven their interest. The department should be able to assign an aftercare worker who will perform the advocacy role described above and who will generally attempt to support the youths as they try to reorient themselves to the public or alternative school setting.

Correctional personnel have special experiences and skills that help them to work with youths in trouble. These are experiences and skills that teachers frequently do not have. Many teachers, however, may desire to be better prepared to work with such youngsters. It seems reasonable to suggest, then, that the correctional agency make available to public schools training programs that would focus on the issues of delinquency and the juvenile justice system and the skills required to work with delinquents. An agency might coordinate its efforts with other groups such as Teacher Corps Activity II, which is a nationally based organization founded to provide assistance to schools and correctional agencies in meeting the educational needs of youths in trouble.

Systematic Work with the World of Work. Because many of the youths in the correctional system under study were 16 or 17 and because many of these youths had been out of school for over a year, it does not seem reasonable that all would find it palatable to return to school. Yet each must somehow find a legitimate means to earn income, to survive without continually being at odds with the law. Correctional agencies can provide a link between these youngsters and legitimate jobs.

We found that many youths had very low job expectations, which may in part have made criminal careers attractive even with their obvious risks. Others seemed to possess unrealistically high expectations. Many seemed to lack knowledge of a range of occupations, thinking only in terms of the stereotypical menial labor jobs. Programs should be able at least to expose youngsters to a realistic range of job possibilities. Readiness for jobs could be enhanced by providing the rudimentary educational skills plus some skill training that goes beyond work with arts and crafts. Placement in vocational schools is certainly one option—again with the continued support of a staff advocate. Another option to be explored would be participation in day or evening programs with vocational training departments within the public schools. Apprentice-type jobs that provide on-the-job training would also be desirable. We would also urge a reduction in the minimum hourly rate for teenagers under 18 in order to provide incentives for employers to hire and train these young people. Or as an alternative, one could at least subsidize employers who are willing to develop work training programs for youths.

Sequencing of Programs and Aftercare. It is unfortunate that much intense, hard work is devoted to youngsters while they stay in a program, only to be wasted after the youths leave because little attention is paid to the continuity of services. We have found that short-run gains accomplished by programs are frequently lost within the first six months after the youths return to the community. During this period, these youths have the nominal services of a parole officer. While some parole officers most certainly provide a dedicated and worthwhile service to the youths, many spend very little time with them: a phone call or two or a visit once a month. On many occasions, as we sought to track the youths during the final six-month period, parole officers did not know where their parolees were, and parents reported that they had had no contact with the parole officers.

We view this aftercare function as extremely critical and not as an add-on to treatment. The aftercare worker should have responsibility for establishing that the youngsters are adequately plugged into existing community resources and should work closely with the youths, their families, and any other significant persons in their networks. Where possible the worker should be advocating or helping others advocate on the youngsters' behalf.

Youths who have been in secure care programs should be placed in nonresidential programs before being placed on parole. We have found that youths who are sequenced through a nonresidential service program do somewhat better in terms of recidivism than those who are placed back on the street with only parole services.

We would also strongly suggest that youths who are doing well in nonresidential programs, be they oriented toward education, work, or recreation, be allowed to continue voluntarily as long as they wish. This additional service can be purchased at a relatively low cost. If such a service can make a difference, the state should find some way of continuing that support. The voluntary nature of this continued support should be underscored, for we are not suggesting that this continuation should excuse the exercise of control over a youngster's life for longer periods of time.

Youths' Participation in Decision-Making. Wherever possible youths should be encouraged to take responsibility for their own actions and what happens to them within the correctional arena. This is particularly important at the time of placement in a program. Commitment to a program and to a particular group of staff members increases the likelihood that the youths will more fully participate in the program, and from observation it seems to reduce the runs that most frequently occur during the first two weeks of entry into a program. One of the advantages of a purchase-of-service system is that youths can be presented with some treatment options. Parameters, of course, always surround choice. In this case if a youngster is given (say) five options and rejects each of them, staff will still have to place the youngster somewhere.

Nevertheless, youth participation is to be encouraged, as it at least to some degree reduces feelings of alienation and gives each youth some sense of control over his or her own destiny. Furthermore it is through a youth's exercise of responsibility that staff can point out how the youth is either managing or mismanaging his or her opportunities. Increasing a youngster's participation has its risks—a youth may fail time and again; however, failure is an integral part of life, and youngsters must be taught to learn from it in order to avoid similar failures in the future.

Punishment and Reward Patterns. From our interviews with youths and from observing their interactions with staff, it is clear that they expect to be punished and rewarded for their behavior. It is equally clear that they share a belief that each person should be punished or rewarded for his or her own actions, not for the actions of others. The rather common practice of punishing a group of youths for what one or a few do is viewed as grossly unfair, and those persons who engage in such practice lose respect of their charges. This perception particularly has implications for the group-centered programs that frequently adapt the model of holding everyone in a group responsible for each individual's behavior. While they may be inculcating a sense of social responsibility, they seem to be also contributing to the youngsters' feeling that the system has been and continues to be unfair, because it addresses not who they are as individuals but what they represent as a group.

Earlier chapters of this book and another book in this series have dealt extensively with the fact that supervision within community-based programs is different from supervision within the more isolated residential programs [1]. Free access to the community means that the youngsters are under more pressure to conform to the wishes of their peers in the community. Sometimes these pressures encourage a youth to participate in deviant behavior. The interplay with people outside the program also diminishes the "we" spirit of some of the better group-oriented programs while also diminishing the control of youths by staff through internal group pressures. This should not be interpreted straightforwardly as a negative consequence of community-based programming. Supervision will have to be designed on a more individualized basis. For example, some of the nonresidential programs have a low staff-youth ratio. In the more intensive tracking programs, a counselor may be responsible for only two youths, thus having an opportunity to supervise the activity of these charges very closely. Rather than relying on group pressures, the counselor is able to negotiate behaviors on a one-to-one level. Frequently acting in an advocacy role, the counselor is able to negotiate with the youngster and other persons, such as teachers or policemen, around the youth's behavior.

While the group "togetherness" may suffer because of contact with the community, the major objective of the correctional program is not to develop programs in which youths simply feel good about the staff. Rather, the goal is to facilitate the youths' efforts to reestablish themselves in the community. Frequently, the pleasant atmosphere of a group-oriented program is obtained at the cost of isolating the group from the community, thus creating a utopian but unrealistic facsimile of the real world. The youngsters must eventually learn to cope with the pressures of their community living situation; that can best be accomplished while they have the support of staff as they seek to negotiate the pressures of those forces competing for their allegiance and commitment.

Feeling Good about Oneself Is Not Enough. To conclude this section on policy implications for program development, we believe it is important to remind the reader that simply making youngsters feel good about themselves is not enough. Certainly it is important for each person to reach a point where the person can respect who he or she is and recognize that he or she is a unique individual of value and worth. But such self-respect can also be a sham. Some youths are misled by staff who overidentify with them. When staff place all the blame for the youngster's difficulties on others, they are generally doing a disservice to the individual and are denying that person's sense of power and responsibility for the person's own life.

Furthermore, youths, particularly in some of the group programs, have been misled about what they can immediately accomplish in the real world. In the microcosm of an isolated program they may be well-respected leaders. But these experiences generally do not follow them back into the community. Some youths consequently may feel that they have been set up. Others may feel even more alienated as they return to the community. Still others may not want to return, or they will immediately get into further trouble in order to be sent back to the place where they experienced the flush of power.

We are not arguing that youths should be simply acted upon and not given power and responsibility. However, we *are* arguing that such power and responsibility should be realistic and should take place where the youths must ultimately succeed—in their network of relationships in the community. It is our belief, based on observation, that youths in the more community linked programs are better able to grapple realistically with who they are while at the same time forging a lasting place for themselves in the community.

IMPLICATIONS FOR MANAGING
A COMMUNITY-BASED
CORRECTIONS SYSTEM

Diversity and Flexibility Through Purchase of Service. One of the major advantages of the Massachusetts community-based system has been the diversity of placement options for its youths. The community-based approach, with its emphasis on purchase of service from private vendors, seems best able to enlarge the range of program options. A particular service, such as a group home, can be ontained through contract for a set number of youths or very specialized services such as job training or psychiatric care can be purchased on a case-by-case basis. Such an approach to service delivery can take into account the individual needs of specific youths while avoiding the traditional mode of segregating youths by age and sex into large training schools.

Reliance on a diverse range of programs allows youths to be more broadly dispersed across a state, thereby reducing their concentration in central locations and making it more feasible for them to receive services closer to home. It is desirable for youths to receive services in programs as close to home as possible. This allows easier access for youths and program staff to the home community, thus facilitating the effort to support any existing linkages that the youths may already have with a supportive network. For two reasons, however, it is not realistic for all youths to be served in or near their communities of origin. First, some may require very specialized and costly services that cannot be expected to be developed in each community. And second, some may come from family situations that are so deteriorated that parents have totally rejected them or they have totally rejected their parents. In such cases it may be more desirable to locate the youngster in a new community with the goal of setting him or her up in an independent living situation with a new supportive network.

Not only do these purchase-of-service arrangements provide flexibility through individualized service; they also provide flexibility to system administrators for controlling the kinds of services being offered. Corrections, like other human service fields, is frequently caught up in the latest treatment fads. By relying on a great number of vendors to provide services, administrators can more readily avoid the tendency to place all their eggs in one basket. If they already have enough guided group interaction programs, they can simply avoid funding any more. If certain kinds of programs do not provide quality services, they can cease funding them. If a new approach seems worthy of trial, they can experiment with it without making a long-range financial commitment. If program administrators are not willing to work with the kinds of youths the department wants to place there, it can simply get someone else to provide the service.

The diversity and flexibility of community-based services, particularly those purchased through private vendors, seems to provide a situation that allows for individualized service, opportunity for innovation without always changing the entire system, and creative management.

Working with the Hard-core Delinquent.   One of the subtle advantages of viewing community corrections as a continuum and recognizing that a system must have programs at more than one point on the continuum is that the "difficult to handle, hard-core, aggressive offender" is not forgotten. It is imperative in some cases to provide a secure setting while maximizing community contact, either by allowing clients to leave the setting under close supervision or by permitting community groups and residents to enter the setting. To think that all offenders can be handled in the same kinds of open community setting is naive, and such thinking can be the Achilles heel of a community-based system. To focus only on the youths who can be easily handled in the open community and ignore the needs of the more difficult individual is irresponsible and paves the way for the creation (or re-creation) of small maximum security institutions. Although the "hard-core" individuals make up a very small percentage of the total population served, they should not be forgotten.

Three kinds of youths have emerged in the secure settings in the Massachusetts system. First is the repetitive assaultive offender; this is the sort of youngster one would most reasonably expect to find in secure settings. Second, one finds a small number of youths who are severely disturbed mentally. Many of them have suicidal tendencies and really should not be in the corrections department in the first place. These youngsters should be handled in the mental health department where they ought to be able to receive more appropriate attention. But the frequent complaint from the mental health department is that such youths are "too violent." It is this type of youngster, therefore, who often "falls between the cracks" of existing services. One would hope that a coordinated effort between the two agencies could better handle the special needs of mentally disturbed youngsters. Third, one finds a number of youths who can best be described as "system nuisances." These youths have not committed serious offenses, but they have not adjusted to the expectations of program staff. Some of them frequently run from programs or act out in programs. That they ultimately wind up in secure care has to be viewed as a negative indicator of the department's ability to handle them. This is a classic example of the way our attempts to help may actually work against the youngsters' long-run chances. Their major "crime" is not against society but against the correctional system. DYS has taken steps to closely monitor intake into secure care, which should reduce the numbers of "system nuisances" entering secure care. Pressure needs to be applied on the private vendor to insure that secure care is not simply being used as a dumping ground for youths who are not easily handled in the initial program placement.

The Massachusetts experience has shown that only a small proportion, about 10 percent, of the youngsters in placement on a given day need to be in secure care [2]. In the past nearly all the youngsters were in such secure programs. While those requiring secure care have been more carefully sorted out in recent years, the problem of what to do with them remains. An opportunity exists to set up several small demonstration projects using several alternative treatment strategies. One of the promising alternatives is the intensive nonresidential tracking programs referred to earlier.

Although the secure care issue should not be neglected, one should remember that the vast majority of youths served can be handled in more open programs. To overemphasize the secure care issue is to allow the advances being made in other areas to be smothered and eventually neglected.

Handling the Less Serious Offender. On the other end of the client spectrum, a different sort of danger exists. Community-based services, as part of a broader diversion effort, become viewed as benign and potentially helpful and therefore something in which even more people should participate and benefit. Thus more persons are encouraged or coerced by the court, sometimes quite subtly, to become involved in these programs. This process is potentially quite dangerous because once again in our desire to help we have identified and urged more individuals to penetrate and be handled in the system. We know that penetration into that system unavoidably stigmatizes a youngster.

This is just one of the possible unintended consequences of community-based reform efforts. Three other related consequences may occur. First, we may become so convinced that what we have to offer is beneficial that we are willing to coerce the *nonadjudicated* into accepting services. In accomplishing the objective of providing more services to more people, agencies frequently disregard individual rights. If a person must be coerced to accept services, then that person's criminal case should be heard in court on its merits.

Second, across the country we see a number of efforts to divert people from the criminal justice system to the mental health systems or to departments of family and children's services. It is frequently assumed that once the individuals are diverted they are necessarily better off, and their cases are therefore obliterated from memory. Those people enamored of diversion ought to be as interested in what the client is being diverted *to* as they are in what the client is being diverted *from*. Are youths diverted to systems that provide better quality services or are they being confined in less humane places for longer periods of time? If the latter is the case, the reform is not complete.

Third, specifically in terms of advocacy and community involvement there is a danger of diluting advocacy until it means simply one private agency advocating on behalf of an individual to another private agency; that is, clients are referred only from one private agency to another. If advocacy does not involve local community groups and residents, the institutionalized client is simply being transformed into an "agency client." This is possibly an improvement over institutionalization, but it is quite removed from the concept of community-based services advanced here.

Community Control or Community Participation.   Given our notion of community-based correction with its emphasis on extent and quality of community relationships, genuinely community-based programs depend upon active community participation. To improve substantially upon the record of institutions, one must do a better job at developing legitimate community ties for youths. These links will to a considerable extent depend upon the responsiveness of local community groups and residents. Thus participation of the local community (professionals and lay persons) in the location, development, implementation, and monitoring of a community-based program is imperative—this should not really surprise anyone. Let us turn, then, to the more thorny issues of local community control.

Local community control (the power to absolutely determine whether a program will be established and to dictate program policy) poses a potentially dangerous situation for community-based corrections. Frequently, local interest groups will coalesce to thwart efforts to establish a group home. Where a real need exists, this action constitutes an abdication of local community responsibility. A common position is that such programs are good for "other communities" but not for "ours." In order to build a case for community services, one must be able to convince powerful community groups that certain needs exist and that they must be met. One of the richest counties in the country, for example, failed to acknowledge that a large proportion of its teenagers were involved in drug abuse. Some people in the county wanted to construct a combination live-in and outpatient drug rehabilitation center. Many families in the county could afford private care. The plan for the rehabilitation center was defeated. In its place a brand new jail was built to protect the community from "drug addicts" of the lower class. Local community control in this case meant blocking services from those who could not afford to purchase them privately. On a much larger scale this is one of the apparent problems with the California Probation Subsidy programs, where state monies are channeled to the counties. While the state system's institutional population is decreasing, new county jails are being built and filled [3].

Shared community participation with a state-wide public agency offers two distinct advantages. First, links with the state-wide agency permit access to special services that it may not be practical to provide in each local community. Second, while allowing for community participation, the links also permit the exertion of pressure from outside if local communities fail to recognize and meet the special needs of their less powerful residents.

Large Vendors vs. Small Vendors. It should be recognized that the delivery of services through purchase from private vendors is characterized by competition. These vendors are not only engaged in helping youths; they are also operating businesses. In most instances, competition is a healthy condition. The vendor must be constantly trying to improve the quality of the service offered relative to other vendors or the vendor may find that there is nothing to sell. The competitive system offers an environment in which innovation is rewarded. However, in actual practice, purchase of service from private vendors has its own difficulties that must be guarded against.

A few of the private vendors in Massachusetts have become very large, providing nearly a complete range of services including foster care, nonresidential programs, group homes, and secure care. With increased revenues and large numbers of youths being served comes considerable power. While it has not yet occurred in this state, one must be concerned about a few agencies' developing a near monopoly of youth service programs. Such a monopoly could wreak havoc for the correctional agency and ultimately for the youths being served. One could imagine one or two agencies' becoming so powerful that they could dictate policy to a department. They could determine what kinds of youths they would handle and which treatment alternatives they would use. Thus, such a monopoly could deal a severe blow to the diversity and flexibility of the service delivery system. It is certainly not unrealistic to foresee one or two agencies garnering enough power to influence legislative decisions around a department's budget and executive appointments.

Because of their size such agencies enjoy some fiscal advantages over the small grass-roots vendor who is attempting to operate a single program. The small vendor does not have the cash flow that provides up-front money for taking on a new program, and without that kind of fiscal support, it is difficult for the vendor to borrow money until the program is in operation. This condition contributes much to the squeezing out of the small vendor and reinforces the trend toward monopoly by the larger agencies.

The threats to the control of one's system and the need for continued innovation in programming lead us to consider options that permit the system to take advantage of the services of the larger vendors while providing opportunities for the smaller vendors to compete. One option is simply to limit the percentage of one's purchase-of-service budget that any one agency can obtain. A second and more creative option is to set aside a portion of the purchase-of-service monies as high-risk monies. These funds would only be available to small grass-roots groups. One would expect some failures in this group, but the seed money allows for new, innovative ideas to be tried. Without this breath of fresh air, the system will most certainly ossify over time and require yet another major reform effort.

Quality Control. Evaluating the quality of service is one of the most critical pitfalls for a system that uses program services purchased from private vendors. Lack of an adequate quality control system could allow the community-based system to deteriorate to a point where clients would be better off placed in institutions. We have indicated all along that there is nothing inherent in the small facility that prevents it from becoming an institution. Abuses are abuses whether they occur in a training school or in a "community-based" program.

Disbursement of monies and quality control are the two principal mechanisms for maintaining control over what happens to youths in a community-based system, particularly if the bulk of services are purchased from private groups. The state agency must have the determination to drop a poor program even if it is operated by a powerful private vendor. The state agency must therefore be able to assess the quality of life within the program. And this must be done routinely— not just after a crisis has already arisen. Our own experience indicates that programs can change dramatically even over a six-month period. The state agency must be able to determine if the program is holding on to the easy clients and quickly discharging the difficult ones. These evaluations must provide preliminary, defensible answers quickly, long before recidivism checks are feasible. Responsible administrators cannot wait two or three years to determine if a program facilitates or hinders reintegration.

Information for quality control purposes can be gained in a variety of ways. Caseworkers visiting their clients can make systematic observations of the program. While this is frequently done, the information is seldom handled systematically and forwarded to the central office. A special quality control unit from the central office can make routine visits to interview staff and youths about the program. At least some of these visits should be unannounced. Evaluators can follow treatment efforts for samples of individual youths to insure that what they are told is actually being done. For example, did the staff actually work with the parents? Did they really try to get the youngster a job? Did they really intervene on the youngster's behalf at the school? Answers to these questions can frequently be obtained by phone.

It is of value to the programs as well as to the youths that those programs offering poor services be weeded out. Only routine monitoring can provide the kind of accountability required. However, quality control should also be seen as a potential service to programs that are having difficulties. A good quality control effort should be able to identify, with the help of program staff, weaknesses that can benefit from technical assistance provided either directly by the department or by outside sources. Tying quality control into technical assistance avoids some of the "executioner" overtones that are almost inevitable with any serious quality control effort.

Staff Hiring and Training. Debates have raged for some time in this field about the use of professional versus paraprofessional staff. Our own observations make us suspect that these debates are being overemphasized. Certainly there is a pla.e for both. The trained social worker brings a particular set of skills to the system. However, the streetwise paraprofessional also brings an important set of skills. The three characteristics that we have found most consistently helpful are: caring, resolve, and high energy. The first is almost a given; if the staff person does not care about young people, that person will probably not be able to work effectively with them or on their behalf. This is as true for system administrators as it is for program staff. Resolve is particularly important to balance off caring. Resolve means that staff people have the determination to establish limits for youngsters; it means that they are willing to take risks to advocate for their clients in the community; it means that they can see beyond their own efforts with the youngsters and recognize that reintegration can only be achieved if they share their efforts with the youths and other actors in the community. The third characteristic—high energy—is needed because work with youngsters and advocacy with community groups is of a high intensity. It is also time-consuming. A time clock is not punched—the needs of a particular client and that client's situation dictate the work load.

Hiring staff with these characteristics and other specialized skills is not enough. The correction agency has an obligation to continue supporting them through training efforts. Training can range from instruction in the general issues of understanding youths in trouble, to the teaching of specific skills such as how to advocate for youths in the community, to providing updates on resources available in various regions of the state. Trainers can come from the private agencies as well as from the department and from outside resources such as universities. Training sessions can serve to remind staff that they are not alone but are performing their tasks in a much larger network. They should provide staff with an opportunity to share their failures as well as their success and in general to maintain their enthusiasm and energy.

Staff Burn-out. One of the consequences of the high intensity of youth work is that staff members frequently "burn out" after two or three years. Some structural changes could be implemented to at least reduce this effect. Frequently, staff members work for weeks without a day off and for months without a weekend off. One reason for this is egotistical in nature—program staff often believe that the program would surely fail if they were not there all the time.

Another reason, however, is that many of these programs are minimally funded or underfunded. Not enough staff can be hired to provide for flexible staffing patterns. Shaving costs at the point of funding contributes to the eventual burn-out of staff and quite possibly the demise of a good program and therefore creates situations that can harm youths rather than help them.

Some of the university-based programs are able to overcome these burn-out difficulties by relying heavily on undergraduate and graduate students under the supervision of permanent staff. The students work intensively for a year or so and then move on to other things, but new students are easily recruited to take their places. The use of work study students in nonuniversity-based programs has also worked out well, providing at least some flexibility for staffing patterns.

One of the contributing factors to staff burn-out is boredom: staff simply get tired of performing the same tasks day in and day out. A creative system administrator may be able to adopt a sabbatical strategy similar to those employed by universities, or a rotation of jobs could be helpful. A program staff person could be rotated to a regional position or a central office position for six months to a year. Similarly, people in those positions could be rotated to program positions. If done sparingly, such rotations could provide individuals with new experiences while maintaining continuity of effort at each of the three levels mentioned. Furthermore, such rotation would enhance the understanding by staff of the various components of the system in which they work.

Maintaining an Openness to Change. One of the paramount dangers of any reform is that it sees in itself the entire solution of an issue or a problem. There seems to be an inevitable tendency to solidify and consolidate gains of reform in order to fend off counterattack. If such consolidation is overdone, it will lead to stagnation and ossification. The "reformed system" will become the entrenched system, and some years later it will require yet another reform effort.

Are there ways by which one can organize a corrections system that will enhance the likelihood that it will remain open to change and innovative ideas without requiring another major reform effort? We believe there are. First, there must be a philosophical conviction that the primary objective of the agency is to help youths work out their difficulties in their community networks. The maintenance of any particular agency structure must always be balanced against this primary objective. Second, close linkages should be maintained between this philosophy and the program development, program management, and quality control functions of the system. If these functions are not integrated and provided with feedback possibilities, the system will not be in a position to judge adequately what kinds of programs it has and why it has them. A system with such integration can afford to admit that it has an imbalance in its range of programs or that a new idea is worth experimenting with to determine where it fits into the overall system.

SUMMARY

The radical step of closing training schools in Massachusetts has shaken the very roots of the youth corrections field. Deinstitutionalization has become an accepted objective in many states, although where such policies are being implemented administrators are generally trying to avoid some of the more disruptive tactics used in Massachusetts.

While they were certainly not entirely successful, the reform efforts in Massachusetts have given us cause to rethink our basic approaches to juvenile corrections. The analysis presented here has shown that the move toward establishing programs in community settings is a step in the right direction. However, even the dramatic shift experienced in Massachusetts has not gone far enough. New ways need to be devised to link delinquent youths in constructive ways to community resources. Our analysis contends that the logical extension of things that seem to work in the Massachusetts system would require attention to working systematically with youths in their total life situations.

Appendixes

Methods of Sampling
and Regression Analysis

Sampling

The sampling of youths for each cohort was accomplished in the following way. The seven administrative regions of the youth services system in Massachusetts were divided for the purposes of the study into four sets: three containing two regions and the fourth containing one very populous region. Beginning in one set, all youths staying longer than two days in detention were interviewed, and all youths committed or referred to the department were followed through the complete sequence of interviewing. This process was continued until we reached the point of having approximately 70 committed or referred youths in each region and twice that number in the very populous region. The 70 committed or referred youths from each region were the contribution of a set of regions to the projected sample of 400 committed or referred youths across the state for the cohort, allowing for attrition of the sample over time. Then the youths constituting the contribution of a set of regions to the comparison sample were selected. Youths neither committed nor referred but going through detention were represented by 12 such youths in each region, 24 in the very populous region. Thus the comparison sample for the entire state was expected to reach approximately 80 after attrition.

The result of all this yielded samples of predetermined size of referred or committed youths and of comparison youths plus a very large sample of detained youths who were not followed up because they did not continue under the care of the department. These detained youths had to be interviewed because we could not predict which detained youths would continue and become part of the sample of committed or referred youths. As a side benefit, we know a great deal about youths who are detained but then not placed under the care of the department.

Figure A–1 gives a schematic view of the location of the regions throughout the state. Region I consists of the western part of the state, with the Springfield area being its most populous center. Region II is composed of the middle of the state, including the Worcester area. Region III includes Cambridge and Somerville and extends northward and westward, including such towns as Lexington and Concord. Region IV is the North Shore area, including at its southern tip part of the Boston area. Region V is the South Shore area, including Quincy and Framingham. Region VI is Boston proper, and region VII is the Cape Cod area, which also includes Fall River and New Bedford.

Regression Analysis

Much of the data analysis in this book has been accomplished with stepwise multiple regression techniques.[a] These techniques enable us to predict an individual's score on one variable, called the dependent variable, from that person's scores on other variables, called independent variables. The regression analysis produces for each dependent variable a number called the regression *constant*, which is the average value of the dependent variable when all the independent variables equal 0, and a series of numbers called regression coefficients, each of which represents the increase or decrease in the dependent variable when one of the independent variables increases by one unit without the other independent variables changing at the same time.[b] The regression coefficients are the most important results because they represent the effect of each independent variable, controlling or holding constant all the rest.

In this book we frequently represent these results in tables. Each column of a table represents the results for a dependent variable. The dependent variable is indicated at the head of the column, the rows

[a]Some readers will be surprised that we use these techniques even with dichotomous dependent variables. However, it happens that multiple discriminant function analysis reduces in the case of a dichotomy to the multiple regression, and thus what we are actually doing in the case of the dichotomous dependent variable with multiple regression is a discriminant function analysis.

[b]The regression coefficients are expressed in the raw score units of the independent and dependent variables rather than in standard score units (Beta weights) in order to enhance the comparability with analyses in other populations and in order to make it easy to compare the practical effects of raw unit changes in different independent variables in our own population.

Figure A–1. Schematic Diagram D.Y.S. Regional Boundaries

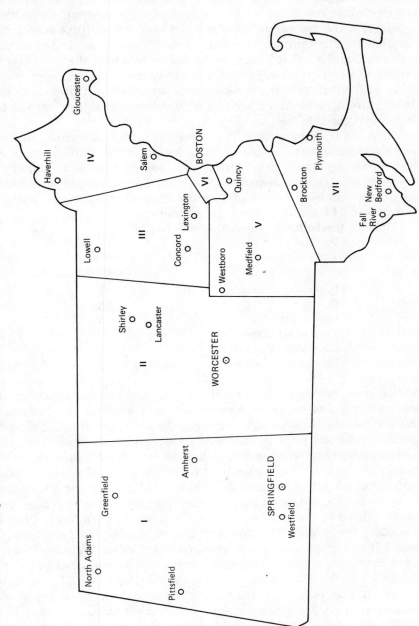

represent the independent variables, and the numbers in the cells are the regression coefficients. At the foot of each column, we indicate in addition the regression constant and also the *multiple correlation* coefficient. The multiple correlation coefficient is a number varying between 0 and +1 that indicates the degree to which the independent variables in combination predict accurately the dependent variable. A value of 0 means that the independent variables are of no help in predicting the dependent variable. A high value means they predict the dependent variable well.

When a variable consists of several unordered categories, like the seven administrative regions of the Massachusetts youth correctional system, we represent each category as a separate variable, scored 1 if a person is in that category, 0 otherwise. Thus a person who was in region I would have a score of 1 on the region I dichotomous variable and a score of 0 on the other region variables.

Consider the following hypothetical results:

	School Placement
Region I	.4
Region II	.5
Region VII	−.3
Years of schooling	.2
Regression constant	.1
Multiple correlation	.78

Notice that regions I, II, and VII are included and the other regions are omitted. The omission means that the regression coefficients of the omitted regions are not significantly different from 0. The regression constant gives the predicted value of the dependent variable school placement when a youth has no schooling and is not in regions I, II, or VII (has scores of 0 on all these variables) or in other words has no schooling and is in regions III, IV, V, or VI. The regression coefficient for years of schooling indicates how much the predicted value for school placement increases for each year of schooling the youth has. The negative regression coefficient for region VII indicates how much the predicted value for school placement *decreases* if the youths were in region VII, compared to what it would be if the youths were in regions III, IV, V, or VI. Similarly, the positive regression coefficients for regions I and II indicate how much the predicted value for school placement would *increase* if the youths were in regions I or II, compared to regions III, IV, V, or VI. The higher the predicted value for school placement, the more likely the youths will be put into a school placement. The multiple correlation of .78 indicates that the independent variables—region and years of schooling—predict school placement rather well.

Finally, we add a column of standardized coefficients or beta weights. These coefficients, essentially the regression coefficients re-expressed with the variables measured in standard score units (deviations from the mean divided by the mean), provide an indication of the relative predictive strength of the different independent variables in our sample. The square of the beta weight is the ratio of variance explained by the particular independent variable if it varies as it does in our sample while other variables remain constant to the total observed variance in the dependent variable. When the equation includes a series of dichotomous variables representing the categories of a variable such as region, as in our example, these standardized coefficients can still be interpreted as increases or decreases in the dependent variable per unit increase in the independent variable. While this interpretation is perfectly legitimate, it becomes clumsy. We therefore used these coefficients in this analysis only as an indicator of relative predictive importance of the various independent variables in our sample and rely on the raw regression coefficients to represent the specific nature and pattern of the predictive relationship.

We indicate the degree of statistical significance of the standardized coefficients by asterisks. One asterisk indicates the .05 level, two of the .01 level, and three the .001 level.[c] Thus, the more asterisks, the more significantly the coefficient is different from 0.

Occasionally we refer to partial correlations. Where they are particularly theoretically interesting, we discuss those partial correlations that would have entered the regression equation next.

[c]Significance tests with dichotomous dependent variables are frequently considered a problem. However the F test associated with the multiple correlation coefficient appears to be the same as Hotelling's T^2, a test used in discriminant function analysis. This would suggest that the significance test associated with the multiple correlation is appropriate even with a dichotomous dependent variable as long as there are continuous variables among the independent variables or as long as the dichotomous independent variables are numerous enough to add up to a discriminant function that is approximately continuous. Significance tests for the individual independent variables are probably accurate for continuous independent variables but only approximate for dichotomous independent variables.

 *Appendix B*

Selected Background Characteristics on Completed Cohort Sample

Variable	Percent	$\overline{X}$	SD	N
Sex				
Female	82			493
Male	18			493
Race				
White	77			493
Black	20			493
Other	3			493
Age at Entry		15.6	1.38	461
Region				
I	11			493
II	14			493
III	11			493
IV	12			493
V	13			493
VI	26			493
VII	13			493
Adult Head of Household				
Two parent	51			487
Single parent	38			487
Adult head but neither parent	7			487
No adult head	4			487

Variable	Percent	$\overline{X}$	SD	N
Father's Occupation				
White collar	22			354
Skilled	32			354
Semiskilled	28			354
Unskilled	11			354
Unemployed/welfare	6			354
Mother's Occupation				
White collar	18			448
Skilled	5			448
Semiskilled	9			448
Unskilled	14			448
Housewife	23			448
Unemployed/welfare	30			448
Father's Schooling		12.02	3.13	306
Mother's Schooling		12.59	2.09	348
Prior Commitment or Referral to DYS				
No	46			
Yes	54			
Current Offense				
Drugs	3			448
Car theft	21			448
Property	29			448
Property and Person	10			448
Person	10			448
Status offenses	18			448
Public misbehavior	3			448
Other	6			448
Don't Use Drugs	36			489
Use Alcohol Regularly	59			490
Go to School Regularly				
Never	42			488
Almost everyday	45			488
Highest Grade in School		8.53	1.40	464
Age First Juvenile Court Appearance		13.15	1.87	458
Number Prior Court Appearances		2.7	4.01	459

Notes

NOTES TO INTRODUCTION

1. Robert D. Vinter, George Downs, and J. Hall, *Juvenile Corrections in the States: Residential Programs and Deinstitutionals* (Ann Arbor, Mich.: National Assessment of Juvenile Corrections, 1975); Rosemary C. Sarri and Robert D. Vinter, "Justice for Whom? Varieties of Juvenile Correctional Approaches," in Malcolm W. Klein, ed., *The Juvenile Justice System* (Beverly Hills, Calif.: SAGE Publications, 1976), pp. 161–200.

2. Andrew Rutherford and Osman Bengur, *Community-Based Alternatives to Juvenile Incarceration* (Washington, D.C.: National Institute of Law Enforcement and Criminal Justice, Law Enforcement Assistance Administration, U.S. Department of Justice, 1976).

3. Vinter, Downs, and Hall, *Juvenile Corrections in the States*.

4. Craig A. McEwen, *Designing Correctional Organizations for Youths: Dilemmas of Subcultural Development* (Cambridge, Mass.: Ballinger Publishing Co., 1978) and Barry C. Feld, *Neutralizing Inmate Violence: Juvenile Offenders in Institutions* (Cambridge, Mass.: Ballinger Publishing Co., 1978).

NOTES TO CHAPTER 1

1. The basic conceptualization of community-based corrections described here was originally developed by Coates while teaching a course on community-based corrections at the University of Maryland in 1969–1970. That original work was influenced by the ideas and works of Peter P. Lejins and LaMar T. Empey. The conceptualization has been refined and operationalized during the course of this research to the point where it has become a pivotal concept for evaluating the outcomes of the DYS reform effort. Much of this section was first prepared as a paper presented at the Massachusetts Standards and Goals Conference, November 18, 1974. It was later revised and published as Robert B. Coates,

"Community Based Corrections: Concept, Impact, Dangers," in Lloyd E. Ohlin, Alden D. Miller, Robert B. Coates, eds., *Juvenile Correctional Reform in Massachusetts* (Washington, D.C.: National Institute for Juvenile Justice and Delinquency Prevention, Law Enforcement Assistance Administration, U.S. Department of Justice, 1977).

2. Neil J. Smelser, *Sociology* (New York: John Wiley and Sons, 1967), p. 95.

3. The use of such factors as frequency and duration represent an adaptation of Edwin H. Sutherland's differential association theory of delinquency causation. See Edwin H. Sutherland and Donald R. Cressey, *Principles of Criminology* (Philadelphia: J.B. Lippincott, 1955).

4. The conceptualization of community-based corrections as developed to this point was adopted and used in recent studies. For example, Rutherford and Bengur found it useful in differentiating among programs for juveniles. See Rutherford and Bengur, *Community-Based Alternatives to Juvenile Incarceration.*

5. Robert D. Vinter, ed., *Time Out: A National Study of Juvenile Correctional Programs* (Ann Arbor, Mich.: National Assessment of Juvenile Corrections, 1976); Donnell M. Pappenfort, Dee Morgan Kilpatrick, and Alma M. Kuby, *A Census of Children's Residential Institution in the United States, Puerto Rico, and the Virgin Islands: 1966.* 7 vols. (Chicago: School of Social Service Administration, University of Chicago, 1970).

6. The perspective of delinquency causation underpinning this work stems largely from a broadly conceived interactionist tradition reflected in: (a) the community-oriented work of Clifford R. Shaw. See Clifford R. Shaw, *Delinquency Areas* (Chicago: University of Chicago Press, 1929); Clifford R. Shaw, *The Jack-Roller* (Chicago: University of Chicago Press, 1930); Clifford R. Shaw and Henry D. McKay, "Social Factors in Juvenile Delinquency," in *Report on Causes of Crime*, vol. 2, no. 13, National Commission on Law Observance and Enforcement (Washington, D.C.: 1931); (b) the differential association perspective developed by Edwin H. Sutherland. See Edwin H. Sutherland and Donald R. Cressey, *Principles of Criminology* (Philadelphia: J.B. Lippincott, 1955). (c) the subculture traditions of Albert Cohen and Richard Cloward and Lloyd Ohlin. See Albert K. Cohen, *Delinquent Boys: The Culture Gang* (Glencoe, Ill.: The Free Press, 1955); Richard A. Cloward and Lloyd E. Ohlin, *Delinquency and Opportunity: A Theory of Delinquent Gangs* (New York: The Free Press, 1960). (d) the clearly dominant interactionist perspective reflected in the writings of David Matza and John Lofland. See David Matza, *Delinquency and Drift* (New York: John Wiley and Sons, 1964); David Matza, *Becoming Deviant* (Englewood Cliffs, N.J.: Prentice Hall, 1969); and John Lofland, *Deviance and Identity* (Englewood Cliffs, N.J.: Prentice Hall, 1969). (e) these perspectives on delinquency causation are tempered some by our interest in the societal reaction perspective. See Edwin M. Lemert, *Human Deviance, Social Problems and Social Control* (Englewood Cliffs, N.J.: Prentice Hall, 1967); Edwin M. Lemert, *Social Pathology* (New York: McGraw-Hill, 1951); and Howard S. Becker, *Outsiders: Studies in the Sociology of Deviance* (New York: Free Press, 1963).

7. Hubert Blumer, *Symbolic Interactionism* (Englewood Cliffs, N.J., Prentice Hall, 1969), p. 8.

8. Lofland, *Deviance and Identity*.

9. Aaron Cicourel, "The Social Organization of the High School and Deviant Adolescent Careers," in Earl Rubington and Martin S. Weinberg, eds., *Deviance: The Interactionist Perspective* (New York: McMillan, 1968), p. 132.

10. Erving Goffman, *Asylums* (Garden City, N.Y.: Anchor Books, 1961) p. 4.

11. Goffman, *Asylums*, p. 5.

12. Hubert H. Moos notes that the social climate perspective assumes that environments, like people, have unique characteristics or "personalities" and that environments can be described in detail to sort out those that are most supportive. See Hubert H. Moos, *Evaluating Correctional Settings* (New York: John Wiley and Sons, 1975). Since this book was published at about the time our data-collection efforts on programs were ending, we were precluded from adopting many of its research suggestions.

13. Gresham Sykes, *The Society of Captives* (Princeton: Princeton University Press, 1958); Donald Clemmer, *The Prison Community* (New York: Rinehart and Company, 1958).

14. Lofland, *Deviance and Identity*, pp. 162–163.

15. Gresham Sykes, *The Society of Captives*.

16. For a description of the day-to-day pressures of establishing positive subcultures in community-based programs see Craig A. McEwen, *Designing Correctional Organizations for Youths: Dilemmas of Subcultural Development* (Cambridge, Mass.: Ballinger Publishing Co., 1978).

17. Paul Lerman has commented on the subtleties of treatment as control in Paul Lerman, *Community Treatment and Social Control: An Analysis of Juvenile Correctional Policy* (Chicago: University of Chicago Press, 1975).

18. Lerman, *Community Treatment and Social Control*; Paul Lerman, "Evaluative Studies of Institutions for Delinquents," *Social Work*, 13 (December 1968); Robert Martinson, "What Works?—Questions and Answers about Prison Reform," *The Public Interest* 35 (Spring 1974): 22–54.

19. American Friends Service Committee, *Struggle for Justice* (New York: Hill and Wang, 1971); David Fogel, ". . . We are the Living Proof . . ." (Cincinnati: W.H. Anderson Co., 1975).

20. Paul C. Friday and Jerold Hage, "Youth Crime in Postindustrial Societies: An Integrated Perspective," *Criminology* 14, 3 (November 1976): 350.

NOTES TO CHAPTER 2

1. For a detailed historical account of the reform effort see Lloyd E. Ohlin, Robert B. Coates, and Alden D. Miller, *Reforming Juvenile Corrections: The Massachusetts Experience* (Cambridge, Mass.: Ballinger Publishing Co., 1978). Also for a formal analysis of the change process see Alden D. Miller, Lloyd E. Ohlin, and Robert B. Coates, *A Theory of Social Reform: Correctional Change Processes in Two States* (Cambridge, Mass.: Ballinger Publishing Co., 1977).

2. For a detailed account of the University of Massachusetts Conference see Robert B. Coates, Alden D. Miller, and Lloyd E. Ohlin, "A Strategic Innovation in the Process of Deinstitutionalization: The University of Massachusetts Conference," in Yitzhak Bakal, ed., *Closing Correctional Institutions* (Lexington, Mass.: D.C. Heath, 1973), pp. 127–148.

3. For a discussion of strategies for setting up group homes see Robert B. Coates and Alden D. Miller, "Neutralization of Community Resistance to Group Homes," in Bakal, ed., *Closing Correctional Institutions*, pp. 67–84.

4. For a more detailed discussion of this period see Alden D. Miller, Lloyd E. Ohlin, and Robert B. Coates, "The Aftermath of Extreme Tactics in Juvenile Justice Reform: A Crisis Four Years Later," in David F. Greenberg, ed., *Corrections and Punishment* (Beverly Hills, Calif.: SAGE Publications, 1977) pp. 227–246.

5. Statistics for fiscal 1968 came from *Delinquency Trends in Massachusetts Fiscal Years 1954–1968*, Massachusetts Department of Youth Services, no date.

6. For a fuller description of the institutional and staging cottages see Barry C. Feld, *Neutralizing Inmate Violence: Juvenile Offenders in Institutions* (Cambridge, Mass.: Ballinger Publishing Co., 1978).

7. Items in this table were adapted from LaMar T. Empey and Stephen Lubeck, *Silverlake Experiment* (Chicago: Aldine, 1971).

NOTES TO CHAPTER 3

1. Portions of this chapter first appeared in Robert B. Coates and Alden D. Miller, "Evaluating Large Scale Social Service Systems in Changing Environments: The Case of Correctional Agencies," *Journal of Research in Crime and Delinquency* 12, 2 (July 1975).

2. See Clarence D. Sherwood, "Methodological Measurement, and Social Action Considerations Related to the Assessment of Large Scale Demonstration Programs." Paper presented at the 124th Annual Meeting of the American Statistical Association, Chicago, Illinois, December 1964; and Clarence Sherwood and Howard E. Freeman, "Research in Large-Scale Intervention Programs," *Journal of Social Issues* 21, 1 (January 1965): 11–27.

3. Perry Levinson, "Evaluation of Social Welfare Programs," *Welfare in Review* 5 (February 1967): 5–12. See also Herbert C. Schulberg and Frank Baker, "Program Evaluation Models and the Implementation of Research Findings," *American Journal of Public Health* 58, 7 (July 1968): 1248–1255.

4. Norman K. Denzin, *The Research Act* (Chicago: Aldine, 1970).

5. The arbitrary period of three months was set because (1) the typical stay during the early period of reform in residential programs was approximately 3 to 4 months, and (2) youths in nonresidential and foster care could remain in programs for long periods, but for our purposes they were exposed to similar community pressures as youths who were terminated from residential programs.

6. Five hundred and eighty-six youths comprised a pool of youths who were committed or referred to the department during our intake period. We were able to obtain a complete set of interviews on 493 youths. We were unable to obtain a complete set of interviews on 93 youths for the following reasons: (1) 17 refused at least one interview; (2) 11 were officially AWOL; (3) 24 could not be located; (4) 26 had moved out of the New England region; (5) 3 had died; and (6) 10 were not identified as eligible for the pool during the intake period. The cohort of 493 is the basic group on which this analysis is based with two exceptions. First, 586 were used to generate scores for the institutionalization-normalization continuum, and second it was also used to generate systems recid-

ivism rates for comparisons across the training-school and community-based systems. The background characteristics, detention experience, and type of placement within DYS of the incompleted youths are comparable to the youths who completed the full set of interviews. Incompleted youths were not retained in the regression analysis because of the missing data problems that they posed.

7. For the same reason, we would suggest that anyone attempting to adapt questions from our instruments should pretest them thoroughly in order to be sure that the language is appropriate for the time.

8. Total full-time staff numbered thirteen during the peak of the project. In addition, generally two to three part-time staff members were also employed from time to time. Field staff had a minimum of a BA; some had already completed their MA; most were using their experience at the center as a way of deciding in which direction their careers should go. Academic backgrounds included sociology, political science, psychology, education, and business administration. Over half of the staff had had at least a year's experience working in some type of social service program for youths. We firmly believe that this latter experience greatly influenced our ability to develop and maintain access with individual programs as well as remaining sensitive to the needs of youths and staff in the programs.

NOTES TO CHAPTER 4

1. Donnell M. Pappenfort and Thomas M. Young, *Use of Secure Detention for Juveniles and Alternatives to Its Use* (Washington, D.C.: Office of Juvenile Justice and Delinquency Prevention, Law Enforcement Assistance Administration, 1977).

2. Margaret K. Rosenheim, "Detention Facilities and Temporary Shelters," in Donnell M. Pappenfort, Dee Morgan Kilpatrick, and Robert W. Roberts, eds., *Child Caring: Social Policy and the Institution* (Chicago: Aldine, 1973).

3. Gresham M. Sykes and David Matza, "Techniques of Neutralization: A Theory of Delinquency," *American Sociological Review* 22 (December 1957): 664–670.

4. While we were able to look at detention decisions and consequences of detention for youths who were committed or referred to DYS, a full-scale study of detention would require a research design that sampled all youths appearing before the court. We have focused soley on the youths who are generally considered to be the most intractable requiring a commitment or referral to DYS.

5. National Advisory Commission on Criminal Justice Standards and Goals, "Juvenile Intake and Detention," in *Corrections* (Washington, D.C.: National Advisory Commission on Criminal Justice Standards and Goals, 1973), pp. 247–272; Rosenheim, "Detention Facilities and Temporary Shelters"; Rosemary C. Sarri, *Under Lock and Key: Juveniles in Jails and Detention* (Ann Arbor, Mich.: National Assessment of Juvenile Correction, 1974).

6. Foster care detention, although in use at the conclusion of the study, was not in use as an alternative when we gathered our data on detention.

7. For a map of the states, its seven regions, and a brief description of each region see Appendix A.

8. Pappenfort and Young, *Use of Secure Detention for Juveniles and Alternatives to Its Use.* For studies showing little or no relationship and for studies indicating that system characteristics are more to the point than youth characteristics see Elyce Zenoff Fenster and Thomas F. Courtless, "Juvenile Detention in an Affluent County," *Family Law Quarterly* 6 (Spring 1972): 21–32; Helen Sumner, "Locking Them Up," *Crime and Delinquency* 17 (April 1971): 168–179; Sarri, *Under Lock and Key: Juveniles in Jails and Detention*; Edward J. Pawlak, "Differential Selection of Juveniles for Detention," *Journal of Research in Crime and Delinquency* 14 (July 1977): 152–165.

9. Heddy Bookin, *Juvenile Detention Decisions*, dissertation in progress, Department of Sociology, Harvard University.

10. Given our theoretical interest of interaction with significant others as it bears on successful socialization (in this case reintegration of delinquent youths into law-abiding activity), we sought to explore these relationships both as dependent and independent variables. We report on data derived by asking direct questions of youths regarding how they perceived certain significant others, such as parents or judges, relating to them. By using indices derived from a series of semantic differential scales we were able to ascertain how youths felt about themselves and significant others and how youths believed those others felt about them. In addition, we were able to add the youths' own self-perceptions to how they perceive others seeing them to give us an indication of how they perceive themselves through the eyes of others—thus we have a picture of the reflexive self-image.

Because of time and space limitations, we necessarily had to be selective about whom we asked youths about. In short, we wanted a diverse set of people, ranging from people who had the most direct and intimate relations with youths to those who would be generally regarded as distant, but nevertheless significant, particularly for youths in trouble with the law.

Three groups emerged theoretically and empirically. The first group, or *primary group*, consisted of mother, father, friends, and DYS program staff. One might express some surprise at the inclusion of program staff in this group, but they are so categorized because of the intensity of relationships in the programs observed. Their inclusion is also justified empirically because, as a group, program staff members were rated only slightly less favorably than mother. (Mother received the highest ratings.) The second group, or *secondary group*, was comprised of school teachers and other DYS youths in programs. The third group, or *public officials*, was composed of police and DYS as an agency.

11. Edwin M. Lemert, *Social Pathology* (New York: McGraw-Hill, 1951); Edwin M. Lemert, *Human Deviance, Social Problems and Social Control* (Englewood Cliffs, N.J.: Prentice Hall, 1967); Howard S. Becker, *Outsiders: Studies in the Sociology of Deviance* (New York: Free Press, 1963). For an overview of this position, see Edwin M. Shur, *Labeling Deviant Behavior* (New York: Harper and Row, 1971). For a specific application of the labeling perspective to corrections, see Robert B. Coates, Alden D. Miller, and Lloyd E. Ohlin, "The Labeling Perspective and Innovation in Juvenile Correctional Systems," in Nicholas Hobbs, ed., *Issues in the Classification of Children* (San Francisco: Josey-Bass, 1975), pp. 123–149.

12. Charles Wellford, "Labelling Theory and Criminology: An Assessment," *Social Problems* 22 (February 1975): 332–345.

13. Anne Rankin Mahoney, "The Effect of Labeling upon Youths in the Juvenile Justice System: A Review of the Evidence," *Law and Society* 8 (Summer 1974): 583–614.

14. Jerome G. Miller, "The Politics of Change: Correctional Reform," in Yitzhak Bakal, ed., *Closing Correctional Institutions*, pp. 3–8.

NOTES TO CHAPTER 5

1. Individual questions, some of which have been slightly modified, come from two sources: LaMar T. Empey and Stephen Lubeck, *Silver Lake Experiment* (Chicago: Aldine, 1971); Donald R. Fessler, "The Development of a Scale for Measuring Community Solidarity," *Rural Sociology* 17 (1952): 144–152.

2. One of the unintended consequences of deinstitutionalization could have been an increase in the numbers of youths being handled as adults and processed into the adult criminal justice system. Such was not the case in Massachusetts. In 1968 365 youths 16 and under were held in jail awaiting court disposition and 6 were held in houses of correction for custody. For 17 year olds the figures were 999 and 249; for 18 year olds they were 1,093 and 491. In 1974 respective figures were: 16 and under—55 and 3; 17 year olds—1,002 and 255; and 18 year olds—1,084 and 457.

3. A "no program" category was necessary for two reasons. First, some youths were immediately placed on traditional parole status with no additional supportive services. Second, a few youths never stayed in a program for a period of a month. Both kinds of youths therefore comprise the "no program" category.

4. The apparent discrepancy between the DYS census data indicating where youths are on a given day (reported in Chapter 2) and the initial placement data reported here can be explained in part by the way we handled youths "awaiting placement" and by our designation of a "no program" category. Also, the differences are influenced by the length of stay in various program types. The average length of stay for secure care was three months. However, youths in foster care and nonresidential placements remained for much longer periods, often exceeding nine months. The fact that nonresidential placements continued to receive services for longer periods of time would inflate the daily counts without influencing the initial placement data.

NOTES TO CHAPTER 8

1. McEwen, *Designing Correctional Organizations for Youths.*

2. Using our definition of secure care, the department has consistently placed approximately 10 percent of its placement population in secure facilities. An extensive study of the secure care issue conducted jointly by the department and the attorney general's office concluded that secure placements were needed for 11.2 percent of the DYS youths. See Final Report of the Task Force on Secure Facilities; the Issue of Security in a *Community-Based System of Juvenile Corrections*, Commonwealth of Massachusetts Department of Youth Services, November, 1977.

3. Lerman, *Community Treatment and Social Control.*

Index

About the Authors

Robert B. Coates, Associate Director of the Center, has been Associate Project Director of the Juvenile Correctional Reform Project since 1971. He holds a doctorate in sociology from the University of Maryland. He has been a Visiting Lecturer on Ministry and Juvenile Justice at the Harvard Divinity School. His research interests have been complemented by numerous national and local community activities. Co-author of three of the five books in the project series, Dr. Coates has also published many articles and reports and is co-author of *Juvenile Correctional Reform: A Preliminary Report* (LEAA, 1977).

Alden D. Miller is Associate Director of the Center for Criminal Justice and Associate Project Director of the Juvenile Correctional Reform Project. He holds a doctorate in sociology from the University of North Carolina and taught at Indiana University and Boston University before joining the staff of the Center in 1971. He is the author of numerous articles on corrections and sociological methodology, co-author of *Juvenile Correctional Reform in Massachusetts: A Preliminary Report* (LEAA, 1977), and is co-author of three of the five books in the project's series.

Lloyd E. Ohlin, Roscoe Pound Professor of Criminology and Research Director of the Center for Criminal Justice, joined the Harvard Law School faculty in 1967. In addition to his academic work, Professor Ohlin has had a variety of practical experiences in public services. He has worked as a sociologist at the Illinois State Penitentiary

in Joliet and for the Illinois Parole and Pardon Board. He directed
the work of the Center for Education and Research in Corrections at
the University of Chicago from 1953 to 1956. From then until his
appointment at Harvard, Professor Ohlin was a member of the faculty
of the Columbia University School of Social Work, and for part of
that time also served as director of the school's research center. During two leaves of absence from Columbia he served as special assistant
to Abraham Ribicoff, Secretary of the Department of Health, Education, and Welfare (1961–1962) and as associate director of the
President's Commission on Law Enforcement and Administration of
Justice (1965–1967).

In addition to numerous articles, Professor Ohlin has published
Selection for Parole (1951); *Sociology and the Field of Corrections*
(1956); *Delinquency and Opportunity* (1960) with Richard A. Cloward; and edited *Prisoners in America* (1974). He is also co-author of
Juvenile Correctional Reform in Massachusetts: A Preliminary Report (1977), and of three of the five books in the juvenile correctional reform series.